Nordic Party Members

Nordic Party Members

Linkages in Troubled Times

Edited by
Marie Demker, Knut Heidar
and Karina Kosiara-Pedersen

ecpr
PRESS

Published by the European Consortium for Political Research, Harbour House, 6–8 Hythe Quay, Colchester, CO2 8JF, United Kingdom

British Library Cataloguing in Publication Data

A catalogue record for this book is available from the British Library

ISBN: HB 978-1-78552-325-0

Library of Congress Cataloging-in-Publication Data Available
ISBN: 978-1-78552-325-0 (cloth)
ISBN: 978-1-5381-5687-2 (pbk)
ISBN: 978-1-78552-326-7 (electronic)

ecpr.eu/shop

Contents

Acknowledgements

This book originated with a conference in Oslo in January 2016, where most of the Scandinavian contributors to this book were present. Later, we met for planning and discussions in Gothenburg and Oslo, and in the spring of 2017, Icelandic and Finnish colleagues joined us, making it a Nordic project.

We had subsequent meetings in Gothenburg in 2017 and 2018, discussing draft chapters. New member and voter surveys in all five Nordic countries provided the empirical basis for the project. The completion of these surveys made it possible, for the first time, to do comparative analyses of party members and their relations to voters in all Nordic countries.

We are grateful to our colleagues who supported and worked enthusiastically to carry out the project, and for the support provided by our respective universities, in particular the University of Gothenburg, which supported most of our meetings. Thanks also to the respective national research councils, research funds and universities for support in carrying out the member surveys. For the voter surveys, we relied on the various national election studies.

Thanks also to Tor Gaute Syrstad (MA), who helped edit the manuscript.

Finally, the project had been developed in a good collegial spirit and we had productive and interesting discussions along the way.

Gothenburg, Oslo, Copenhagen, 4 March 2019
Marie Demker, Knut Heidar and Karina Kosiara-Pedersen

Figures

CHAPTER 2

CHAPTER 5

CHAPTER 10

CHAPTER 11

Tables

CHAPTER 4

CHAPTER 6

CHAPTER 7

CHAPTER 8

CHAPTER 9

CHAPTER 10

CHAPTER 11

1

Nordic Party Democracies

Marie Demker, Knut Heidar and Karina Kosiara-Pedersen

The Nordic countries are party democracies. But in what sense? In the system-level analyses of Schumpeter (1942) and Schattschneider (1942), all democracies are 'party democracies' (e.g. see Allern and Pedersen 2007). Democracy is based on the *voters' opportunity to choose* between different parties competing for votes at free elections. The power-seeking elites will offer alternative programmes. They will also seek to adjust their policies according to voter preferences in order to win elections (Downs 1957). In this model of party democracy, it does not matter *how* the elites develop their policies just as long as the voters are offered alternatives.

There is, however, another conception of party democracy, sometimes labelled the 'European model' as opposed to the American one (Wright 1971). The European model adds that parties should practise internal democracy when developing their policies (e.g. Duverger [1954] 1972). Parties build *organized linkages between the voters and the political decision makers* – with the party members as intermediate actors. In this version of party democracy, the party organizations and their members *supplement* the electoral market in channelling voter preferences into political institutions. Nation-level democracy – the European way – therefore has two pillars: electoral competition and party-organized linkages. Despite its name, however, the model is not necessarily exclusively European (Cross and Katz 2013) nor are all European democracies by default party democracies in terms of offering working party linkages.

No doubt, the Nordic countries are 'party democracies' in the electoral sense. The question is whether they are also 'linkage democracies' in the European, two-pillar way. Membership figures in Nordic parties have declined substantially since the 1950s, but they are still high as compared to most European democracies and above average when looking at Western Europe only (Kölln 2015; Poguntke et al. 2016; van Biezen, Mair and Poguntke 2012; van Haute and Gauja 2015). Nominal membership figures, however, are only one indication of a viable grass-roots connection. It takes more than a certain number of party members to create linkage, just as it takes more than a high number of voters to create electoral democracy. The party members must also be representative of the party voters, they must be active in the policy-making processes inside the parties and, not least, these active members must be influential. We know that the Nordic countries generally have strong political parties that control the parliaments (Esaiasson and Heidar 2000), but we do not know *to what extent* parties organize effective member-based linkages between civil society and the state. Therefore, the general question addressed in this book is:

> *Do members in political parties today, despite the fading of party membership numbers, provide Nordic party democracy with the kind of linkage that will support a sustainable democracy?*

In this introductory chapter, we first elaborate on parties' linkage function before turning to some of the current challenges of parties and their membership organizations. We then present the analytical framework for the study of organized party linkage in democracies and its four dimensions: parties' reach, members' representation, member activism and member influence. Next, we present the Nordic cases and parties included in the analyses. Thereafter, the data on which the chapters are mainly based, namely, the party member surveys in Denmark (2012), Finland (2016), Sweden (2015) and Norway (2017), as well as the electoral survey in Iceland (2013), are presented. Last, we present the main results of the chapters and the book outline.

PARTY LINKAGE

Linkage is the raison d'être of political parties (Lawson 1988). Parties traditionally link citizen preferences with government through vote structuring at elections, forming a channel of participation, recruitment, training and socialization of political leadership, government organizing, policy formulation and interest aggregation (King 1969). However, political parties are not the sole providers of democratic political linkage as other collective actors, such as interest organizations, pressure groups and social movements as well as mass media and opinion polls, may also provide some kind of political linkage.

Nevertheless, parties offer a unique linkage between voters and elected representatives as they are the only actors carrying out activities both in the electoral arena and in the parliamentary arena. 'Parties are *the* central intermediate and intermediary structure between society and government' (Sartori 1976, ix, emphasis in original), or in other words, 'the great intermediary which links social forces and ideologies to official governmental institutions and relates them to political action within the larger political community' (Neumann 1956, 396). They provide linkage between the rulers and the ruled, between the government and the electorate.

One of the most influential theorists of democracy (or 'polyarchy', as he terms it) in the twentieth century, Robert A. Dahl, did not elaborate much on political parties. He groups parties with other needed 'political associations', like interest groups and lobbying organizations, that are free from state interference and provide voters with a choice at elections (Dahl 1998, 98). The internal life of political parties is not central to democracy. Dahl gives words to the 'American' party perspective.

In Giovanni Sartori's work, we find the 'European' view (1976). Sartori distinguishes between 'factions' and 'parties'. Factions are divisive elite groups, fighting for privilege and power in their own interest. Parties, on the other hand, are kin to the liberal project after the Enlightenment: they are expressions of diversity; they facilitate progress. To Sartori, parties are instruments for 'representing the people by expressing their demands', they have a 'voice function' (1976, 27–28). Parties not only *express*, but they also *channel*. Parties are two-way channels; communication flows downwards from the elites as well as upwards from the citizens. But on the whole, a party 'lends itself to expressions from below far more than to manipulation from above' (1976, 29). At the same time, as an early indication of the 'cartel party' model, he claims that parties may well 'relapse into something resembling faction' (1976, 25).

Dalton, Farrell and McAllister (2011, 7) identify five forms of linkage between parties and voters: campaign linkage (recruit candidates), participatory linkage (activate citizens during elections), ideological linkage (inform voters on policies, voters vote according to policy interests), representative linkage (ensure good congruence between citizens' policy preferences and party policies) and policy linkage (parties deliver the policies advocated at elections). There is clearly variation in how the linkage between the elected representatives and the electorate is enhanced by, for example, the societal elite, membership organizations, affiliated organizations, traditional one-way media or newer social media and political marketing tools.

Party organizations provide linkage in several different ways, as indicated by the plethora of party models or types depicted in the literature (Katz and Mair 1995, 2018; Krouwel 2006). In the classic left-of-centre 'mass parties', linkage was established through membership organizations as well as affiliated labour unions (Duverger [1954] 1972). The 'catch-all' (Kirchheimer 1966) or 'electoral professional' parties (Pancbianco 1988) maintained membership organizations but linked to broader segments of society. In the 'cartel party' model, membership organizations are maintained for legitimacy, and intra-party democracy is constrained by stratarchy and individualization of membership rights as well as by blurring the distinction between members and supporters (Katz and Mair 1995, 2018). In more top-ruled elite parties, membership tends to be disregarded in party decision-making processes, and it is the party elite, consisting of elected representatives and employees in party headquarters, who create linkage to the electorate through mass and social media and with the aid of political marketing tools (Ignazi 2018; Krouwel 2012; Schumacher and Giger 2017).

CHALLENGES TO PARTY MEMBER ORGANIZATIONS

Since the 'frozen' West European party systems began melting in the 1960s and 1970s, the old parties have lost their strong grip on members and voters alike (Dalton 2014). Electoral volatility is on the rise, and voters decide closer to the elections whom to vote for. This volatility among voters reduces the chance that they will enrol in a party. However, it is not only party membership as such but also group membership in general (e.g. collective trade union affiliation) that is declining (van Biezen and Poguntke 2014). Political engagement, like sports and various other group activities, has become individualized (Putnam 2000).

Political parties are also challenged by the personalization of politics. The personalization of politics implies an emphasis on persons instead of the party (Cross, Katz and Pruysers 2018; Rahat and Kenig 2018). Centralized personalization implies an increased focus on the party leadership, but also at the lower levels within the organization it may have an impact on the character of the party member organization. Individual party members may locally gain importance at the expense of the party as a collective.

Parties have responded in several ways to contextual challenges and opportunities and to membership decline. These responses challenge party membership linkage either because they change its character directly or because they replace it. First, party members have in several ways been (partly) replaced in a number of tasks within the parties. This challenges the incentives for engaging in party membership as well as the circumstances in which party membership linkage may be performed. In particular, party member funding has been replaced or supplemented by public financing. While members in mass parties provided a substantial part of the party funding, membership dues and voluntary contributions now make up a smaller share; parties rely increasingly on public financing (Bardi, Calossi and Pizzimenti 2017; Kölln 2015, 2016; van Biezen and Kopecký 2017).

Second, some parties have individualized member rights regarding important decisions on candidate nomination and party programmes (Cross and Katz 2013; Cross and Pilet 2015). This could be through member referenda or all-member meetings at the expense of representative assemblies. In this way, parties want to make membership more attractive for individual rank-and-file members. However, by individualizing intra-party democracy, parties may also be weakening the impact of their members as this bypasses the active and involved members, the mid-level elite, who stand a better chance of opposing the party leadership than rank-and-file members have on their own (cf. Katz and Mair 2009).

Third, parties have opened up for other kinds of affiliation than the traditional dues-paying party membership (Achury et al. 2018; Faucher 2015; Gauja 2015; Kosiara-Pedersen, Scarrow and van Haute 2017; Scarrow 2015). These newer supporters are, to different degrees, granted rights and opportunities for participation and decision-making within the parties that were previously reserved for party members. This blurs the distinction between members and other supporters (Hooghe and

Kölln 2018; Kosiara-Pedersen, Scarrow and van Haute 2017; Webb, Poletti and Bale 2017). One particular way in which parties have blurred the distinction between members and other supporters is by introducing primaries (Bernardi, Sandri and Seddone 2016; Cross et al. 2016; Sandri, Seddone and Venturino 2015).

Fourth, party bureaucracies have increased in size (Bardi, Calossi and Pizzimenti 2017), and these professionals have supplemented and replaced party members when it comes to such diverse tasks as keeping membership files, designing campaign materials, getting input from voters, formulating party policies and communicating messages. Parties have become professionalized in the sense that communication, campaign, policy and organizational experts are hired to take on these tasks. In addition, parties have professionalized their fundraising by, for example, opening up for the US-style political contributions from supporters and seeking out corporate and organizational funders. Trends towards professionalization of politics also have implications for how party member organizations are administered. Party members are to a larger extent handled like any other assets in an organization, where organizational consultants work on recruiting, mobilizing and keeping members, streamlining dues payment and so forth. Similarly, the digitalization of society opens up new ways of recruiting and mobilizing members as well as new ways for members to participate.

Fifth, while labour-intensive campaigning was essential to traditional mass parties, in particular those without ties to corporate money, capital-intensive campaign methods (including various aspects of political marketing tools such as advertisements and social media campaigns) have now supplemented or even replaced this. Parties are able to campaign without their members. Party members have also been supplemented or replaced by political marketing tools such as focus groups, opinion polls and the 'big data' available on social media in regard to interest aggregation (Gibson and Römmele 2009; Kosiara-Pedersen 2011). Local chairs are no longer the primary 'eyes and ears' of their parties.

In addition, the Internet, social media and so on have further facilitated parties' direct communication with the electorate between elections. In the 'golden age' of class-based politics, the parties had close links with specific media, which allowed them to communicate to their segments. When these party-linked newspapers declined and the more neutral (if not completely non-political) broadsheets grew, parties did not have newspapers available for unmediated communication. Party membership organizations provided a viable channel of communication from party to electorate (and vice versa). However, digitalization put an end to this exclusivity of the party members. Now party leaders, candidates and other party personnel may communicate directly to supporters without the intermediation of members.

European party systems have been strongly affected by the rise of new parties. While almost all of these new parties uphold the tradition of establishing a party member organization, they are not able to enrol as many members as the classic mass parties did in their 'golden age' in the 1950s and 1960s. Moreover, the dominant mode of party organization today is leadership-centred, publicly financed, media-oriented and strongly influenced by professional electioneering. These trends may have strengthened the ever-present 'oligarchic tendencies' within parties (Michels [1911] 1962). Hence, the question is whether party members' presence and activism within the parties, even today, provide linkage between the voters and the party elites. It is a question of whether the general decline in party membership, the changing media setting and mediatization of politics, along with tendencies to professionalization, individualization, personalization and digitalization of politics, have undermined this linkage and the way 'European' party democracies used to work.

Party Member Linkage Research

Party organizations as a channel of citizen participation, voter representativity and elite communication have not been at the forefront of comparative political research. There are, however, projects and studies discussing and monitoring party organizations in general which are highly relevant (Katz and Crotty 2006). Many of these are based on official records as found in the broad, comparative data archives organized by Katz and Mair for 1960–1990 (1994) and, more recently, extended and developed in the political parties database initiated by Scarrow, Webb and Poguntke (2017; see also www.politicalpartydb.org).

Studies of membership linkage are few and seldom comparative (Allern, Heidar and Karlsen 2016). One reason is that surveys of party members and parties' organizational elites have been rare. Seyd and Whiteley conducted the early British studies around 1990 (Seyd and Whiteley 1992, 2002; Whiteley and Seyd 1998; Whiteley, Seyd and Richardson 1994), and Dutch party researchers had a series of party member surveys from 1986 onwards (den Ridder, van Holsteyn and Koole, 2019). Heidar organized the first of four Norwegian studies in 1991 (Allern, Heidar and Karlsen 2016; Heidar 1994; Heidar and Saglie 2002), and Irish and Danish party member surveys followed around the turn of the century (Bille and Elklit 2003; Gallagher and Marsh 2002, 2004; Pedersen 2003; Pedersen et al. 2004). Since then we have seen a (growing) interest in several European democracies (see the country chapters in van Haute and Gauja 2015). However, prior to the ongoing project on 'Members and Activists in Political Parties' (www.projectmapp.eu), party member surveys have not been conducted across countries.[1] Hence, comparative analyses of party membership linkage have been limited to other kinds of data.

Another reason for the lack of membership studies is that the dominant US political science milieu has no such actor to study. Party membership hardly exists as a meaningful category in the US (Aldrich 2011). There is, of course, US research focusing on activists, organizers and volunteers. When survey data are analysed, focusing on voter-party congruence, 'the party' is generally taken to be the party elite, that is, the candidates or members of Congress/MPs (e.g. Dalton 2017). This is of course highly relevant from the point of view of the 'one-pillar' democracy models, as this focuses on electoral linkage, but it is insufficient when looking at parties as channels of organized linkages. In the latter case, party member organizations have (or had) a democratic linkage role worth studying.

FOUR DIMENSIONS OF PARTY MEMBERSHIP LINKAGE

In light of these changes and challenges to parties, our main interest lies with the parties' linkage to voters through the membership organizations. Consequently, we look at the members as actors through whom parties link to the electorate. In our analytical framework, we distinguish between four dimensions that together add up to a comprehensive description of how party member organizations may channel citizen involvement and preferences into party policies and representatives. These four dimensions of linkage cover the extent of the membership reach of parties, the degrees of member representativity (compared to the voters), the level and character of members' activities and, finally, the level and type of internal party democracy.

Reach: Membership Trends and Recruitment

The first aspect of linkage concerns size. This is an organizational characteristic and indicates the extent of party reach within civil society. The broader the reach, the stronger the potential for party linkage. This dimension is different from the three that follow as they require member surveys in order to describe characteristics of the members and by default the party membership. Party members play an important role in channelling channel citizen opinions into the party organization. The members constitute the 'citizen assembly' of the party's electoral segment, a potential deliberative assembly on behalf of their voters. By and large, the members are also better informed and more engaged than the average party voter. No doubt, party elites may commission voter surveys and set up focus groups to help develop winning electoral coalitions, but these will be top-down-generated linkages belonging to the one-pillar democracies. It is difficult to determine what number (or share) of members are needed to have an operative party linkage. Are there thresholds or absolute levels that indicate a sufficient, a good, or a satisfactory number of members? A high member/voter ratio is obviously a better platform for linkage than a low ratio, even if a high number in itself does not guarantee the participation and influence of party members. At the other end of the scale, also, absolute standards are difficult to set, perhaps beyond the number displayed for the Dutch 'Partij voor de Vrijheid' party (PVV). Even though the PVV has a substantial party group in the Dutch parliament, it formally has only one member, namely, the party leader himself (den Ridder, van Holsteyn and Koole 2015). Without a big-enough group of rank-and-file party members, a party will have problems providing organized linkage between the electorate and the elected with the party members as intermediaries. But clearly, even a high number of members do not in itself guarantee linkage.

Membership figures and the member/voter ratios show the extent to which parties have recruited and kept members. How effective 'reach' is for linkage, however, depends in part on why members enrol in the party. Do they join to be active, to create linkage, intending to take part in the internal political processes? Alternatively, do they join to signal passive support only? Members' motivations are also important when assessing the reach of Nordic party organizations. Hence, to assess this dimension of linkage, we analyse membership figures as well as members' motivations.

Representation: Social and Ideological

The social and ideological profile of party members is central to linkage as it shows how well parties are anchored socially and politically in society. To analyse the congruence or match between members and their voters, we look at theories of representation (Allern, Heidar and Karlsen 2016; Pitkin 1967). Party members are of course not representatives of voters in the same way that party representatives in public office are, since they are not elected. However, *member representativeness* is important when it comes to establishing party linkage.

We distinguish between two dimensions in representativity: social and ideological. First, social representativeness is an important aspect of an assessment of parties' linkage through party membership organizations since it shows whether the social base of the party is reflected – or mirrored – in the party membership. Are party members' backgrounds and experiences similar to those of the voters they represent? Which groups within the electorate are offered a linkage through parties? Is the parties' descriptive linkage representative of party voters, or is it skewed? Second, the ideological representativeness is relevant in particular due to parties' role in interest aggregation and policy formulation. Is the party membership representative of the political or ideological opinions of the voters? Will members bring forward the political preferences of the party voters in internal debates? Representative members – both socially and politically – are an important aspect of party linkage as this shows the extent to which party members in intra-party decision-making processes can articulate the political interests and views of a party's support base.

Hence, when analysing the extent to which party member organizations provide representative linkage, we first analyse the socioeconomic characteristics of parties' grass roots and the extent to which they differ from voters. Then, in order to assess the effectiveness of the internal representation, we also analyse the ideological representativeness and members' policy agreement.

Activity: Participation and Activism

The number of members has traditionally been a measure of parties' participatory linkages. High membership/electorate ratios indicate an extensive reach among the electorate at large. Similarly, parties mobilizing a large share of their voters potentially have a strong link to (their part of) society and to their voters through their members. A focus on membership figures as an indicator of participation rests on the premise that signing up for membership actually indicates member activism inside the party. But party membership has a polymorphic nature, and party member activism varies, as do other types of participation, in degree, type and quality both within and among parties and over time (Heidar 1994). This variation implies that parties with few members may have a higher number of activists, if they activate a larger share of their members, than parties with low rates of internal participation (Pedersen 2003). Similarly, a party that primarily loses inactive members – not the active ones – may retain its level of activism on a smaller base.

This means that both mere enrolment in the party ('reach') and members' internal participation ('activism') must be included when studying parties' *participatory* linkage. Hence, we discuss both the membership figures, why party members join (dimension one) and the level and type of participation (dimension three). We also discuss different explanations for members' participation. Taken together, these provide a comprehensive assessment of the extent to which parties offer a participatory electoral linkage and the character of these linkages.

Influence: Power Relations and Decision-Making

As we have seen, parties may easily bypass their members. Hence, whether party elites pay attention to and are willing to adjust their policies on the basis of internal party decision-making is essential for parties as organized linkages. Internal democracy within parties is not a necessary condition for representative democracy at the national level since the latter is based on the electoral competition between parties. However, intra-party democracy is essential when considering party linkage through their membership organization.

The challenges to intra-party democracy are not new, as indicated by the century-old debate on Michels' 'iron law of oligarchy' (Michels [1911] 1962). Recent studies point to increased centralizing within the parties, with less of a say for the active middle-level elites, although there is no definitive verdict on this (Cross and Katz 2013; Katz and Mair 2009). Even though Nordic parties generally have a tradition of strong organization with internal party democracy, giving members a say in policy formulation, leadership selection and candidate nomination, these centralizing tendencies may also have reached the Nordic countries in spite of formal arrangements (Bolin et al. 2017).

In our assessment of how party member organizations provide linkage, we look at how members perceive the degree of intra-party democracy within their own party and to what extent there is a link between ideological disagreement and demands for intra-party democracy.

THE NORDIC COUNTRIES AND THEIR PARTIES.
Contexts And Explanations

How might a comparative study of Nordic countries contribute to the scholarly and public debates on the role of members within political parties and the role of parties in democracies? Generally, the design of this study is based on a traditional most similar systems approach. Not that we ignore the differences, but the similarities make it easier to compare and contrast membership in the Nordic countries while discussing possible explanations in terms of party characteristics rather than cultural and institutional differences. In order to highlight the usefulness of studying the Nordic region, we first briefly describe the evolution of the Nordic party systems. This will help us understand the macro- and meso-level comparisons across countries and parties made in the subsequent chapters. We then discuss the selection of the Nordic countries, their similarities and differences and whether they are exceptional and more likely than other countries to establish working party membership linkages. Finally, we move from the system level to the party level, presenting the parties included in the empirical analyses and the categorizations of these as applied throughout the book.

The Nordic Polities and Their Party Systems

The Nordic party systems have often been characterized as five-party systems (Berglund and Lindström 1978) on the basis of the seminal work of Lipset and Rokkan (1967). In the Nordic countries, the traces of the national and industrial revolutions consisted of one dominant reformist socialist party, one smaller revolutionary socialist party, one agrarian party, one liberal party and one conservative party. According to Lipset and Rokkan, the prominent social cleavages from the 1920s, when parliamentary democracy was introduced and stabilized, produced a party system that was frozen for several decades. In the Nordic countries, this heritage was the five-party system.

This was for a long time prominent in descriptions of the Nordic party systems (Demker 2006; Petersson 1991). More recent studies, however, show that the five-party model was a contingent phenomenon, appearing at a certain moment of time, and not a lasting order (Demker and Svåsand 2005; Hansen and Kosiara-Pedersen 2017; Jónsson 2014; Jungar and Jupskås 2014). The five-party model has been challenged and has, in reality, collapsed. Today, it is more accurate to maintain that there is a development away from a homogeneous Nordic party system, even if we still find important similarities. The agrarian parties have been a perennial force, making the Nordics different from European party systems in general. In Denmark and Finland, these parties have been dominant in certain periods. The Danish 'Venstre' (Liberals), traditionally an agrarian party, has, since the 1980s, developed into a liberal-conservative party, making labelling difficult. The Swedish Centre Party has increasingly taken a turn towards pro-EU policies and adopted points of view that are more liberal. The social democratic parties have been uniquely strong. In Sweden, Denmark and Norway, they were in government for most of the time from the Second World War to the 1970s. Conservative forces have not been as prominent as in Great Britain, Germany or France. Christian parties have until recently played a peripheral role in the party systems, except in Norway.

The challenges to the Nordic party systems all come from the new forces that also have affected other West European countries: radical right and green parties. All Nordic countries except Iceland now have radical, 'populist', right parties influencing the party systems in one way or another. In Finland and Norway, these parties are today governing partners, and in Denmark, a parliamentary support party for the minority government up till the 2019 election. In Sweden, the Swedish Democrats hold the parliamentary balance between the centre-left and the centre-right governmental alternatives, but neither bloc wants to cooperate with the party. All Nordic parties also have green – or red-green – parties influencing government by either being coalition partners or providing the parliamentary majority for the government from time to time.

(The Myth of?) Nordic Exceptionalism

In order to assess how a comparative study of Nordic countries can contribute to the debates on party membership linkage, we must address two questions. The first is whether the Nordic cases are more alike than different, and the second is whether they are exceptional compared to other party democracies. We are looking for similarities or differences that may have an effect on party membership linkages.

The Nordic countries are all parliamentary democracies with multiparty systems and many similarities in constitutional structure and political settings. This is particularly the case for the Scandinavian countries, although Finland and Iceland are not very different. In many comparative analyses, the Nordic countries are presented within a most similar system design setting as they share religious, economic and social characteristics. However, despite many similarities, there are also relevant differences. To give some examples, radical right parties have developed within the five countries to different degrees, and religion plays a larger role in Norway and Iceland. Hence, while we do regard the five Nordic countries as similar, the contexts they provide for party membership linkage are not identical. We expect to find that both country and party differences in party membership linkage can be explained to some extent by the finer details of history, social structure and politics.

Next, the question is whether the Nordic countries are exceptional. The Nordic countries are certainly not anything like a random sample of democracies. They are all old, enduring democracies with uninterrupted free parliamentary elections, except for the Second World War period. Nordic parties are formally democratic organizations with members taking part in decisions on the party programme and in the nomination of candidates for public office (Bolin et al. 2017), while applying the parties' election pledges seems to be the prerogative of the parliamentary party groups (Heidar and Koole 2000). The parliamentary party groups may have good reasons to discard or moderate such pledges, having to cope with changing realities, public debates, negotiations with coalition parties and expected voter reactions. Still, these changes must be justified by the party elites when they subsequently face party members and, ultimately, voters. In addition, as noted earlier, membership figures in Nordic parties are slightly above average when looking at Western Europe. This points towards conditions favourable to party membership linkage in what are still predominantly traditionally organized 'mass' parties. The message is that if party linkage is crumbling in the Nordic parties, linkage may also be at risk in most other developed democracies.

However, while the Nordic countries share religious, economic and social characteristics that set them apart from other countries in Europe and in the West more generally (Arter 2015), they are not necessarily as exceptional (anymore) as suggested by the (older) literature (Heidar 2004, 59). As pointed out in a recent comparative analysis of electoral behaviour, Nordic exceptionalism has by and large been found to be a myth (Bengtsson et al. 2013). Party membership figures are not very different from the general European levels (except for Iceland). Similarly, the changes in the Nordic party systems, in particular (but not only) the rise of populist and green parties and declining support for mainstream parties, are much like changes occurring elsewhere (see Lisi 2018).

Studying the Nordic countries means that we analyse party linkage in five similar but not identical systems. The Nordics are not exceptional cases compared to other European countries. They do, however, offer a transparent setting for explicit discussions of causal impact of a number of relevant factors, even if we are not able to control systematically for critical factors like public party finance, media structure and electoral system. Parties' participatory linkages have favourable conditions in the Nordic countries due to the historically strong party membership organizations and participatory traditions. However, they are not 'critical cases' in the sense that negative findings here indicate that linkage in other countries is impossible. Nevertheless, we find that useful lessons may be drawn from the Nordic comparisons, lessons that are relevant for parties in other societies with a well-educated, affluent and highly volatile electorate.

The Nordic Parties

A total of thirty-six parties across the five countries are included in this study. Due to differences in the data available, however, the eleven empirical chapters vary in terms of which parties are included. In each chapter, the authors base their analyses on the most recent party member surveys (see next).[2] In order to explore differences between parties, we distinguish between parties on the basis of their ideology/party family, size and age.

We include parties from almost all party families and hence cover a broad ideological spectrum. This enables us to explore whether there are differences across the political landscape. The overall expectation is that parties to the left of centre emphasize linkage through membership organizations more than parties to the right of centre. This is based on the history of party organizational development and the emergence of different party types. Mass parties developed on the left in the wake of newly enfranchised workers, although, over time, this proved to be 'contagious' to the right-of-centre elite parties (Duverger [1954] 1972; Epstein 1967; Katz and Mair 1995; Panebianco 1988).

In table 1.1, we list the Nordic parties according to their party families and (approximate) left-right placement. Parties not included in the member surveys used in this book are marked by parentheses. It is a general picture, and some would disagree with the details. For example, the Danish Liberal Party (Venstre), with its agrarian origin and right-oriented liberalism, is notoriously difficult to place. Is this party agrarian, liberal or conservative? The greens generally resist placement on the left-right scale as they regard this dimension as irrelevant or at least old-fashioned. Some green parties, however, label themselves 'left-green', like the Icelandic 'Left Green Movement', making the placement easier. Another example is the radical right parties, which, like the Norwegian Progress Party, may be right-wing on both the redistributive and the value dimensions, while

Table 1.1. Nordic political parties: Party family and left-right order.

	DENMARK	FINLAND	ICELAND	NORWAY	SWEDEN
Left Socialist	Red-Green Alliance, Socialist People's Party	Left Alliance	Left-Greens	Socialist Left	Left Party
Social Democrats	Social Democrats	Social Democrats	Social Democrats	Social Democrats	Social Democrats
Greens		Green League		Green Party	Green Party
Agrarians		Centre Party	Progressive Party	Centre Party	(Centre Party)
Other	Social Liberal Party		Pirate Party, Bright Future		Feminist Initiative
Christian Democrats	Christian Democrats			Christian Democrats	Christian Democrats
Liberals	Liberals Liberal Alliance			Liberal Party	Liberal People's Party/ Liberal Party
Conservative	Conservative Party	Coalition Party	Independence Party	Conservative Party	Moderate Party
Radical Right	Danish People's Party	The inns (Blue Future)		Progress Party	(Sweden Democrats)

Note: Party names and their English translations are found in table A1.1 in the appendix.

the Danish People's Party has been moving to the left on redistributive issues (Jungar and Jupskås 2014).

As noted earlier, size, measured by membership figures, indicates the 'reach' of the party, and this is explored in more detail in chapter 2. Party size and age are to some extent related, even though some old parties never grew big (like the Danish Social Liberals and the Norwegian Liberals) or have declined markedly (like the Swedish Liberals and the Danish Conservatives).

We distinguish between old and new parties with the overall expectation that the older parties are more likely to provide linkage through party membership organizations than newer parties. Old parties have the advantage of being established at a time when parties had closer links to classes, organizational networks and socio-cultural groups (cf. Lipset and Rokkan 1967), and when party membership was more common and one of few channels for political participation. New parties were established in contexts where the links between class and party were weakened due to social mobility and the saliency of new issues (Inglehart 1977), higher volatility and the emergence of newer channels of political participation such as social movements and social media. Most operationalizations of old versus new will be somewhat arbitrary. We have chosen to set 1960 as the cut-off point since this is where mass parties reached their peak and the frozen party systems began thawing. Hence, the terms 'old' and 'new' should be seen relative to the long timespan of the Nordic party systems. This cut-off point has previously proved useful in research on new parties (Bolin 2012; Harmel and Robertson 1985; Tavits 2006). Table 1.2 shows the categorization of old and new parties based on the year that the party was established.

Table 1.2.　Old and new Nordic political parties included in this book.

	OLD	NEW
Denmark	Socialist People's Party, Social Democrats, Social Liberals, Liberals, Conservative People's Party	Red-Green Alliance, Christian Democrats, Liberal Alliance, Danish People's Party
Finland	Social Democrats, Centre Party, Coalition Party	Green Alliance, Left Alliance, The Finns
Iceland	Progressive Party, Independence Party, Social Democrats	Left-Green Movement, Pirates, Bright Future, Reform
Norway	Labour Party, Centre Party, Christian Democratic Party, Liberal Party, Conservative Party	Socialist Left Party, Green Party, Progress Party
Sweden	Social Democrats, Liberal People's Party/Liberal Party, Moderate Party	Feminist Initiative, Green Party, Christian Democrats

Note: The Danish Socialist People's Party was founded in 1959 and had many of the 'new party' characteristics. It could well have been grouped among these. The Icelandic Social Democrats is listed as an old party, although formally the party was formed through an amalgamation of the main established parties on the left in 2000.

Of the 36 parties, only the Danish Christian Democrats and the Swedish Feminist Initiative were not represented in the national parliament at the time of the surveys. Of all parties represented in parliament at the time of the surveys, only the Swedish Centre Party and the Sweden Democrats are not included in these analyses.

THE PARTY MEMBER SURVEYS

There is a long-standing tradition of party member studies in the Scandinavian countries. The Norwegian party member survey of 1991 was followed by surveys among parties across the political spectrum in 2000, 2009 and 2017 (Allern, Heidar and Karlsen 2016; Heidar and Saglie 2004). In Denmark, the first party member survey across all parties was conducted in 2000/2001 (Bille and Elklit 2003; Hansen 2002; Pedersen 2003; Pedersen et al. 2004) and followed up by a similar one in 2012 (Kosiara-Pedersen 2015, 2017; Kosiara-Pedersen and Hansen 2012). In Sweden, Widfeldt in the 1990s studied party member activism on the basis of various population surveys that included questions on membership and party activity (Widfeldt 1999). The first Swedish party member survey similar to the ones conducted in Norway and Denmark was done in 2015 (Kölln and Polk 2015).

There are only a few cross-country comparisons of Nordic party members. Some studies involving Danish and Norwegian party members have been done, focusing on gender differences (Heidar and Pedersen 2006), the use of technology in communication (Pedersen and Saglie 2005) and party member activism (Heidar, Kosiara-Pedersen and Saglie 2012).

Besides the most recent party member surveys carried out in Norway in 2016–2017, in Sweden in 2015 and in Denmark in 2012, there are some matching data available for Iceland and Finland. The Iceland election studies include a sufficiently large number of party members to allow for analyses of the member subgroup. In Finland, the first member survey was done in 2016 (Keipi et al. 2017). Although the purpose of this differs from that of the Scandinavian surveys, it includes questions enabling analyses of the members' socio-demographic profiles and the representativity of party members compared to party voters. Table 1.3 sums up the five surveys used in the empirical analyses.

To the extent that we compare party members to party voters, the data for the voters are from the national election surveys. In most countries, the party member surveys were conducted within a year before or after the election surveys. In Norway, however, the party members of 2016-2017 are compared to the voters at the 2013 general election (Aardal and Bergh 2015).[3] In Denmark, the closest election to the 2012 party member survey is the general election of 2011 (Stubager, Hansen and Andersen 2013). In Sweden, the 2015 membership is compared with the voters at the 2014 election (Tryggvason and Hedberg 2015), and comparisons in Finland are made on the basis of the national election survey from the same year as the member study (Grönlund and Wass 2016).

Table 1.3. The party member surveys.

	DENMARK 2012	FINLAND 2016	ICELAND 2013	NORWAY 2017	SWEDEN 2015
Type of survey	Party member survey on all parliamentarian parties. Online survey using SurveyXact	Party member survey on six biggest parliamentarian parties. Greens and NCP (e-mail). SDP, Centre, Left, Finns (e-mail and mail)	Election survey. 27% of voters also report party members. Self-reported members sub-sample used in the analyses of party members	Party member survey on all parliamentarian parties. Online survey using Questback	Party member survey to six parliamentarian parties plus the Feminist Initiative. Online survey by Laboratory of Opinion Research
Principal investigators	Karina Kosiara-Pedersen and Kasper Møller Hansen	Arttu Saarinen, Aki Koivula, Teo Keipi and Ilkka Koiranen	Ólafur P. Harðarson	Knut Heidar and Anders Ravik Jupskås	Ann-Kristin Kölln and Jonathan Polk
Period conducted	Apr.–May 2012	Apr.–Sep. 2016	May–Sep. 2013	Nov.–Feb. 2017	May–early July 2015
Sample	Random samples (8,000) from the Liberals and Social Democrats. All members with e-mail addresses registered by the seven others. In total, about 63,000 members.	*Greens:* Total sample from e-mail register covering 87% of the members. SDP, Centre, Left, Finns: Random sample from mail and e-mail register separately. *NCP:* Random sample solely from e-mail register covering approximately 60% of the members.	Random sample of 2,595 voters. Interviews conducted by telephone.	Random selection of 1,000 members in eight parties, in total 8,000 invitations.	Random sample of 7,000 members from the Social Democrats. All members with e-mail addresses in five of the other seven Riksdag parties, plus Feminist Initiative. In total, 84,000.

Response rates	36% overall. EL: 47.4% SF: 39.4% SD: 43.9% RV: 7.6% KD: 46.7% V: 40.3% DF: 49.2% KF: 46.3% LA: 7.1%	24.4% overall. Greens: 27.4% SDP: 30.8% Centre: 18.0% Left: 35.2% Finns: 32.1% NCP: 19.0%	Net response rate was 59%.	33% overall. SV: 34.2% AP: 34.6% MDG: 36.9% SP: 30.5% KRF: 28.5% V: 39.7% H: 28.7% FRP: 31.9%	12% overall. V: 14.0% S: 17.6% Mp: 11.7% Fl: n.a. KD: 9.5% Fp/Lib: 9.9% M: 12.3%
Total survey N	22,415	12,427	382 party members answered the survey	2,606	10,392
Reference	Kosiara-Pedersen (2017)	Keipi et al. (2017)	Önnudóttir and Björnsdóttir (2014)	Heidar et al. (2017)	Kölln and Polk (2017)
Members compared to voters in the NES	2011	In ch. 4, tables 1–2 and 4–9 based on 2015 NES. Table 3 on 1917 'Everyday life and participation' survey	2013 (same survey as for members)	2013	2014

BOOK CHAPTERS AND OUTLINE

The first two empirical chapters analyse the *parties' reach* as a basis for creating linkage to civil society. In chapter 2, Bolin, Kosiara-Pedersen and Kristinsson analyse trends in the party membership figures in the Nordic parties. They find membership decline among the old, cleavage parties, with the exception of the Icelandic parties. These old parties, however, generally still have many more members than the new left and right parties in spite of the latter's stable or increasing membership. In chapter 3, Heidar and Kosiara-Pedersen examine party members' recruitment background and motivations for enrolment. Scandinavian party members join mainly out of political interest, although social networks – in particular family – are important catalysers.

Part II includes three chapters on *social and political representation*. In chapter 4, Heidar, Kristinsson, Saarinen, Koivula and Keipi analyse who the Nordic party members are and the extent to which they are socially representative of their parties' voters. In general, men dominate among the members, although more so in right than left parties. Apart from gender, radical right parties have a better match between members and voters than the radical left and green parties. In chapter 5, Polk and Kölln compare political profiles of party voters, members and party candidates in order to analyse how representative the members are. They find a mixed picture of political congruence and conflict across the three party levels. Candidates for office are often more left-leaning than members and voters, but on the whole, the authors report rather high figures for left-right agreement between the party levels. In the third chapter in Part II (chapter 6), Blombäck, Jupskås and Hinnfors find internal member agreement high for a range of other issues also. Still, new issues, such as immigration, are challenging the internal party harmony in old parties, while new radical right party members disagree on economic issues.

Part III of the book focuses on *party member activities*. In chapter 7, Heidar and Kosiara-Pedersen analyse member participation within and outside of the parties, and in chapter 8, they look at different types of party members. Scandinavian party members are generally very active both internally and externally as party ambassadors – more so in the new parties than the old ones. The main group of 'party workers' engage in a broad range of activities. A smaller group of 'veterans' are characterized by having taken their turn in office (primarily in the past). Finally, there is a group of members who are not so active inside the party but very much engaged in promoting their party's standing in the media and in face-to-face interactions among the voters. In chapter 9, Jupskås and Kosiara-Pedersen explore explanations for party member participation along various dimensions of party activism. They find that individual resources are important, likewise a participatory party culture and satisfaction with intra-party democracy. Most important in explaining participation, however, is integration in organized civil society, that is, engagement and trust in other organizations.

Part IV focuses on *influence*, in particular party members' perceptions of and demand for intra-party democracy. In chapter 10, Bolin and Kosiara-Pedersen study how party members perceive the level of intra-party democracy and what may explain this perception. They find that members in general are quite satisfied with intra-party democracy. This is not dependent on activity level or former office holding. In chapter 11, Kölln and Polk combine party membership surveys in Denmark, Norway and Sweden with data from the Comparative Candidate Surveys to study the extent to which the chain of representation within parties is connected to demands for intra-party democracy. They find that a large gap between members and candidates goes together with demands for more internal party democracy. In other words, disagreements on policies lead to demands for a stronger voice.

Finally, in chapter 12, we conclude with a discussion on how party members make a difference in democracies. We discuss what the ten empirical chapters contribute to our understanding of how party organizations supplement the electoral linkage in democracies. We also discuss the generalizability and implications of these findings. Finally, we elaborate on how parties may be able to sustain or even improve the linkage provided by their member organizations in troubled times and how future studies may contribute to a better understanding of what the changes to party organizations mean for democracy in general.

NOTES

1. See also Heidar and Wauters (2019).
2. With one exception: in chapter 11, the 2009 Norwegian survey is used in order to maximize comparability with the candidate survey from 2009.
3. The 2017 national election survey was not available for analysis at the time of writing.

BIBLIOGRAPHY

Aardal, Bernt and Johannes Bergh, eds. 2015. *Valg og velgere. En studie av stortingsvalget 2013*. Oslo: Cappelen Damm Akademisk.

Achury, Susan, Susan E. Scarrow, Karina Kosiara-Pedersen and Emilie van Haute. 2018. 'The Consequences of Membership Incentives: Do Greater Political Benefits Attract Different Kinds of Members?' *Party Politics*. https://doi.org/10.1177/1354068818754603.

Aldrich, John H. 2011. *Why Parties? A Second Look*. Chicago: University of Chicago Press.

Allern, Elin Haugsgjerd and Karina Pedersen. 2007. 'The Impact of Party Organisational Changes on Democracy'. *West European Politics* 30 (1): 68–92.

Allern, Elin Haugsgjerd, Knut Heidar and Rune Karlsen. 2016. *After the Mass Party Continuity and Change in Political Parties and Representation in Norway*. Lanham, MD: Lexington Books

Arter, David. 2015. *Scandinavian Politics Today*, 3rd ed. Manchester: Manchester University Press.

Bardi, Luciano, Enrico Calossi and Eugenio Pizzimenti. 2017. 'Which Face Comes First? The Ascendancy of the Party in Public Office'. In *Organizing Political Parties: Representation, Participation, and Power*, edited by Susan E. Scarrow, Paul D. Webb and Thomas Poguntke, 62–83. Oxford: Oxford University Press.

Bengtsson, Åsa, Kasper Møller Hansen, Olafur Hardarson, Hanne Marthe Narud and Henrik Oscarsson. 2013. *The Nordic Voter: Myths of Exceptionalism*. Colchester: ECPR Press.

Berglund, Sten and Ulf Lindström. 1978. 'The Scandinavian Party System in Transition'. *European Journal of Political Research* 7 (3): 187–204.

Bernardi, L., G. Sandri and A. Seddone. 2016. 'Challenges of Political Participation and Intra-Party Democracy: Bittersweet Symphony from Party Membership and Primary Elections in Italy'. *Acta Politica* 52: 218–40.

Bille, Lars and Jørgen Elklit, eds. 2003. *Partiernes Medlemmer*. Aarhus: Aarhus Universitetsforlag.

Bolin, Niklas. 2012. *Målsättning riksdagen. Ett aktörsperspektiv på nya partiers inträde i det nationella parlamentet*. Umeå: Umeå universitet.

Bolin, Niklas, Nicholas Aylott, Benjamin von dem Berge and Thomas Poguntke. 2017. 'Patterns of Intra-Party Democracy across the World'. In *Organizing Political Parties: Representation, Participation, and Power*, edited by Susan E. Scarrow, Thomas Poguntke and Paul Webb, 158–84. Oxford: Oxford University Press.

Cross, William and Jean-Benoit Pilet, eds. 2015. *The Politics of Party Leadership: A Cross-National Perspective*. Oxford: Oxford University Press.

Cross, William P. and Richard S. Katz, eds. 2013. *The Challenges of Intra-Party Democracy*. Oxford: Oxford University Press.

Cross, William P., Richard S. Katz and Scott Pruysers, eds. 2018. *The Personalization of Democratic Politics and the Challenge for Political Parties*. Oxford: Oxford University Press.

Cross, William P., Ofer Kenig, Scott Pruysers and Gideon Rahat. 2016. *The Promise and Challenge of Party Primary Elections: A Comparative Perspective*. Montreal/Chicago: McGill-Queen's University Press.

Dahl, Robert A. 1998. *On Democracy*. New Haven, CT: Yale University Press.

Dalton, Russell J. 2014. *Citizen Politics: Public Opinion and Political Parties in Advanced Industrial Democracies*, 6th ed. Washington, DC: CQ Press.

———. 2017. 'Party Representation along Multiple Issue Dimensions'. *Party Politics* 23 (6): 609–23.

Dalton, Russell J., David M. Farrell and Ian McAllister. 2011. *Political Parties and Democratic Linkage: How Parties Organize Democracy*. Oxford: Oxford University Press.

Demker, Marie. 2006. 'Essor et déclin du modèle nordique à cinq partis'. *Revue internationale de politique comparée* 13 (3): 469–82.

Demker, Marie and Lars Svåsand. 2005. *Partiernas århundrade. Fempartimodellens uppgång och fall i Norge och Sverige*. Stockholm: Santérus förlag.

den Ridder, Josje, Joop van Holsteyn and Ruud Koole. 2015. 'Party Membership in the Netherlands'. In *Party Members and Activists*, edited by Anika Gauja and Emilie van Haute. London: Routledge.

———. 2019. 'Something for Everyone? Political Parties, Party Members and Representation in the Netherlands'. In *Do Parties Still Represent?* edited by Knut Heidar and Bram Wauters. London: Routledge.

Downs, Anthony. 1957. *An Economic Theory of Democracy*. New York: Harper and Row Publishers.

Duverger, Maurice. (1954) 1972. *Political Parties: Their Organization and Activity in the Modern State*. London: Methuen.

Epstein, Leon D. 1967. *Political Parties in Western Democracies*. New York: Frederick A. Praeger.

Esaiasson, Peter and Knut Heidar, eds. 2000. *Beyond Westminster and Congress: The Nordic Experience*. Columbus: Ohio State University Press.

Faucher, Florence. 2015. 'New Forms of Political Participation: Changing Demands or Changing Opportunities to Participate in Political Parties?' *Comparative European Politics* 13: 409–59.

Gallagher, Michael and Michael Marsh. 2002. *Days of Blue Loyalty: The Politics of Membership of the Fine Gael Party*. Dublin: PSAI.

———. 2004. 'Party Membership in Ireland: The Members of Fine Gael'. *Party Politics* 10 (4): 407–25.

Gauja, Anika. 2015. 'The Construction of Party Membership'. *European Journal of Political Research* 54 (2): 232–48.

Gibson, Rachel K. and Andrea Römmele. 2009. 'Measuring the Professionalization of Political Campaigning'. *Party Politics* 15: 265–93.

Grönlund, Kimmo and Hanna Wass, eds. 2016. *Poliittisen osallistumisen eriytyminen – Eduskuntavaalitutkimus 2015*. Helsinki: Ministry of Justice.

Hansen, Bernhard. 2002. *Party Activism in Denmark*. Aarhus: Politica.

Hansen, Kasper M. and Karina Kosiara-Pedersen. 2017. 'Nordic Voters and Party Systems'. In *Routledge Handbook on Scandinavian Politics*, edited by Peter Nedergaard and Anders Wivel, 114–23. London: Routledge.

Harmel, Robert and John D. Robertson. 1985. 'Formation and Success of New Parties: A Cross National Analysis'. *International Political Science Review* 6 (4): 501–23.

Heidar, Knut. 1994. 'The Polymorphic Nature of Party Membership'. *European Journal of Political Research* 25: 61–86.

———. 2004. 'Parties and Party Systems'. In *Nordic Politics: Comparative Perspectives*, edited by Knut Heidar, 40–59. Oslo: Universitetsforlaget.

Heidar, Knut and Bram Wauters, eds. 2019. *Do Parties Still Represent?* London: Routledge.

Heidar, Knut and Jo Saglie. 2002. *Hva skjer med Partiene?* Oslo: Gyldendal.

———. 2004. 'A Decline of Linkage? Intra-Party Participation in Norway, 1991–2000'. *European Journal of Political Research* 42: 761–86.

Heidar, Knut and Karina Kosiara-Pedersen. 2006. 'Party Feminism: Gender Gaps within Nordic Political Parties'. *Scandinavian Political Studies* 29 (3): 192–218.

Heidar, Knut and Ruud Koole. 2000. 'Parliamentary Party Groups Compared'. In *Parliamentary Party Groups in European Democracies: Political Parties behind Closed Doors*, edited by Knut Heidar and Ruud Koole, 248–70. London: Routledge.

Heidar, Knut, Anders Jupskås and Marit Kværnenes. 2017. *Partimedlemsundersøkelsen 2016. Dokumentasjonsrapport*. Project Report, Department of Political Science, University of Oslo.

Heidar, Knut, Karina Kosiara-Pedersen and Jo Saglie. 2012. 'Party Change and Party Member Participation in Denmark and Norway'. In *Democracy, Elections and Political Parties: Essays in Honor of Jørgen Elklit*, edited by Jens Blom-Hansen, Christoffer Green-Pedersen and Svend-Erik Skaaning, 155–63. Aarhus: Politica.

Hooghe, Marc and Ann-Kristin Kölln. 2018. 'Types of Party Affiliation and the Multi-Speed Party: What Kind of Party Support Is Functionally Equivalent to Party Membership?' *Party Politics*. Online first. https://doi.org/10.1177/1354068818794220.

Ignazi, Piero. 2018. 'The Four Knights of Intra-Party Democracy: A Rescue for Party Delegitimation'. *Party Politics*. Online first. https://doi.org/10.1177/1354068818754599.

Inglehart, Ronald. 1977. *The Silent Revolution*. Princeton, NJ: Princeton University Press.

Jónsson, G. 2014. 'Iceland and the Nordic Model of Consensus Democracy'. *Scandinavian Journal of History* 39 (4): 510–28.

Jungar, Ann-Cathrine and Anders Ravik Jupskås. 2014. 'Populist Radical Right Parties in the Nordic Region: A New and Distinct Party Family?' *Scandinavian Political Studies* 37: 215–38.

Katz, Richard S. and Peter Mair, eds. 1994. *How Parties Organize: Change and Adaptation in Party Organizations in Western Democracies*. London: SAGE.

———. 1995. 'Changing Models of Party Organization and Party Democracy: The Emergence of the Cartel Party'. *Party Politics* 1: 5–28.

———. 2009. 'The Cartel Party Thesis: A Restatement'. *Perspectives on Politics* 7: 753–66.

———. 2018. *Democracy and the Cartelization of Political Parties*. Oxford: Oxford University Press.

Katz, Richard S. and William Crotty, eds. 2006. *Handbook of Party Politics*. London: SAGE.

Keipi, Teo, Ilkka Koiranen, Aki Koivula and Arttu Saarinen. 2017. 'A Deeper Look at Party Members: Assessing Members' and Supporters' Social Structure'. *Research on Finnish Society* 10 (2): 166–72.

King, Anthony. 1969. 'Political Parties in Western Democracies: Some Sceptical Reflections'. *Polity* 2 (2): 111–41.

Kirchheimer, Otto. 1966. 'The Transformation of the Western European Party System'. In *Political Parties and Political Development*, edited by Joseph Lapalombara and Myron Weiner, 177–200. Princeton, NJ: Princeton University Press.

Kölln, Ann-Kristin. 2015. 'The Effects of Membership Decline on Party Organisations in Europe'. *European Journal of Political Research* 54 (4): 707–25.

———. 2016. 'Party Membership in Europe: Testing Party-Level Explanations of Decline'. *Party Politics* 22 (4): 465–77.

Kölln, Ann-Kristin and Jonathan Polk. 2015. *2015 Svenske partimedlemsundersökingen. Resultatredovisning*. University of Gothenburg, Department of Political Science. http://pol.gu.se/partiforskningsprogrammet/Forskning+om+partier/partimedlemsundersokning.

———. 2017. 'Emancipated Party Members: Examining Ideological Incongruence within Political Parties'. *Party Politics* 23 (1): 18–29.

Kosiara-Pedersen, Karina. 2011. 'Forandres partimedlemskab af partiernes anvendelse af politisk marketing?' In *Politisk Marketing. Personer, Partier & Praksis*, edited by Sigge Winther Nielsen, 87–105. Copenhagen: Karnov Group.

———. 2015. 'Party Membership in Denmark: Fluctuating Membership Figures and Organizational Stability'. In *Party Members and Activists*, edited by Emilie van Haute and Anika Gauja, 66–83. London: Routledge.

———. 2017. *Demokratiets ildsjæle. Partimedlemmer i Danmark*. Copenhagen: DJØF Publishing.

Kosiara-Pedersen, Karina and Kasper M. Hansen. 2012. *Danske Partimedlemmer – Dokumentationsrapport fra projektet: Moderne Partimedlemmer*. Aarhus, Denmark: Institut for Statskundskab, Københavns Universitet.

Kosiara-Pedersen, K., Susan E. Scarrow and Emilie van Haute. 2017. 'Rules of Engagement? Party Membership Costs, New Forms of Party Affiliation, and Partisan Participation'. In *Organizing Representation: Political Parties, Participation, and Power*, edited by Susan E. Scarrow, Paul D. Webb and Thomas Poguntke, 234–58. Oxford: Oxford University Press.

Krouwel, André. 2006. 'Party Models'. In *Handbook of Party Politics*, edited by Richard S. Katz and William Crotty, 249–69. London: SAGE.

————. 2012. *Party Transformations in European Democracies: Multi-Layered Governance in Europe and Beyond (MLG)*. Albany: State University of New York Press.

Lawson, Kay. 1988. 'When Linkage Fails'. In *When Parties Fail: Emerging Alternative Organizations*, edited by Kay Lawson and Peter Merkl, 13–40. Princeton, NJ: Princeton University Press.

Lipset, Seymour M. and Stein Rokkan. 1967. 'Cleavage Structures, Party Systems, and Voter Alignments: An Introduction'. In *Party Systems and Voter Alignments*, edited by Seymour M. Lipset and Stein Rokkan, 1–64. New York/London: Free Press.

Lisi, Marco, ed. 2018. *Party System Change, the European Crisis and the State of Democracy*. London: Routledge.

Michels, Robert. (1911) 1962. *Political Parties: A Sociological Study of the Oligarchic Tendencies of Modern Democracies*. New York: Free Press.

Neumann, Sigmund. 1956. *Modern Political Parties: Approaches to Comparative Politics*. Chicago: Chicago University Press.

Önnudóttir, Eva H. and Ágústa Edda Björnsdóttir. 2014. *Icelandic National Election Study (ICENES) 2013 Election: Sample Design and Data Collection Report*. http://fel.hi.is/sites/fel.hi.is/files/islenska_kosningarannsoknin/ICENESSecondrelease/2014/ICENES_2013/icenes_2013_design_report_english.pdf.

Panebianco, Angelo. 1988. *Political Parties: Organization and Power*. Cambridge: Cambridge University Press.

Pedersen, Karina. 2003. *Party Membership Linkage: The Danish Case*. Department of Political Science: University of Copenhagen.

Pedersen, Karina and Jo Saglie. 2005. 'New Technology in Ageing Parties: Internet Use in Danish and Norwegian Parties'. *Party Politics* 11 (3): 359–77. doi: 10.1177/1354068805051782.

Pedersen, Karina, Lars Bille, Roger Buch Jensen, Jørgen Elklit, Bernard Hansen and H. J. Nielsen. 2004. 'Sleeping or Active Partners? Danish Party Members at the Turn of the Millennium'. *Party Politics* 10 (4): 367–84.

Petersson, O. 1991. *Nordisk Politik*. Stockholm: Allmänna förlaget.

Pitkin, Hanna Fenichel. 1967. *The Concept of Representation*. Berkeley: University of California Press.

Poguntke, Thomas, Susan E. Scarrow, Paul D. Webb, Elin H. Allern, Nicholas Aylott, Ingrid van Biezen, Enrico Calossi, Marina Costa Lobo, William P. Cross, Kris Deschouwer et al. 2016. 'Party Rules, Party Resources and the Politics of Parliamentary Democracies: How Parties Organize in the 21st Century'. *Party Politics* 22 (6): 661–78.

Putnam, Robert D. 2000. *Bowling Alone*. New York: Touchstone.

Rahat, Gideon and Ofer Kenig. 2018. *From Party Politics to Personalized Politics? Party Change and Political Personalization in Democracies*. Oxford: Oxford University Press.

Sandri, Giulia, Antonella Seddone and Fulvio Venturino. 2015. *Party Primaries in Comparative Perspective: Party Primaries in Comparative Perspective*. Farnham: Ashgate.

Sartori, Giovanni. 1976. *Parties and Party Systems: A Framework for Analysis*. Cambridge: Cambridge University Press.

Scarrow, Susan E. 2015. *Beyond Party Members: Changing Approaches to Partisan Mobilization*. Oxford: Oxford University Press.

Scarrow, Susan E., Paul Webb and Thomas Poguntke, eds. 2017. *Organizing Political Parties: Representation, Participation, and Power*. Oxford: Oxford University Press.

Schattschneider, E. E. 1942. *Party Government*. New York: Rinehart.

Schumacher, Gijs and Nathalie Giger. 2017. 'Do Leadership Parties Change More?' *Journal of Elections, Public Opinion and Parties* 28 (3): 349–60.

Schumpeter, Joseph. 1942. *Capitalism, Socialism and Democracy.* New York: Harper & Row.

Seyd, Patrick and Paul Whiteley. 1992. *Labour's Grass Roots: The Politics of Party Membership.* Oxford: Clarendon Press.

———. 2002. *New Labour's Grassroots: The Transformation of the Labour Party Membership.* Basingstoke: Palgrave Macmillan.

Stubager, Rune, Kasper Møller Hansen and Jørgen Goul Andersen. 2013. *Krisevalg – Økonomien og folketingsvalget 2011.* Copenhagen: Dansk Jurist-og Økonomforbundets Forlag.

Tavits, Margit. 2006. 'Party System Change: Testing a Model of New Party Entry'. *Party Politics* 12 (1): 99–119.

Tryggvason, Per Oleskog and Per Hedberg. 2015. *Swedish National Election Studies Program Method Report: Super Election Edition.* Report 2015:02 Swedish National Election Studies Program, Department of Political Science, University of Gothenburg.

van Biezen, Ingrid and Petr Kopecký. 2017. 'The Paradox of Party Funding: The Limited Impact of State Subsidies on Party Membership'. In *Organizing Political Parties: Representation, Participation, and Power*, edited by Susan E. Scarrow, Paul D. Webb and Thomas Poguntke, 84–105. Oxford: Oxford University Press.

van Biezen, Ingrid and Thomas Poguntke. 2014. 'The Decline of Membership-Based Politics'. *Party Politics* 20 (2): 205–14.

van Biezen, Ingrid, Peter Mair and Thomas Poguntke. 2012. 'Going, Going, . . . Gone? The Decline of Party Membership in Contemporary Europe'. *European Journal of Political Research* 51: 24–56.

van Haute, Emilie and Anika Gauja, eds. 2015. *Party Members and Activists.* London: Routledge.

Webb, Paul, Monica Poletti and Tim Bale. 2017. 'So Who Really Does the Donkey Work in "Multi-Speed Membership Parties"? Comparing the Election Campaign Activity of Party Members and Party Supporters'. *Electoral Studies* 46 (1): 64–74.

Whiteley, Paul and Patrick Seyd. 1998. 'The Dynamics of Party Activism in Britain: A Spiral of Demobilization?' *British Journal of Political Science* 28 (1): 113–37.

Whiteley, Paul, Patrick Seyd and Jeremy Richardson. 1994. *True Blues: The Politics of Conservative Party Membership.* Oxford: Clarendon Press.

Widfeldt, Anders. 1999. *Linking Parties with People? Party Membership in Sweden 1960–1994.* Aldershot: Ashgate.

Wright, William. 1971. 'Comparative Party Models: Rational-Efficient and Party Democracy'. In *A Comparative Study of Party Organization*, edited by William Wright, 17–54. Columbus: Merrill.

Appendix

Table A1.1.   English and original party names.

	ENGLISH NAME	ORIGINAL NAME, ABBREVIATION
Denmark	Social Democrats	Socialdemokratiet, S
	Danish People's Party	Dansk Folkeparti, DF
	Social Liberal Party	Radikale Venstre, RV
	Socialist People's Party	Socialistisk Folkeparti, SF
	Red-Green Alliance	Enhedslisten, EL
	Liberal Alliance	Liberal Alliance, LA
	Conservatives	Konservativt Folkeparti, KF
	Liberals	Venstre, V
	Christian Democrats	Kristendemokraterne, KD
Iceland[i]	Progressive Party	Framsóknarflokkurinn, B
	Independence Party	Sjálfstæðisflokkurinn, D
	Social Democratic Alliance	Samfylkingin, S
	Left Green Movement	Vinstrihreyfingin – grænt framboð, V
	Bright Future	Björt framtíð, A
	Pirate Party	Píratar, P
Finland	Left Alliance	Vasemmistoliitto, Vas.
	Social Democratic Party of Finland	Suomen sosiaalidemokraattinen puolue, SDP
	Green League	Vihreä liitto, Vih.
	Centre Party	Suomen Keskusta, Kesk.
	The Finns	Perussuomalaiset, PS
	National Coalition Party	Kansallinen kokoomus, Kok.
Norway	Socialist Left Party	Sosialistisk Venstreparti, SV
	Labour Party	Arbeiderpartiet, Ap

(*Continued*)

Table A1.1.   (Continued)

	ENGLISH NAME	ORIGINAL NAME, ABBREVIATION
	Green Party	Miljøpartiet de Grønne, MDG
	Centre Party	Senterpartiet, Sp
	Christian Democratic Party	Kristelig Folkeparti, KrF
	Liberal Party	Venstre, V
	Conservative Party	Høyre, H
	Progress Party	Fremskrittspartiet, FrP
Sweden	Left Party	Vänsterpartiet, V
	Social Democrats	Socialdemokraterna, S
	Green Party	Miljöpartiet – de gröna, Mp
	Feminist Initiative	Feministiskt Initiativ, FI
	Christian Democrats	Kristdemokraterna, KD
	Centre Party	Centerpartiet, C
	Liberal People's Party	Folkpartiet/Liberalerna, Fp/Lib
	Moderate Party	Moderaterna, M
	Sweden Democrats	Sverigedemokraterna, SD

Note: The parties have one official list letter (listabókstafur), which is the letter voters mark when they wish to vote for them. This is the letter in the table. This is not necessarily the most commonly used abbreviation of their name. Thus, Framsóknarflokkurinn is usually Frams.; Sjálfstæðisflokkurinn, Sj. or Sjálf.; Samfylkingin, Sf.; Vinstrihreyfingin grænt framboð, VG; and Píratar, P.

I

REACH

Party Membership and Member Recruitment

2

Nordic Party Membership Trends

Niklas Bolin, Karina Kosiara-Pedersen
and Gunnar Helgi Kristinsson

The general trend of overall decline in party membership is massively supported by empirical research (Mair and van Biezen 2001; van Biezen, Mair and Poguntke 2012; van Haute, Paulis and Sierens 2017; Whiteley 2011). At the turn of the century, Mair and van Biezen were already arguing that 'parties in contemporary Europe are rapidly losing their capacity to engage citizens' (2001, 5).

The number of members a party has is not as significant as it was in the heyday of the mass parties (Duverger 1964). As argued by van Biezen, Mair and Poguntke, 'Membership has now reached such a low ebb that it may no longer constitute a relevant indicator of organizational capacity' (2012, 24). The strength of party organizations is determined not by membership figures but by finances, staff and other measures (Webb and Keith 2017). In addition, parties reach out to society not only through members but also through other types of affiliates (Faucher 2015; Gauja 2015; Kosiara-Pedersen, Scarrow and van Haute 2017).

However, membership figures are still relevant for membership linkage as the number of members indicates parties' reach within civil society. The more members a party has, the larger its base for participatory linkage. It is not possible to set an absolute level above which parties provide participatory linkage. But a party with a high membership figure could be argued to provide more participatory linkage than parties with lower figures. In addition, we have witnessed parties without traditional party members, such as the Dutch Partij voor de Vrijheid and the Swiss Lega dei Ticinesi (Mazzoleni and Voerman 2017), which are not providing any membership linkage; hence, there is a minimum.

Mere membership figures are insufficient to provide linkage, as argued in chapter 1 and elaborated upon in the remaining chapters. However, they provide a base for participatory party linkage, and the purpose of this chapter is to map and explain the level and change in Nordic party membership figures.

We first sketch out our expectations on membership developments, and then we present the measures and data applied. In the following four sections, we first uncover variations in party membership over time across the five Nordic countries, including a small section devoted to the exceptionalism of the Icelandic parties. In the second part of the analysis, we consider how membership development varies across party families. The third part is devoted to analyses of differences across old and new parties, and the fourth briefly discusses the issue of government and opposition parties. We finish with a conclusion and a short discussion of new forms of party affiliation.

THE DYNAMICS OF MEMBERSHIP CHANGE

In the following, we discuss what we could expect from an empirical assessment of variations among the Nordic countries, across party families and between old and new parties.[1]

The aggregate membership figures at the level of each country show the extent to which the party channel as such is able to mobilize the electorate. Cross-country differences in political culture, democratic development, party system and so forth may explain variations in party membership, such as variations that have been found in membership developments between small and large systems as well as new and old ones (Mair and van Biezen 2001; van Biezen, Mair and Poguntke 2012; Weldon 2006). However, given that our sample of countries, perhaps with the small exception of Iceland, resembles a most similar system design, we refrain from generating any explicit expectations about country-level variations. We expect that parties in general have witnessed a decrease in membership numbers, but we have no a priori expectation about variations across countries.

We focus mainly on variation at the party level. One problem with the broad generalizations of the declining party membership trend is that aggregate country figures may not reveal underlying variations within systems, across party types or from one juncture to another, for example (Kölln 2016; Kosiara-Pedersen 2013). When membership decline is studied primarily at the country level, it may not adequately reflect the causal mechanisms at work.

During the heyday of mass party membership organizations, in the early postwar era, Duverger (1964) presented the European mass party as the typically modern form of party organization, brought on by universal suffrage and the central role of parties in electoral competition. He suggested that the socialist model of party organizations was sufficiently effective in electoral competition to bring about 'contagion from the left', whereby middle class, centre-right parties would imitate their left-wing competitors. This would lead to the predominance of mass party structures in developed democracies. Duverger's study laid the foundation for subsequent research into party organization.

His work, nonetheless, attracted criticism from American scholars such as Epstein (1980), who suggested that party organizations might develop in different directions depending on the specific contexts in different democratic systems. In particular, the European and American traditions differ in regard to party members; the US parties may be seen as 'empty vessels' (Katz and Kolodny 1994). Successive models of party organizations, such as the catch-all, electoral-professional and cartel parties, have since undermined the central place of the membership organization in party theory as parties are believed to have become more leadership-controlled, professionalized and dependent on state subsidies (Katz and Mair 1995; Kirchheimer 1966; Panebianco 1988).

Parties' organizational change also changes the incentives for potential members to enrol as well as for party members' participation and involvement. The growing professionalization of politics and political marketing tools have reduced parties' need for ordinary members for campaigning (e.g. Farrell and Webb 2000; Katz and Mair 1994) and communication (Whiteley 2011). Instead of relying on members to perform voluntary campaign work, such as door-to-door canvassing and leaflet delivering, parties increasingly pay professionals. New technologies enable the party leadership to skip the detour through members and aim directly at communication with the voters. At the same time, development in the media system has given voters several channels of information besides the classic party-controlled newspapers. This implies that parties are no longer the main source of information about society and politics. In other words, not only have parties' incentives to keep members decreased, members' incentives to enrol or stay have also become weaker.

Parties differ to the extent to which they encourage party membership (Scarrow 1996). The institutional path, party principles and ideology matter for how parties organize their membership organizations. Parties to the left of centre have generally been more likely than parties to the right of centre to emphasize participatory democracy and encourage enrolment by granting party members more influence on important decisions (Bolin et al. 2017). This would imply that left-of-centre parties should have larger membership organizations than their counterparts to the right.

In regard to change over time, however, there might be slightly different processes at play. Shortly after Lipset and Rokkan (1967) had noted that the party systems of the 1960s appeared in most cases to reflect the cleavage structures of the 1920s, the first cracks appeared in the frozen party landscapes where new concerns provided the impetus for new types of mobilization (Dalton 1996; Inglehart 1977; Mudde 2004). This was starkly apparent in the Danish and Norwegian landslide elections of 1973. The traditional bonds between parties and social groups waned, and in some cases, new alignments were created. Volatility increased, and the looser bonds between social groups and parties made joining a political party less of a natural thing to do. This trend has been accelerating as parties increasingly distance themselves from citizens and turn to the state as their main provider of resources. According to the cartel party thesis (Katz and Mair 1995), parties are likely to rely less on the membership and more on a professional organization and financial resources for campaigning. This makes parties more dependent on the state and less dependent on members.

The defrosting of the frozen party system has had a larger impact on the classical mass parties created by, and firmly based in, the traditional economic cleavage structures, such as the social democratic and agrarian parties, than parties with other roots, such as the liberals. Hence, while parties based on the cleavages originating in the Industrial Revolution, primarily those to the left, are expected to show relatively high party membership numbers, they are also expected to have lost members to a higher degree than other parties.

As previous research suggests, the lifespans of parties may matter (Pedersen 1982) as do their levels of institutionalization (Harmel and Svåsand 1993), hence, we derive expectations pertaining to the age of parties. The differences between older and newer parties may reflect the relative attractiveness of parties across generations. Older parties existed in an age with close links between class and party, and where party membership was one of the few channels for political participation between elections. Newer parties cater to different social groups. They are formed in an age where new cleavages gain increased attention at the expense of old and established ones (Inglehart 1977). Ties between social groups and parties have been cut. A smaller proportion of the electorate is engaged in manual labour or primary industry, and secularization and polarization on religious issues have undermined the support of liberal and conservative parties. Other issues attract the attention of many voters, including immigration and the environment. Hence, the political agenda, and thereby the issues around which parties mobilize, has changed.

Party organizations are likely to undergo life-cycle transformations, where they are more reliant on party members in the formation stage than later, when institutionalization has set in more fully. Old and established parties are less dependent on ordinary party members than they used to be for effective electioneering, and their organizational strategies may therefore focus on different things, such as obtaining state subsidies or other financial support as well as colonizing the public sector in strategically important areas (Kölln 2016; Kopecký, Mair and Spirova 2012). However, new parties may also have access to at least some of these resources. In the Nordic countries, public financing is not favourable to the established parties but is provided on the basis of votes (Bolin 2012; Pedersen 2004). While the context is to some extent similar for established and new parties, new parties are not expected to have the kind of access to external funding that the classic mass parties – with their ties to employee, business or agrarian interest organizations – have. In addition, due to the norm of membership parties, new parties may also need to run some kind of membership organization for legitimacy reasons.

To sum up, we explore party membership trends in the five countries, in the party families (see chapter 1) and across old and newer parties. We do not have expectations about country differences, but in regard to differences among parties, we expect, first, the traditional mass parties that played a role when the party systems were formed on the basis of the traditional cleavages, in particular the social democrats and agrarians, to enrol a larger share of the electorate than other parties. Second, we expect that older parties more generally will enrol more members than newer parties. Even though the historic advantage may wane, the classic mass parties are expected still to have the upper hand. However, the advantage only concerns their rate of mobilization. Concerning the trends, we expect older parties to be in decline and newer parties to have a modest increase.

MEASURES OF PARTY MEMBERSHIP AND DATA

Before turning to the presentation and analyses of membership figures, we address four methodological issues. First, one of the problems in assessing membership developments is that membership may mean different things in different parties and may vary across time. Members may be counted in different ways or not be counted at all with any kind of precision. All Scandinavian parties enrol individual members. However, some have also enrolled members collectively through links with ancillary organizations. The invention of different types of membership and ancillary organizations is by no means new (Duverger 1964, 107; Scarrow 2015). In the Nordic countries, collective membership and separate youth and women's organizations have always played a large role. In the Swedish Social Democratic Party, collective membership provided around three-quarters of the membership for a long time, while in the Norwegian Labour Party, it had already begun to decline during the 1950s, standing at 59 per cent in 1963 (Elvander 1980; Widfeldt 1999). The organizational relationship between parties and unions continued to weaken, although at a different phase, and by the 1990s, it had reached a point where formal collective membership was completely phased out, although important contacts remained, especially in Sweden (Allern, Aylott and Christiansen 2007). The Icelandic Social Democratic Party was always much weaker organizationally than its Scandinavian counterparts. Although it was formed with an indirect structure by the labour unions in 1916, the social democratic leadership of the unions was strongly challenged by both communists and conservatives in the 1930s, and organizational ties were severed in 1940–1942. Even though we would prefer to include only individual members, we have to rely on the available data.

The second point to make is that we rely on data on the five Nordic countries in the MAPP data set. This covers 397 parties in 31 countries between 1945 and 2014 (cf. van Haute, Paulis and Sierens 2017).[2] In order to be as up to date as possible, we have collected data for additional years for the Nordic parties.[3] The data are mainly collected from the parties. Different methods of estimating membership may yield different outcomes (Ponce and Scarrow 2016; Scarrow 2015). However, according to Scarrow and Gezgor (2010), the difference between survey data and party data is not great. In some cases, however, it may be considerable. An example of this seems to be Iceland, where party figures seem less reliable than survey data. In the Icelandic parties there were no formal records of members, or only rather inaccurate ones since parties relied extensively on informal networks and patronage rather than internal party democracy (Kristinsson 1991). The absence of formal rights and duties associated with membership eased the way in Iceland for the development of open, or partially open, primaries from around 1970. The open primaries had the effect of boosting party membership figures, as candidates made major efforts to mobilize supporters and draw them to the polls. For comparability, in this chapter, we rely on the MAPP data on Iceland dating back to the early 1980s rather than survey material.

Third, dependent on the research question, once a membership figure is available there are several ways in which it can be presented. The absolute number of members provides a good measure for the actual number of heads that parties may count on as potential candidates and campaign activists (see chapters 7 and 8 in this volume). However, when comparing over time and across countries, it does not take into consideration what share of potential members parties are enrolling. The member/voter (M/V) ratio is an adequate assessment of the share of party supporters a party is able to enrol, but this measure is too sensitive to fluctuations in electoral support. Hence, when assessing the *membership density*, we rely on the most conventional measure, which is the member/electorate (M/E) ratio. Due to the slow changes in the size of the electorate, this provides a more stable measure of changes in membership density. The downside is that a small party with a low M/E ratio may provide a highly effective channel of communication for its few voters, that is, the M/V ratio may be high even if the M/E ratio is low. However, the M/E ratio enables comparison across countries of various sizes, as we do here.

Finally, parties are included in the analysis from the time their membership figures are available. However, once included, the figures are 'smoothed' where real data are missing between two points in time. This may create minor errors in cases where data are missing, but overall the reporting should be fairly accurate. 'Smoothing', however, requires two data points, which means that our coverage is limited to the latest date for which we have actual entries.

PARTY MEMBERSHIP OVER TIME
ACROSS THE NORDIC COUNTRIES

Studies show that in an international comparison, the Nordic countries have an average or above-average M/E ratio, although the details vary according to measurement method (Poguntke et al. 2016; Scarrow 2015; van Biezen, Mair and Poguntke 2012; Whiteley 2011). For example, van Biezen, Mair and Poguntke (2012) find in their study of twenty-seven countries that while Finland scores well above average (third highest M/E ratio), Norway (ninth place), Denmark (thirteenth place) and Sweden (fourteenth place) are all average performers. In the Political Party Database project as presented in Webb and Keith (2017), another recent study based on data collected from the parties, the Scandinavian countries score roughly in the middle. In the comparison of eighteenth countries, Norway (fifth place) scores a somewhat higher M/E ratio than Denmark (seventh place) and Sweden (eighth place). Although the overall pattern holds, data from survey-based studies show slightly different results. Whiteley (2011), for example, using data from the ISSP survey of 2004, finds that among thirty-six countries, Norway has the highest M/E ratio (sixth place), followed by Sweden (thirteenth place), Finland (eighteenth place) and Denmark (twentieth place).

However, even if at an (above) average level in a European comparison, the aggregate long-term trend in the northern part of Europe is also that of decline. Figure 2.1 shows the long-term trends in M/E ratios in Denmark, Finland, Norway and Sweden. During the early postwar period, party organizations were strongest in Denmark, with close to 30 per cent of the electorate belonging to political parties; however, only Danish data cover all major parties. Denmark shows the most stable long-term decline in party membership over the whole period, ending at below 5 per cent after the turn of the century. Due to their large share of aggregate membership, the steady decline of the Danish Social Democratic membership organization since around 1950 has been the driving force behind this development. The decline was also significant for agrarian Liberals, and from around 1970 also the Conservatives, that is, for all three established parties.

The Finnish membership organizations gained strength at a fast rate during the early post–Second World War years, reaching close to 20 per cent of the electorate during the 1960s. Since then there has been a slow and steady rate of decline ending at about 5 per cent in the late 2010s. The organizational mobilization of the agrarian Centre Party played a large role in the growth in membership figures in the early postwar period, while in recent decades all traditional parties have lost members.

Party membership figures in Norway only include Labour and the Conservatives in the early period, while the figures from 1957 on include all of the major parties. By the late 1950s Labour's membership had begun to decline while that of the

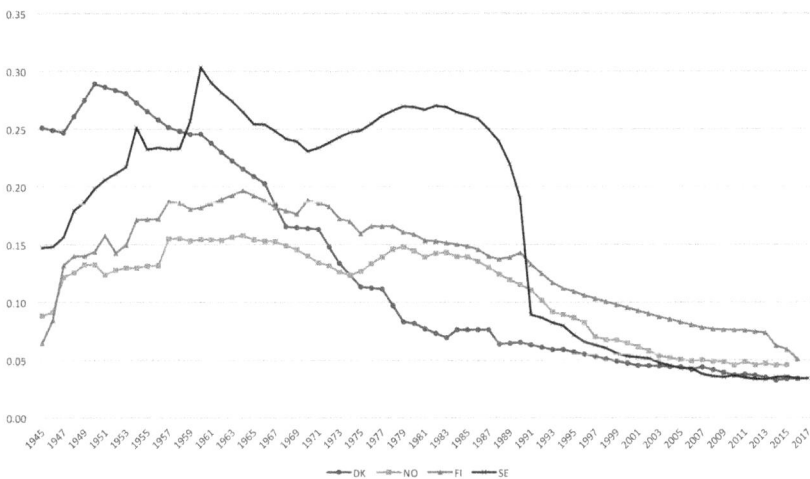

Figure 2.1. Member/electorate ratios across the Nordic countries 1945–2017.

Conservatives was still increasing. This indicates a certain amount of mobilization within the non-socialist electorate. Since the 1980s, membership of all established parties has declined. Figure 2.1 shows, however, that this trend has not continued after the turn of the century, and both Labour and Conservatives have actually increased their membership slightly in recent years.

The early figures for Sweden are mainly based on membership figures for the Social Democrats and Conservatives. The membership of both parties was growing at that time. In 1960, other parties were added. Despite ups and downs for individual parties, the overall trend was stable until around 1990. The year 1991 marks a turning point since at that time the formal organizational ties between the Social Democrats and labour movement were discontinued (Allern, Aylott and Christiansen 2007), leading to a marked decline in membership figures.

No data exist on membership in the Icelandic parties prior to the 1980s. This is partly because the parties were secretive about their members while at the same time inquisitive concerning members of their competitors in a system where patronage rewards were closely associated with party affiliation (Kristinsson 1996). Moreover, their membership records – to the extent that they existed at all – were incomplete or misleading. Membership rights and duties were not well defined. The introduction of the primaries from around 1970 may actually have helped bring some order to the membership records. The primaries are also likely to have helped to mobilize party supporters and bring them into the party fold. Thus, Icelandic parties have a much higher proportion of the electorate enrolled than parties in other Nordic countries.

In figure 2.2, we reach the period (since 1982) where we are able to include Iceland. The trend in Iceland stands out in stark contrast to that of the other

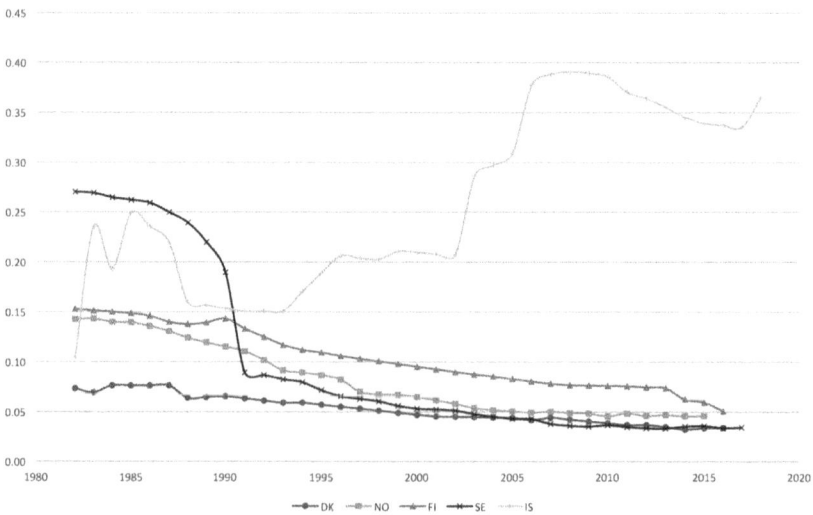

Figure 2.2.   Member/electorate ratios in the Nordic region 1982–2018.

countries. While the Icelandic mobilization rate in the first part of the period lies within the levels of the other countries, the Icelandic trend since 1990 has been an increase, moderately at first and then more marked since 2002. As for the remaining four countries, the trend is clearly a decline. For almost twenty years, the three Scandinavian countries have had quite similar M/E ratios in a slowly declining trend from just above to just under 5 per cent. The trend in Finland has been similar, although the decline took place at a slightly higher level of membership until the late 2010s.

In sum, the M/E ratios of Norway, Finland and Sweden rose until around 1960, and while Norway and Finland followed the same declining trend after that, the Swedish ratios remained stable until 1990, when they declined drastically. The Danish trend is a bit different, with a sharper decline starting a little earlier. During the early postwar period, it seems that the three Scandinavian countries may have had the strongest membership organizations. However, when all that is said, it is important to note that the reliability of membership data from these times can be questioned. Not only are there gaps in coverage but subsequent corrections of figures may account for part of the trends. What remains certain is that all four of the larger Nordic countries enrolled similar, but markedly smaller, proportions of the electorate after the turn of the century than Iceland.

What Explains the Icelandic Exception?

Before continuing the analysis of membership trends across different groups of parties, we will focus on the Icelandic parties a little longer. They contradict the general trend not only among the Nordic neighbours but also among other established democracies (van Biezen, Mair and Poguntke 2012; van Haute, Paulis and Sierens 2017). Party membership figures according to official party statistics have fluctuated between 20 and 40 per cent of the electorate in recent decades, while the Icelandic Election Study shows that between 16 and 30 per cent of respondents self-report to be members of political parties in the same period (Kristinsson 2010). The proportion of party members is uniquely high compared to that of other parliamentary democracies, no matter which figure is taken as a more valid indicator.

To a certain extent, Icelandic exceptionalism reflects kinship with the US parties as well as their Scandinavian counterparts. Thus, the mass party model never set roots in Icelandic party politics to the extent that it did in Scandinavia, especially not among the parties on the centre-right. The Icelandic conservatives and agrarians in many respects continued operating a caucus-style party organization despite the formal adoption of mass party statutes in the interwar period. Power remained with the parliamentary groups and personal networks of parliamentarians, while the formal rights and duties of party members remained vague. To this day, only 40 per cent of those claiming to be party members report paying membership fees, and less than one-third have attended at least two meetings in the previous year (figures from 2013 election study). Membership in the parties is in this sense inexpensive and may not mean the same thing as in the other four Nordic countries.

Even more important may be the primaries, which were introduced with varying degrees of inclusiveness during the 1970s. Introducing relatively open competitions for places on party lists at a time when the power of party elites was increasingly being brought into question had an enormous appeal among voters. It was an incredible mobilizing power for the parties. Although adherents of traditional notions of party democracy are in some cases sceptical concerning their effects on party stability, party managers in general do not doubt the role of primaries in expanding party membership.

In figure 2.3, we compare self-reported membership to self-reported voting in the primaries. In this case, we use self-reported membership because of a denser availability of data and comparability to voting in primaries. In most cases, there is close correspondence between party membership and voting in primaries. The early primaries in some cases created problems of party cohesion and may even have contributed to party splits. However, adaptations of the election formula and the growing practice of making party enrolment a precondition for voting have reduced the risks for the parties (Indriðason and Kristinsson 2015). The level of party cohesion in parliament is generally similar to that in the other Nordic countries (Kristinsson 2011). Candidates in party primaries, however, need financial backing, and money has considerable mobilizing power. Hence, the greatest problem associated with the primaries, which remains to some extent unresolved, is how to deal with political finance in a credible and legitimate manner.

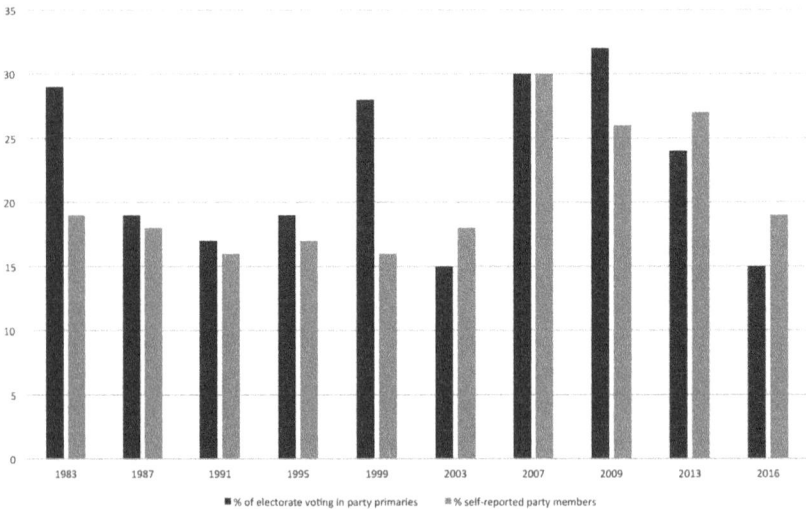

Figure 2.3. Participation in party primaries and self-reported membership of political parties in Iceland 1983–2016.

PARTY FAMILIES

Party families are based on ideology, and we expect party families towards the left to be more inclined towards enrolling members than right-of-centre party families. However, there is another factor to include, namely, the age of party families. Older parties are expected to be in decline and newer parties are expected to grow. Figure 2.4 shows the M/E ratio of party members on average per party family (as operationalized in chapter 1) in the Nordic countries from 1945 to 2015 (see table 2.1 for data on membership by party).

The membership of social democratic parties (Sd) in the Nordic region was growing until around 1980, although developments differed between countries. The Danish party has been characterized by a slow but steady decline, and the same may be said of its Norwegian counterpart, although the decline there was more uneven and seems to have halted after the turn of the century. The Finnish and Icelandic figures are more uneven and display patterns of different trends at different times. But a crucial decline evident in figure 2.4 is due to the development of the Swedish, and to a lesser extent the Norwegian, membership organizations around 1990. Prior to this, the Norwegian and Swedish parties had collective membership (joint membership of unions and party), and the declining membership is due to the decoupling of these organizational ties. In particular, the decision of the Swedish Social Democrats to make all membership individual had a major impact on their membership in 1991, which fell from 840,000 to 260,000 members. Hence, this marked change is not related to voters' decision on whether or not to join but instead to an organizational issue, which nevertheless determines M/E ratios.

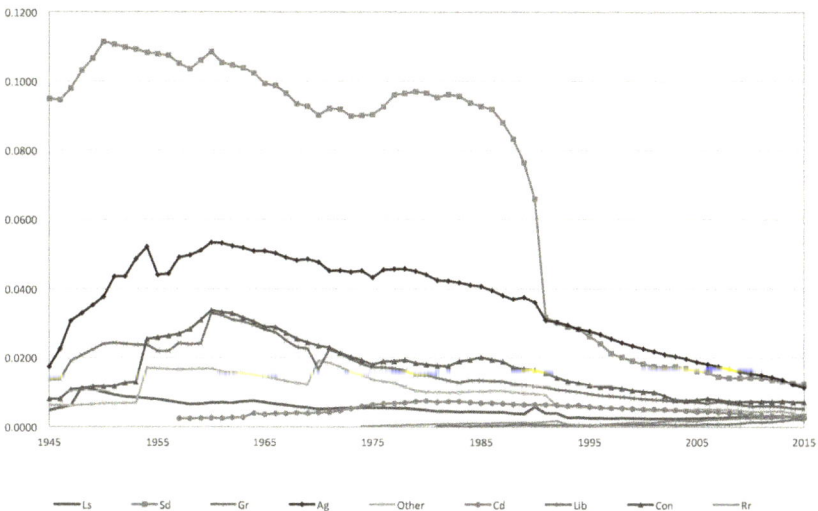

Figure 2.4. Member/electorate ratios on average per party family in the Nordic countries 1945–2015.

Like the social democrats, the agrarians (Ag) during the interwar and early postwar period benefited from close relations between the interest organizations of farmers and their parties. Formal organizational ties, however, did not exist in the period displayed in figure 2.4. Declining numbers in agriculture (i.e. fewer farmers) limited the pool of potential members and inevitably had an impact on party membership. Despite their attempts to appeal to a broader electorate, the rural communities in many respects remain the most vital source of agrarian parties. The downward trend displayed in figure 2.3 is most strongly influenced by a decline in membership of the Finnish and Swedish parties, which always had the largest number of members in absolute terms.

Although the conservative parties (Con) were undoubtedly well represented in employers' organizations throughout the Nordic region, the latter are unlikely to have provided a basis for massive membership recruitment on a scale similar to the social democratic or agrarian parties. Whereas those parties depended on the 'mass' of members and their dues, conservative parties have been able to link to a smaller pool of more well-off party supporters. Conservative membership figures, nonetheless, indicate a recruitment drive in the early postwar period, reaching its zenith at some point in the 1960s or 1970s, which is later than the social democratic and agrarian parties. Then the decline hit the conservatives as well. The Icelandic Independence Party is an exception, with a steadily growing membership from the time data are available in the 1980s from around 25,000 to 50,000 members after the turn of the century.

Liberal parties (Lib) to some extent display a pattern similar to that of the conservatives, with a growing number of party members in the early postwar period but a steady decline after that. By far the strongest liberal party in membership terms is the Danish Liberals, Venstre, which has strong agrarian roots, but its membership development is fairly typical for liberal parties in the region as a whole.

The left socialist parties (Ls) displayed in figure 2.4 are a mixed bag, some of them with a communist past and others reflecting newer trends on the far left. The former have in general declined, while the latter display some capacity for increased membership recruitment. In the case of the Left Party in Sweden (formerly the Left Party Communists), the two go together in the sense that long-term decline after 1960 was followed by a steep increase in the 2010s.

The Christian democratic parties (Cd) in the Nordic region are in many ways different from the large mainstream Christian democrats in Europe, expressing a strong Protestant concern with growing secularization and challenge to traditional religious values. They gained strength during the 1960s and 1970s on political issues like liberalization of abortion and porn in Denmark and the proposal to replace 'Christianity' classes with 'religion' classes in high school in Sweden. Among their organizational resources were undoubtedly networks of Free Church and layman organizations which have existed since the nineteenth century. However, although they have had some political success except in Iceland, they have far from gained the sizes of their 'sister' parties south of the Nordic border. Like most other party families, they have been experiencing long-term membership decline.

Separate green parties (Gr) exist in all the Nordic countries except Iceland (where the Left Greens are generally regarded as more of a left-socialist party than a green party, like the Danish Socialist People's Party). However, the most recent addition – Alternativet in Denmark, which is classified as a green party – is not covered in figure 2.4, having entered parliament only in 2015. The green party family has clearly increased its membership figures in recent decades although the combined number of members remains modest.

Like the green parties, the radical right parties (Rr) show a tendency towards stronger membership organizations, although their total membership figures remain modest. The dive in the early 1990s was caused by dwindling numbers in the Norwegian Progress Party, but the upward trend for the period as a whole remains unmistakable. Furthermore, it could be noted that the Sweden Democrats have increased their membership quite drastically in recent years, reaching more than 25,000 members in the spring of 2018 compared to just 5,000 in 2010.

The 'others' represented in figure 2.4 represent a variety of parties, where the Danish Social Liberals and Swedish People's Party in Finland weigh most heavily. The pattern seems rather typical of other traditional non-socialist parties: growth in the early postwar period followed by a downward trend.

Turning to the more recent trends of the party families, figure 2.5 shows that the trends in 2000 to 2015 are similar across the various party families, with a steady decline except for the greens and radical right. There is a tendency towards convergence of the ratios in two groups: the classic mass parties, social democrats/labour and agrarians, each enrolling around 1.5 per cent of the electorate, and all other party families enrolling less than half of that, mostly half a percentage and less.

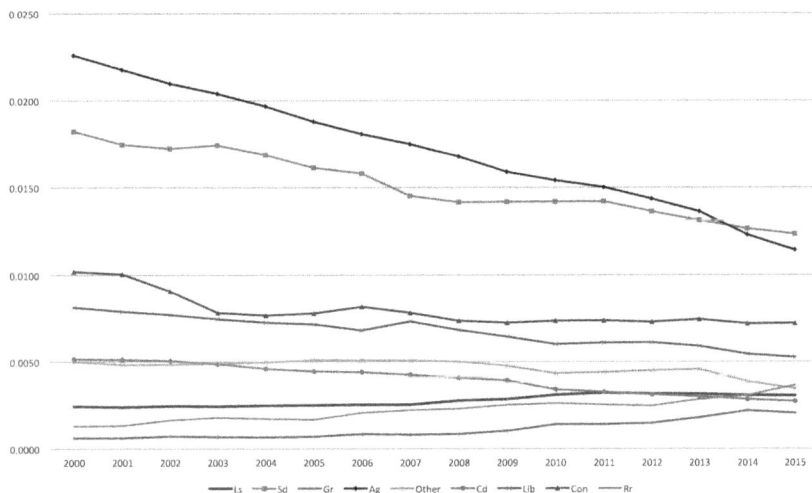

Figure 2.5. Member/electorate ratios of party families 2000–2015.

In sum, whereas the older, traditional party families are in decline, some of the newer party families are experiencing an increase in membership figures. However, the newer parties are not able to make up for the membership decline in the older parties, something we turn to in the next section.

PARTY AGE

Party age appears to be related to membership recruitment in the Nordic parties.[4] Old parties (established before 1960; see chapter 1) have lost members. New parties are gaining members. Figure 2.6 shows that during the early postwar period, old parties were gaining members and the zenith of party membership at this aggregate level was the 1970s and 1980s. Since then there has been a decline in the number of members brought about – judging by our discussion of party types – especially by the dissolution of party-union ties in the Norwegian and Swedish social democratic parties. Since the late 1990s, however, the decline has been more moderate.

New parties have gained members over the past decades despite some fluctuations. This trend is primarily the result of increasing membership of radical right parties and green parties, although in some cases new parties on the far left play a role as well.

Membership ratios of the newer parties are fairly low. They have not been even remotely able to reach the membership levels of the older parties. Hence, established parties' membership losses can in no way be picked up by the younger parties. Party membership is not a common spare-time activity, and there are ample opportunities

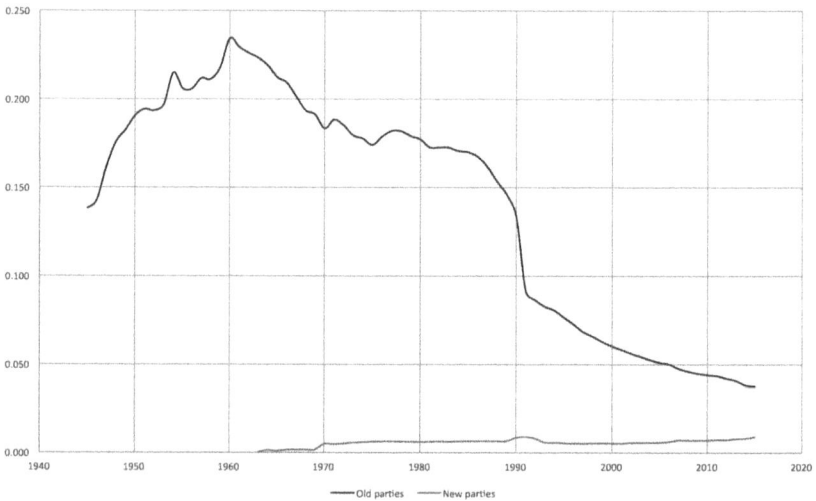

Figure 2.6.   Member/electorate ratios of old and new parties 1945–2015.

for political participation and for influencing political decisions through other channels. Party membership is for a select few.

Old and new parties are converging in the share of party members they enrol. Do we expect that within ten or twenty years, their M/E ratios will be similar? Electorally, the older parties are losing their dominance across party systems. This may be expected at the membership level as well, at least in the longer run. Members who enrolled in the older parties back in the heralded 'golden days of membership parties' when party membership was more common are leaving their parties or are simply dying out. Even though it will be a little while before these members are gone, the enrolment situation is otherwise quite similar for older and newer parties. While older parties may have the advantage of experience and an established organization, newer parties may easily organize in a way that takes current trends into consideration. For example, newer parties may not to the same extent build local chapters across the country in order to be present for potential members. Members enrol via the website, and parties may stay in contact with them from the central office, possibly until membership reaches a sufficient number to warrant a local branch. Or parties may simply choose to establish 'cyber branches' (Scarrow 2015) or organize in networks rather than in geographically based branches (Heidar and Saglie 2002). Hence, newer parties may to a larger extent cater to current demands from potential members, whereas older parties may be stuck with 'yesterday's organization'.

GOVERNMENT AND OPPOSITION

We are not able to systematically address differences and similarities across government and opposition parties. The quality of the data and in some cases irregular reporting of membership figures make systematic evaluations difficult, especially in cases of short-lived governments. Furthermore, since the older and established parties take on government responsibility to a larger extent than newer and smaller parties, the trend will be that government parties have more members than opposition parties. However, anecdotal evidence surely supports that government participation and loss of ministerial offices both may cause party members to enrol in or exit their parties.

A recent case of interest is the rather drastic membership loss of the Swedish Greens during their first term in government from 2014 to 2018. Supposedly due to a combination of internal turmoil and dissatisfaction with how the party leadership was forced to compromise with some of the party's core ideas, the Greens' membership fell from about 20,000 in 2014 to about 10,000 in 2017. In a similar vein, the Danish Socialist People's Party lost a substantial number of members during and following their first, and short, government participation in 2011 to 2013. In Norway, memberships declined for the Socialist Left Party (SV) in their period in government from 2005 to 2013, and for the Progress Party (FrP) in 2013–2017 (latest figures) to a small extent. In both parties, this decline seems, in part, to be an effect of governmental responsibilities. After leaving government, the Socialist Left Party has again increased its membership.

However, having to leave the government may also lead to increasing membership figures. For example, the Danish parties ousted from office in 2001 and their parliamentary support parties (the left-of-centre parties) all saw an increase in their membership figures when the Liberals and Conservatives formed a government, which, together with the Danish People's Party, commanded a majority. Similarly, when the Conservative prime minister in 1993 left the Prime Minister's Office to the Social Democrats due to 'Tamilsagen' without calling for a parliamentary election, which would have electorally hurt the Conservatives and increased the electoral support of the Liberals, the Liberals gained members and overtook the Social Democrats as the largest Danish membership party (Kosiara-Pedersen 2017, 17). Devoted Liberal supporters chose party membership when denied the opportunity to go to the polls.

CONCLUSION

Party membership in the Nordic countries, as in most other parts of the Western world, is in decline. Although the data from the early period of this study are less reliable than later data, it seems safe to conclude that the long-term trend for all Scandinavian countries as well as Finland is negative. However, some important deviations underlie this general trend. At the country level, the Icelandic case stands out. While the M/E ratio at the beginning of the 2010s is well below 10 per cent in the rest of the Nordic countries, the Icelandic counterpart is, at least according to some reports, stunningly close to 40 per cent. The explanation for this seems to be mainly due to the primaries but also to the low cost of party membership.

The analysis also reveals that the decline has been more severe for some groups of parties than others. As expected, parties with roots in traditional economic cleavages, such as the social democrats and agrarians, have lost quite large shares of their memberships. In contrast, the green and the radical right party families are generally on the rise. Similarly, as we expected, we also found that the big losses of members during the past decades are primarily an effect of a decrease among the old parties, that is, those that existed before 1960. In contrast, there is an increase in the membership of newer parties. To a large extent, of course, this increase is due to the aforementioned rise in some of the newer party families.

However, the overall picture is that of decline. So, are we quickly approaching a time where party members become extinct? Dues-paying party members organized in local branches with a say on the party manifesto, candidate nomination and party leader selection may become rarer. However, since parties are transforming the way in which they affiliate their supporters, there is no reason to believe that they will not continue to provide some form of channel for political participation. Several newer studies have pointed to how parties, as depicted in the cartel party model more than twenty years ago (Katz and Mair 1995), blur the distinction between members

Table 2.1. Party membership in the Nordic countries, 1950–2015.

PARTY/YEAR	1950	1960	1970	1980	1990	2000	2010	2015
Denmark								
SD	283,907	259,459	177,507	101,387	76,941	53,484	46,052	38,595
RV	30,500	35,000	25,600	10,100	8,000	5,934	7,600	7,000
KF	80,050	108,751	129,195	44,873	36,610	22,128	13,864	10,500
V	201,429	192,629	136,207	94,754	75,224	76,155	44,361	37,060
SF			4,152	4,668	7,903	6,499	17,883	8,475
CD		3,334	1,230	10,440	9,347	6,248	2,445	2,056
DF						6,252	10,186	17,122
EL						1,975	5,111	9,504
LA							2,200	6,000
A								7,000
Norway								
Ap	200,501	165,096	155,254	153,507	128,109	58,768	49,407	57,602
Høyre	53,249	78,193	81,454	118,424	103,061	53,127	26,172	31,285
Sp	36,776	61,750	70,000	53,517	45,000	30,298	16,977	7,501
KrF		30,008	40,744	69,697	56,176	47,864	27,338	22,282
Venstre		25,045	15,195	12,007	11,345	6,552	8,632	8,886
SV			2,865	9,750	10,272	7,428	7,920	8,394
FrP				8,874	15,553	11,824	22,623	15,820
Rødt						1,365	1,846	2,681
MDG						264	1,195	16,673
Finland								
KESK	143,000	253,000	288,000	305,000	277,000	228,670	167,334	139,486
KOK	73,000	78,000	81,000	77,000	68,000	42,555	40,666	39,000
SDP	67,000	43,000	61,000	100,000	82,000	62,780	50,334	41,607
SKDL	68,000	59,000	52,000	45,668	34,000			
SFP		51,000	49,000	42,000	42,000	34,225	29,334	22,940
SKL/KD			3,000	20,000	17,340	14,335	12,666	9,000
SMP			40,000	20,000	21,800			

(continued)

Table 2.1. (continued)

	PARTY/YEAR	1950	1960	1970	1980	1990	2000	2010	2015
	LKP			8,000	7,250	3,500			
	VAS					34,000	13,225	10,000	10,280
	VIHR					600	1,645	4,332	8,000
	PS							4,332	9,320
Sweden	S	722,073	801,068	890,070	1,205,252	837,870	156,233	105,626	96,065
	C	174,000	179,104	182,437	210,364	171,124	57,417	35,130	28,531
	V	46,640	19,834	14,368	18,157	12,279	13,504	11,030	17,217
	M		206,613	123,251	127,735	118,593	76,732	47,338	47,330
	FP		89,528	77,131	50,553	40,416	20,665	18,100	14,264
	KD			14,587	22,041	25,369	24,005	22,382	21,118
	MP					7,600	6,918	15,544	16,738
	SD							5,846	23,117
	NyD								
Iceland	IP					22,500	33,000	500,00	47,550
	F					5,140	8,545	13,424	12,294
	VG						500	5,796	5,364
	Frj						700		
	Sf							20,328	15,806
	Pir								1,832

and supporters and supplement their party memberships with other kinds of affiliates (Faucher 2015; Gauja 2015; Kosiara-Pedersen, Scarrow and van Haute 2017). Among the Nordic countries, the Icelandic parties stand out. However, the new, green, left-wing Danish party, Alternativet, is also experimenting with other kinds of party attachment (Kosiara-Pedersen and Kristiansen 2016), as are the pirate parties.

The blurring of the distinction between members and supporters, in particular if there is decision-making power involved, may not be popular among traditional rank-and-file members. However, new research points out that it may be advantageous for parties as they may affiliate a larger number when opening up to other kinds of affiliation, even if the number of traditional party members will be smaller (Kosiara-Pedersen, Scarrow and van Haute 2017). Furthermore, there are indications that supporters 'enrolling' when there are smaller costs are more representative of party voters than when costs are high, as with some forms of traditional party membership (Achury et al. 2018). Transferring these results to the Nordic countries, not only do the Icelandic parties have more members, but they are also expected to have more representative members, something that will be returned to in chapter 4 of this volume.

In sum, the party membership figures, while providing an important aspect of how parties provide participatory linkage, by no means tell the whole story. Why members enrol, who they are, how representative they are and how they participate are essential questions to respond to in assessing the character of parties' linkage, and these are the themes for the remaining chapters of this book.

NOTES

1. Thanks to Lára Hrönn Hlynsdóttir, University of Iceland, for research assistance with the data set.

2. See http://www.projectmapp.eu/ for more on the data and other party member surveys.

3. Data for Norway go to 2015, whereas data for Denmark and Finland go to 2016. For Sweden, we have also collected data for 2017, and new data for Iceland were collected from the parties in 2018.

4. Having considered different ways of operationalizing party age, we settled for the simple measure of dividing parties into pre- and post-1960. This reflects the partial thawing of frozen cleavages, which began in the 1960s, and the emergence of new concerns among the electorate. While such a definition inevitably suffers from some degree of arbitrariness, we take comfort in the fact that this specific cut-off point has repeatedly been applied in research on new parties (Bolin 2012; Harmel and Robertson 1985; Tavits 2006).

BIBLIOGRAPHY

Achury, Susan, Susan E. Scarrow, Karina Kosiara-Pedersen and Emilie van Haute. 2018. 'The Consequences of Membership Incentives: Do Greater Political Benefits Attract Different Kinds of Members?' *Party Politics*. doi: 10.1177/1354068818754603.

Allern, Elin Haugsgjerd, Nicholas Aylott and Flemming Juul Christiansen. 2007. 'Social Democrats and Trade Unions in Scandinavia: The Decline and Persistence of Institutional Relationships'. *European Journal of Political Research* 46 (5): 607–35. doi: 10.1111/j.1475–6765.2007.00706.x.

Bolin, Niklas. 2012. *Målsättning riksdagen. Ett aktörsperspektiv på nya partiers inträde i det nationella parlamentet.* Umeå: Umeå universitet.

Bolin, Niklas, Nicholas Aylott, Benjamin von dem Berge and Thomas Poguntke. 2017. 'Patterns of Intra-Party Democracy around the World'. In *Organizing Representation: Political Parties, Participation, and Power*, edited by Susan Scarrow, Paul Webb and Thomas Poguntke, 158–84. Oxford: Oxford University Press.

Dalton, Russell J. 1996. 'Political Cleavages, Issues, and Electoral Change'. In *Comparing Democracies: Elections and Voting in Global Perspective*, edited by Lawrence LeDuc, Richard G. Niemi and Pippa Norris, 319–42. Thousand Oaks, CA: SAGE.

Duverger, Maurice. 1964. *Political Parties: Their Organization and Activity in the Modern State.* London: Methuen.

Elvander, Nils. 1980. *Skandinavisk arbetarrörelse.* Stockholm: Liber.

Epstein, Leon. 1980. *Political Parties in Western Democracies.* New Brunswick: Transaction Books.

Farrell, David M. and Paul Webb. 2000. 'Political Parties as Campaign Organizations'. In *Parties without Partisans: Political Change in Advanced Industrial Democracies*, edited by Russell J. Dalton and Martin P. Wattenberg, 102–28. Oxford: Oxford University Press.

Faucher, Florence. 2015. 'New Forms of Political Participation: Changing Demands or Changing Opportunities to Participate in Political Parties?' *Comparative European Politics* 13 (4): 405–29. doi: 10.1057/cep.2013.31.

Gauja, Anika. 2015. 'The Construction of Party Membership'. *European Journal of Political Research* 54 (2): 232–48. doi: 10.1111/1475–6765.12078.

Harmel, Robert and John D. Robertson. 1985. 'Formation and Success of New Parties: A Cross-National Analysis'. *International Political Science Review* 6 (4): 501–23.

Harmel, Robert and Lars Svåsand. 1993. 'Party Leadership and Party Institutionalisation: Three Phases of Development'. *West European Politics* 16 (2): 67–88.

Heidar, Knut and Jo Saglie. 2002. *Hva skjer med partiene?* Oslo: Gyldendal.

Indriðason, Indriði H. and Gunnar Helgi Kristinsson. 2015. 'Primary Consequences: The Effects of Candidate Selection through Party Primaries in Iceland'. *Party Politics* 21 (4): 565–76. doi: 10.1177/1354068813487117.

Inglehart, Ronald. 1977. *The Silent Revolution.* Princeton, NJ: Princeton University Press.

Katz, Richard S. and Peter Mair, eds. 1994. *How Parties Organize: Change and Adaptation in Party Organizations in Western Democracies.* London: SAGE.

———. 1995. 'Changing Models of Party Organization and Party Democracy: The Emergence of the Cartel Party'. *Party Politics* 1 (1): 5–28.

Katz, Richard S. and Robin Kolodny. 1994. 'Party Organization as an Empty Vessel: Parties in American Politics'. In *How Parties Organize: Change and Adaptation in Party Organizations in Western Democracies*, edited by Richard S. Katz and Peter Mair, 23–50. London: SAGE.

Kirchheimer, Otto. 1966. 'The Transformation of the Western European Party Systems'. In *Political Parties and Political Development*, edited by Joseph LaPalombara and Myron Weiner, 177–200. Princeton, NJ: Princeton University Press.

Kölln, Ann-Kristin. 2016. 'Party Membership in Europe: Testing Party-Level Explanations of Decline'. *Party Politics* 22 (4): 465–77. doi: 10.1177/1354068814550432.

Kopecký, Petr, Peter Mair and Maria Spirova, eds. 2012. *Party Patronage and Party Government in European Democracies*. Oxford: Oxford University Press.

Kosiara-Pedersen, Karina. 2013. 'Party Membership in Denmark'. In *Parteien ohne Mitglieder?*, edited by Ulrich von Alemann, Martin Morlok and Tim Spier, 205–20. Baden-Baden: Nomos Verlagsgesellschaft mbH & Co. KG. (Schriften zum Parteienrecht und zur Parteienforschung; Nr. 46).

———. 2017. *Demokratiets ildsjæle – Partimedlemmer i Danmark*. Copenhagen: Djøf Publishing.

Kosiara-Pedersen, Karina and A. M. Kristiansen. 2016. 'Alternativt partimedlemskab'. In *Statskundskab i praksis. Klassiske teorier og moderne problemer*, edited by Karina Kosiara-Pedersen, Gustav Nedergaard and Emil Lobe Suenson, 33–49. Copenhagen: Karnov Group.

Kosiara-Pedersen, Karina, Susan E. Scarrow and Emilie van Haute. 2017. 'Rules of Engagement? Party Membership Costs, New Forms of Party Affiliation, and Partisan Participation'. In *Organizing Political Parties: Representation, Participation, and Power*, edited by Susan E. Scarrow, Paul D. Webb and Thomas Pogunktke, 234–58. Oxford: Oxford University Press.

Kristinsson, Gunnar Helgi. 1991. *Farmers' Parties*. Reykjavík: Social Science Research Institute.

———. 2010. 'The Greatest Number of Party Members? Membership Structures in Icelandic Political Parties'. *The Icelandic Review of Politics and Administration* 6 (2): 123–50.

———. 1996. 'Parties, States and Patronage'. *West European Politics* 19 (3): 433–57.

———. 2011. 'Party Cohesion in the Icelandic Althingi'. *Icelandic Review of Politics and Administration* 7 (2): 73–96.

Lipset, Seymour M. and Stein Rokkan. 1967. 'Cleavage Structures, Party Systems, and Voter Alignments: An Introduction'. In *Party Systems and Voter Alignments*, edited by Seymour M. Lipset and Stein Rokkan, 1–64. New York and London: Free Press.

Mair, Peter and Ingrid van Biezen. 2001. 'Party Membership in Twenty European Democracies, 1980–2000'. *Party Politics* 7 (1): 5–21.

Mazzoleni, Oscar and Gerrit Voerman. 2017. 'Memberless Parties: Beyond the Business-Firm Party Model?' *Party Politics* 23 (6): 783–92. doi: 10.1177/1354068815627398.

Mudde, Cas. 2004. 'The Populist Zeitgeist'. *Government and Opposition* 39 (4): 542–63.

Panebianco, Angelo. 1988. *Political Parties: Organization & Power*. Cambridge: Cambridge University Press.

Pedersen, Karina. 2004. 'From Aggregation to Cartel? The Danish Case'. In *How Political Parties Respond: Interest Aggregation Revisited*, edited by Kay Lawson and Thomas Pogunktke, 86–104. London and New York: Routledge.

Pedersen, Mogens N. 1982. 'Towards a New Typology of Party Lifespans and Minor Parties'. *Scandinavian Political Studies* 5 (1): 1–16.

Pogunktke, Thomas, Susan E. Scarrow, Paul D. Webb, Elin H. Allern, Nicholas Aylott, Ingrid van Biezen, Enrico Calossi, Marina Costa Lobo, William P Cross, Kris Deschouwer et al. 2016. 'Party Rules, Party Resources and the Politics of Parliamentary Democracies: How Parties Organize in the 21st Century'. *Party Politics* 22 (6): 661–78. doi: 10.1177/1354068816662493.

Ponce, Aldo F. and Susan E. Scarrow. 2016. 'Which Members? Using Cross-National Surveys to Study Party Membership'. *Party Politics* 22 (6): 679–90. doi: 10.1177/1354068814550435.

Scarrow, Susan E. 1996. *Parties and Their Members: Organizing for Victory in Britain and Germany*. Oxford: Oxford University Press.

———. 2015. *Beyond Party Members: Changing Approaches to Partisan Mobilization*. Oxford: Oxford University Press.

Scarrow, Susan E. and Burcu Gezgor. 2010. 'Declining Memberships, Changing Members? European Political Party Members in a New Era'. *Party Politics* 16 (6): 823–43. doi: 10.1177/1354068809346078.

Tavits, Margit. 2006. 'Party System Change: Testing a Model of New Party Entry'. *Party Politics* 12 (1): 99–119.

van Biezen, Ingrid, Peter Mair and Thomas Poguntke. 2012. 'Going, Going, . . . Gone? The Decline of Party Membership in Contemporary Europe'. *European Journal of Political Research* 51 (1): 24–56.

van Haute, Emilie, Emilien Paulis and Vivien Sierens. 2017. 'Assessing Party Membership Figures: The Mapp Dataset'. *European Political Science*. doi: 10.1057/s41304–016–0098-z.

Webb, Paul D. and Dan Keith. 2017. 'Assessing the Strength of Party Organizational Resources: A Survey of the Evidence from the Political Party Database'. In *Organizing Political Parties: Representation, Participation, and Power*, edited by Susan E. Scarrow, Paul D. Webb and Thomas Pogunktke, 31–61. Oxford: Oxford University Press.

Weldon, Steven. 2006. 'Downsize My Polity? The Impact of Size on Party Membership and Member Activism'. *Party Politics* 12 (4): 467–81. doi: 10.1177/1354068806064729.

Whiteley, Paul F. 2011. 'Is the Party Over? The Decline of Party Activism and Membership across the Democratic World'. *Party Politics* 17 (1): 21–44. doi: 10.1177/1354068810365505.

Widfeldt, Anders. 1999. *Linking Parties with People? Party Membership in Sweden, 1960–1997*. Aldershot: Ashgate.

3

Why Do Members Join Parties?

Knut Heidar and Karina Kosiara-Pedersen

The stable cleavage systems of postwar Europe have been gradually undermined by demographic and social changes as well as changes in the media systems (Dalton 2014; Karvonen and Kuhnle 2001). More education, affluence and social mobility have changed political behaviour and attitudes. Critical journalism and the new social media have increased public access to varied political information. Other channels of participation have emerged. Political participation is less stable than it was during the period of 'frozen cleavages' in the 1950s and 1960s. People look for the political involvement that suits their interests and offers the best opportunities – in parties, ad hoc action committees, social movements, online communities and so on. The bonds between social classes and parties have weakened, new parties have emerged and voters have become more volatile.

In order to adjust to these conditions for party membership, parties have adapted their organizational and political strategies for recruiting members and sympathizers. This is reflected in the variety of analytical party models found in the literature. The 'mass party' model (Duverger [1954] 1972) emphasized the role of party members, while the later 'catch-all', 'cartel', 'business-firm' and 'entrepreneurial' parties all appear less focused on the members (e.g. Katz 2017; Krouwel 2006). We can safely assume that the social and political reasons for joining socialist and Christian parties in the interwar period were different from today's (Panebianco 1988; von Beyme 1985). Group identities have declined and individual life projects have become more important. Some argue that the 'personalization of collective action' has been given momentum by new digital media (Bennet and Segerberg 2011). Several parties have individualized party member rights and duties, and some have opened up opportunities for other kinds of affiliation than traditional party membership (Faucher 2015; Gauja 2015; Gibson 2015; Scarrow 2015).

In spite of the 'decline of parties' perspective emerging from studies of membership figures, and the now quite low member/electorate ratios, people still sign up for traditional
membership. Why? Do party members today enrol to spend hours handing out flyers,
attend meetings, participate in debates, take part in recruitment drives and canvass in
their neighbourhoods at election times? Do they enrol with the intention of running for
office or to gain favours? Are they becoming members to meet interesting people, to support democracy and to fight for what they believe in? Or is it quite simply 'a family affair'?

In this chapter, we examine the 'why' question from the individual perspective.[1]
We analyse motivations for enrolment as expressed by party members themselves.
The study is based on party member surveys conducted in Denmark (2012), Sweden (2015) and Norway (2017).[2] First, we briefly discuss likely reasons for joining
a political organization as suggested in the literature. Most researchers base their
analysis on a general typology, looking at political, material and social motivations
for party membership. This will also be our guide here. In the second part, we look
at some background factors that may influence the motivation to join, specifically,
the age when enrolling, member cohort and former party membership. Third, we
analyse members' motivations to see if these differ among countries, party families
and membership generations. Fourth, we look more closely at the extent to which
the social milieu, in particular family, matters for enrolment. Finally, we conclude.

WHY JOIN A POLITICAL PARTY?
Some Expectations

Max Weber noted that there are two basic motives for entering into politics: ideology and material rewards, and that these can operate in combination (Weber 1958).
However, political activists are rarely drawn to politics by one of these factors alone
(von Beyme 1985, 168–75). Hence, James Q. Wilson's (1973) modern classic in the
literature on motives for joining political organizations expands this simple Weberian
model. Wilson's typology combines rational-choice incentives and social psychology
rewards, and it includes four major types of incentives for membership:

1. Material: This includes all rewards that come with a price, such as a job, increased salary or preferential treatment in public services.
2. Specific solidary incentives: Rewards that are enjoyed in a social setting and
   are not available to everyone, like holding public office, receiving invitations
   to exclusive social gatherings and so on.
3. Collective solidary incentives: Rewards that are accessible to all party members,
   like party gatherings, working with others, group identity and so on.
4. Purposive incentive: Working for a common goal, for example, ideological,
   issue-specific goals or a specific 'way of life'.

Scholars have elaborated on the motivating factors (e.g. see von Beyme 1985,
168–75). Richard Katz has written an influential article on the costs and benefits of

party membership (Katz 1990, 154–56). He argued that, on the benefit side, party members could gain political influence, preferential treatment, material benefits, inside information and social and psychic rewards, while the cost side included membership fees and the use of time. In an effort to summarize both rationalistic and socio-psychological motives for party activities, Patrick Seyd and Paul Whiteley (1992) developed a fine-tuned version of different motivations, labelled the 'general incentives theory'. Here they targeted 'selective and collective incentives, group motivations, and affective or expressive motives' (Whiteley and Seyd 2002, 56). This kind of analysis has previously been done on the Danish 2000 data (Hansen 2002).

In this chapter, we study the individual supply side of party member recruitment. Our focus is on the members' *individual* motivations, and our aim is to show the reasons for enrolment as expressed by the party members themselves.[3] Hence, we base our analysis on the Weber-Wilson tradition; we distinguish between political, ideological, social, career and 'passive support' motivations for party membership.

What does previous research tell us about the role of political, social and material incentives for party membership? In a European context, research shows the importance of *political* motives when people join a party (den Ridder, van Holsteyn and Koole 2015; Heidar 2006, 304–35, 2015; van Haute and Gauja 2015). New members join to fight for specific political interests or for a particular ideological perspective (Gallagher and March 2002; Heidar and Saglie 2003; Seyd and Whiteley 1992). *The social influence* from family, friends and colleagues is also important. A study of the Italian Socialist Party in the 1960s showed that about one-third of the members gave this reason for their membership (Barnes 1967). A study of Swedish adolescents found that the development of political interest, which we can assume triggers participation, was influenced both by friends and family, but with family as the strongest and most lasting influence (Shehata and Amnå 2017). Similarly, turnout 'runs in the family' (Dahlgaard 2017). The Norwegian 1991 and 2000 member surveys showed that one in seven listed the social factor (family and network) as the most important (Heidar and Saglie 2003, 778). A comparative analysis of membership in political organizations based on population data concluded that contextual forces were important and that the Scandinavian (and Northern European) countries were characterized by 'extensive but fundamentally passive memberships' (Morales 2009, 63).

On the basis of these previous research results, *we expect that party members give ideology/politics as their most important motivation, but also that influence from their social environment is important, whereas they score low on material incentives. Passive memberships are also frequent.*

Party families have different historical backgrounds. There are likely differences in motivations between members of the traditional, larger mass parties, with a history of local presence and government participation (social democrats, agrarians and conservatives) compared to the members enrolled in small and fairly new parties with more specific ideological platforms (like the left socialists, the greens and possibly the small liberal parties). The large mass parties have traditionally had a strong local presence and closer links with specific social groups. These were often governing parties that controlled public goods and were therefore better able to deliver on material benefits such as positions in public office.

Hence, on this basis, *we expect that ideology is more important in the new niche parties than in the old mass parties, whereas the opposite is the case with social and material incentives.*

On the other hand, a recent, wide-ranging comparative study on the character of party organizations concludes that the difference between individual parties is large, and that party family and country are less important (Webb, Poguntke and Scarrow 2017, ch.13). The specific party factors' will to some extent override the effect of national context and party family background. Differences in national contexts and their party systems are at any rate small in the Scandinavian countries (cf. chapter 1).

We therefore expect large variations among individual parties, variations that cannot be attributed to party family or country but are products of the parties' particular histories.

MEMBER ENROLMENT:
Age, Political Generations And Party Switchers

Member surveys in Denmark, Norway and Sweden give us the data needed to analyse why members join. As in many chapters in this book, cross-country analyses are limited by the differences in the content and timing of the surveys. There are about four years between the Danish and the Norwegian surveys (2012 vs. 2016–2017), and during these years, memberships' political contexts could change, possibly flavouring the responses. Hence, we proceed with caution. However, some of the issues discussed – like age – do not depend much on political context.

Before discussing members' motives for joining, we describe three aspects of the flow of members into the parties since these concern the timing and context of enrolment as well. At what age did the members join? Youth are generally considered more sensitive to ideology than middle-aged and older people. In what decade did they sign up as members? The 1970s is often seen as the decade of a new, rebellious, 'flower-power' generation. Finally, had they been members of any other party before joining? May we assume that party membership is part of the new political volatility? In other words, what kind of social and political experiences did the members bring with them into the parties?

Age

Parties may recruit and organize members of all ages. However, in regard to age of enrolment, it is worth noting parties' particular efforts to bring in the younger generations by organizing youth wings. The odd one out in this regard is Denmark, where parties do not have intra-party youth wings but independent, affiliated political youth organizations. While some choose to enrol in both party and youth

Table 3.1. At what age did Scandinavian party members join their party?*

AGE/COUNTRY	DENMARK	NORWAY	SWEDEN
–29	33	45	33
30–39	24	22	22
40–49	21	16	18
50–	22	17	27
Total	100	100	100

* Weighted figures according to the different parties' share of total number of party members in the country.
Note: Data presented are expressed as percentage.

organizations, these memberships in Denmark are distinct (Kosiara-Pedersen and Harre 2015). Since the Danish youth organizations include some of the potential younger members, we could expect that the share of younger enrolments would be lower in Denmark. In all the Scandinavian countries, however, parties recruit most strongly among the young. As we see in table 3.1, the largest share of members signed up before turning thirty. One-third joined in their teens or in their twenties. Today that would generally mean that many became party members while still in – or fresh from – education and *before* settling down with a job and family.

Parties are not only open to the young, however. We see that one in five joined after turning fifty. Parties recruit new members from different generations. There is a tendency for Norwegian parties to recruit more young people, while the Swedish recruit more from the older cohorts. In the Swedish parties, one in four new members signed up from the fifty-and-up group. These members are disproportionally recruited by the feminist, Christian, liberal and conservative parties, while the traditional left parties are more attractive to the younger cohorts. This could mean that the youth parties are stronger in Norway or that Norwegian parties do not face as strong competition for new members from special-issue groups as in Sweden, but we do not know. The youth movement is generally strong in social democratic parties. However, whether this is more the case in Norway than in Sweden and Denmark is an open question. For the individual parties, some of the older recruits could also be party switchers; an example would be someone who has left an established party as a result of internal disagreements to join a newer one, such as the Swedish Feminist party.

Party Cohorts

In what decades did the members join? The timing of party membership may influence the type and motivations of the new members. The 'rebellious' generation from the 1970s may look different from the 'yuppie' generation of the 1980s and 1990s. Also, the more recently arrived members may be of a different brand compared to the old 'remainers'.

Table 3.2 shows that most Scandinavian party members have joined fairly recently. More than half the membership belongs to the post-2000 cohorts. A party-level

Table 3.2. Decades of members' enrolment.*

AGE/COUNTRY	DENMARK	NORWAY	SWEDEN
–1980s	32	33	27
1990s	16	13	12
2000s	37	19	20
2010s	15	35	41
Total	100	100	100

* Weighted figures. Note: Data presented are expressed as percentage.

analysis (not shown) finds that new and more recently founded parties (not surprisingly) had their highest intake of members in recent years. However, recent intake was also significant for older, radical right parties in Norway and Denmark, as well as left socialist, greens and the Norwegian Liberals (founded and reorganized in the 1970s and 1980s); these parties recruited more than two-thirds of their members after the year 2000.

In some of the parties, many members had signed up more than thirty years ago. This is particularly the case for the old cleavage parties, that is, social democratic, conservative and agrarian parties. These old, well-established parties (with high voting support over time) currently enrol a balanced mix of member cohorts (table on individual parties not shown).

In sum, the party members are a mix of old-timers and a new breed, of experienced people and newcomers. Table 3.2 shows very similar country profiles. The small differences may to some extent be explained by the timing of the surveys. It is unsurprising that the Swedish survey conducted in 2015 includes more members from the 2010s compared to the Danish survey from 2012.

Previous Membership

Electoral volatility is increasing in the Nordic countries (Bengtsson et al. 2013), and even elected parliamentarians at both the municipal and national levels on occasion switch party. The question is to what extent can volatility also be found among party members. Do members switch party? We have data only for Denmark and Norway, but in these countries, the majority of party members had not previously been members of another party. However, there is variation between the parties. In table 3.3, we see a high degree of similarity within several of the party families. The highest share of switchers is found in the Danish left socialist Red-Green Alliance and in the Liberal Alliance, which are, respectively, mergers and splits of existing parties. However, the Norwegian Greens and the radical right parties in both countries also have a high share of members with experience from other parties. Fewer party switchers are found in the old cleavage parties: social democrats, Christians, conservatives and in the Norwegian agrarian and Danish liberal parties.

Table 3.3. Share with previous membership.

	Left Socialist	Social Dem.	Green	Agrarian	Other	Christ. Dem.	Liberal	Conser-vative	Radical Right	All*
Denmark 2012	40/18 **	12	–	–	25 ***	11	13/44 ****	16	26	18
Norway 2017	19	13	29	15	–	10	22	13	29	15

*Weighted; **Enhedslisten/Socialistisk Folkeparti; ***Radikale Venstre; ****Venstre/Liberal Alliance. Note: Data presented are expressed as percentage.

WHY ARE SCANDINAVIAN MEMBERS JOINING PARTIES?

We now turn to the party membership as a whole at the time of the surveys. What reasons do members in the three countries give for their enrolment? A methodological challenge is the fact that the question formulations vary. In Denmark, members were asked to offer up to four reasons for joining. In Norway, the question was about the respondents' most important reason (only one answer possible). The Swedes were asked how important several given reasons had been, and they could answer for each. Moreover, all surveys operated with a fixed set of alternative answers. Table A3.1 (appendix) summarizes the questions, the fixed answers and the methodological choices made.

In table 3.4, at the country level, and in tables 3.5 through 3.7 for the different parties, the reasons for membership are regrouped according to the Wilson typology and standardized to vary between 0 and 100. Our aim has been to make the results as comparable as possible. For the Danish respondents, we did not include alternatives that did not match the relevant categories. For the Swedish members, we only included the 'very important' responses. The percentages ticking off a specific reason in Denmark (on average three) and Sweden ('very important') exceeded 100 in both countries since the respondent could register more than one important motive. We therefore standardize these percentages to sum up to 100. That means that both for Denmark and Sweden, the figures are not the percentage (of members) giving a particular reason for joining, but a weighted measure indicating how important that particular reason was for the members of a particular party. The Norwegian figures are the percentage indicating the fixed motive as the most important.

Political, Social and Material Reasons for Joining

Tables 3.4 through 3.7 all show that the dominant motivation expressed by party members is politics: political issues and ideology. About two-thirds of the members joined their parties primarily for political reasons, and this share is identical across the three countries. Ideology seems more important in Denmark and Norway than in Sweden, where particular political issues count more strongly. Perhaps the political debates – or the potential members – in Sweden are more pragmatic, creating more

Table 3.4. **Scandinavian party members: Reasons for joining the party.***

Country/Reasons	Denmark	Norway	Sweden
Political	17	20	30
Ideological	49	47	38
Social, family, friends and colleagues	14	12	16
Career	5	1	2
Passive, support for democracy	15	15	14
Total	100	95	100

* Weighted and standardized figures. Note: Data presented are expressed as percentage.

interest in policy issues than in ideology. We do not know for certain. However, that the majority of party members join for political reasons is not very surprising. What might be surprising is that a third of the members in political parties actually joined for reasons *other* than political ones.

The remaining third of the responses point to social factors and a motivation to provide general support for the party and for democracy. The social factor, indicated by the importance of family, friends and colleagues, was important for around 15 per cent of the party members. We include those who indicated that membership was 'natural, given my occupational background'. About as many had joined to give general support to the party or, via the party, to democracy. These members had not joined to take part in internal party affairs, run for office or influence policies, but with the intention to signal passive support only.

Material incentives, or the ambition to build a political career, do not come across strongly. In Norway and Sweden, only 1 or 2 per cent give this as a reason for their membership in this way. In Denmark, the figure is 5 per cent. On the one hand, party membership is an unlikely road to wealth, which is apparent from recent studies of patronage, since material gain is not a strong factor in Nordic politics (Allern 2012; Bischoff 2012; Kristinsson 2012). On the other hand, respondents are expected to hesitate to admit to joining the party for career opportunities or material gains – even in an anonymous survey. An affirmative answer is not socially acceptable within the equalitarian Nordic cultures (Graubard 1986). However, even if the figures are deflated, we think they actually do reflect that people by and large do not join parties for career boosting or material benefits. In sum, as expected, party members give ideology and politics as their most important motivation, whereas they score low on material incentives.

Turning to differences across parties and party families, this is shown in tables 3.5 through 3.7. The ideology factor is generally strong in the left socialist, green and Christian parties. Members here join on the basis of a broad 'world view', not only ideology in the traditional sense. The exception among the Christian parties is the Swedish Christian Democrats. This party distinguishes itself by being more of a people's party and less of a (religiously focused) Christian party. The Feminist Initiative Party

Table 3.5. Denmark. Selection of the four most important reasons for joining, 2012.

	Left Socialist		Social Dem.	Other	Christ. Dem.	Liberal		Conservative	Radical Right	All*
	EL	SF	SD	RV	KD	Venstre	LA	KF	DF	
Political issues	13	16	21	17	9	17	10	17	10	17
Ideology	60	50	44	49	63	44	67	46	59	49
Participate in other social party activities	5	5	6	5	2	7	5	7	7	6
Political career opportunities	2	4	5	5	1	6	5	7	6	5
Support for democracy	14	17	14	19	11	15	10	13	14	15
Influence from family	2	4	7	3	6	7	1	6	2	5
Influence from friends	4	4	3	2	8	4	2	4	2	3
Total	100	100	100	100	100	100	100	100	100	100

* Weighted according to party membership strength. N=16,540. Date presented are expressed as weighted and standardized percentages.

Table 3.6. Norway. Most important reason for joining, 2017.

	Left Socialist	Social Dem.	Green	Agrarian	Christ. Dem.	Liberal	Conservative	Radical Right	All*
	SV	Ap	MDG	Sp	KrF	V	H	FrP	
Political issues	20	16	20	28	16	27	22	25	20
Ideology	57	45	51	40	50	41	50	43	47
Org./occupation	5	10	2	9	4	2	2	2	6
Social/family/friends	2	8	2	7	7	4	6	3	6
Political career opportunities	1	1	0	1	2	0	1	1	1
Express passive support	12	14	24	11	17	20	11	23	15
Other	3	6	1	4	4	6	8	3	5
Total	100	100	100	100	100	100	100	100	100

* Weighted. N=2,594. Missing=12. Note: Data presented are expressed as percentage.

Table 3.7. Sweden. Very important reason for joining, 2015.

	Left Socialist	Social Dem.	Green	Other	Christ. Dem.	Liberal	Conservative	All*
	V	S	Mp	F!	KD	Fp/L	M	
Political issues	30	28	31	23	28	32	31	30
Ideology	43	34	45	43	37	38	34	38
Org/occupation	5	11	3	3	3	3	2	5
Social/family/ friends	9	13	10	7	12	12	12	11
Political career opportunities	1	1	2	2	2	2	3	2
Express passive support	12	13	9	22	18	13	18	14
Total	100	100	100	100	100	100	100	100

* Weighted. F! (Feminists) and Liberals are not included in the weighting and are excluded from 'All'. N=9,825–10,282. Missing=110–566. Note: Data presented are expressed as weighted and standardized percentage.

members in Sweden also have a very high score on ideology, as would be expected due to the party's emphasis on feminism.

Motives having to do with occupation, family and friends are categorized as 'social'. Both Norwegian and Swedish social democrats have a particularly high social score. The old 'movement parties' have traditionally recruited from within their socioeconomic cleavage. The same can to some extent be said about the Norwegian agrarian and the Danish liberal parties (the old agrarians). Finally, we note the high level of passive supporters in the Norwegian Greens (founded in 1988). This is a relatively new party, created on the basis of an interest organization for the 'protection of the environment of the future'. This background may have brought a high number of passive members into the new party. Still, this seems to contradict the emphasis on grass-roots democracy often emphasized by green parties themselves (Poguntke 1993).

Overall, there are no striking differences between the three Scandinavian countries. Members in all countries are attracted to the parties for roughly the same reasons. The expectation that politics dominate the horizon of prospective party members is verified. As noted, this is not a stunning discovery, but it contradicts the picture sometimes painted of political activists as careerists primarily looking for material gains. We must of course hold open the possibility that members start out with an interest in politics and then, after climbing the ladder, end up with an interest in a political career. We also, as expected, find that ideology is most important to members joining small niche parties, like the left socialists and the greens. The social factor is important to a number of new members, and we shall probe more into the family side of member recruitment below. Just as common as the social factor is joining in order to signal general (although passive) support for the party or for democracy. These sympathizers increase the external legitimacy of parties in democracies.

Does Party Generation Affect Motivation?

Some members joined years ago, some fairly recently. We expect to find a relationship between party generation and motives for joining due to both the character of the new party generation entering in a particular period and the profiles of members who leave the party. Tables 3.8 through 3.10 show the motivation profiles of party generations at the time of the party member surveys.

There are some differences between party generations, but none are consistent across all the Scandinavian countries. In Sweden, there is virtually no difference in motivation profiles between the party generations. In Norway, we find that the ideological motive is more frequent in the 'oldest' party generations (entering before 1990). In Denmark and Norway, there is also a steady decline in the importance of social factors. This fits the assumption of declining social movement milieus and cleavage politics. However, we are puzzled as to why this is not the case in Sweden. Party generations in Sweden have a stable and high listing of social factors as very important.

Table 3.8. Denmark. Most important reason for joining by party generation. All parties.*

Generation/Motivation	−1979	1980s	1990s	2000s	2010s
Political issues	27	28	28	29	29
Ideology	30	29	29	29	28
Org./occupation	3	3	2	1	0
Social/family/friends	13	10	9	7	6
Career	2	2	4	3	3
Express passive support	26	27	29	32	33
Total	100	100	100	100	100

* Weighted figures. The percentage base is the total number of answers given, not the number of respondents. Note: Data presented are expressed as percentage.

Table 3.9. Norway. Reasons for joining by party generation. All parties, 2017.

Generation/Motivation	−1979	1980s	1990s	2000	2010s
Political issues	19	19	23	20	24
Ideology	56	54	45	46	43
Org./occupation	6	6	10	5	3
Social/family/friends	10	8	3	4	3
Career	0	0	1	1	0
Express passive support	5	10	13	20	22
Other	4	3	5	4	5
Total	100	100	100	100	100

Weighted figures. N=2,530. Missing=9. Note: Data presented are expressed as percentage.

Table 3.10.   Sweden. Most important reason for joining by party generation. All parties.*

Generation/Motivation	−1979	1980s	1990s	2000	2010s
Political issues	30	31	31	31	30
Ideology	35	38	38	37	39
Org./occupation	5	5	5	5	3
Social/family/friends	13	12	12	12	10
Career	1	1	1	2	3
Express passive support	15	13	13	14	14
Total	100	100	100	100	100

* Weighted figures. The percentage base is the total number of answers given, not the number of respondents.
Note: Data presented are expressed as percentage.

Another notable trend in Denmark and Norway, but not in Sweden, is the increase in the share of members enrolling to 'passively support' their party. This is a stronger trend in Norway than in Denmark, but it is difficult to compare cross-country as the figures are sensitive to the questions asked. It is striking that the share of Norwegian members expressing passive support as a main motive increases as we go from generation to generation – from 5 per cent in the pre-1980 generation to 22 per cent among the 2010s. In a supply-side perspective, this could indicate that those party members who remain in the party for a long time did not enrol mainly for passive support. Those who enrolled merely as a token of passive support are more likely to have left the party. In a demand-side perspective, this could also imply that parties today encourage 'passive support' members to a larger extent than they did in the past. Parties don't need members to the same extent that they did in the past in light of the professionalization of party organizations and campaigns, such as the digitalization of membership files, capital-intensive political marketing tools, new channels of direct communication between party elite and electorate and public party financing. In addition, parties may prefer passive members, who provide legitimacy but not the potential programmatic costs of ideologically motivated members (cf. Scarrow 1996). Again, we are not able to explain the Swedish stability in enrolment incentives.

How Important Is the Family?

In the history of modern industrial societies, the notion of individualization is central. Scandinavian citizens today are not part of a collective, a social milieu (locality, class, work sector, religious, cultural networks, etc.) to the same degree as before. It follows that party membership is expected to be more an expression of individual choice than simply a reflection of social environment. Still, we know that family, friends and work colleagues are important for socialization and political beliefs, in particular, the closest of these relations (Bond et al. 2012; Dahlgaard 2017; Hansen 2017; Rolfe 2012; Shehata and Amnå 2017).

The Norwegian and Danish surveys include specific questions on the impact of the social surroundings. The Danish survey asked whether family, friends and colleagues 'close to you' had been members of the party before you joined. The Norwegian survey asked whether any particular social milieu had been important for the members' decision to join. Some differences may be due to these differences in questions, for example, social milieu may be important *even if* the people in this milieu are *not* party members.

Among Danish members, four out of ten responded that family, close friends or colleagues were party members before they joined themselves. In Norway, more than half said that such milieus had been important for their decision to join. This is a strong indication that social milieus weigh heavily for member recruitment. Four out of ten who were recruited to the parties were part of milieus who were much more involved in party work than the general public.

In tables 3.11 and 3.12, we see that the old, cleavage-based parties stand out from the more recently formed ones. The social factor is central in recruitment to the social democratic and Christian parties. In Norway, members of the social democrats, agrarians and Christian democrats listed organizational affiliation as particularly important, reflecting their parties' past as old, movement organizations. More recently organized parties, such as the Liberal Alliance in Denmark and the Greens in Norway, are different in that they have not had the time to build similar supporting milieus. However, there is also a size factor here, as shown in the limited milieu factors found in the also old but smaller Liberals in Norway and the Social Liberals in Denmark.

The importance of family in political socialization is old news. Politically engaged parents, often measured by the political discussions around the dinner table, have an effect on political interest and participation (Shehata and Amnå 2017). Hence, we zoom in on whether one or both parents have been enrolled in a party. Does party membership in Norway and Denmark run in the family? Table 3.13 shows that the answer is yes. The level of party membership in the general population is around 4 to 5 per cent in both countries (see chapter 2), while the share of party members with parents who have been members is 39 and 50 per cent, respectively. Even if party membership in the population is for a specific year, while the parents may have had their membership for a long time, there is obviously a disproportional share of 'party parents' in the member surveys. We may safely assume that the family socialization of new generations of party members is reflected in these figures. Party members pass on party membership to their children. 'Party dynasties' are found not only at the elite levels in the parties but also among party members in general. However, not all children share in this inheritance. Hence, it may be an equally interesting story that around half the party members have not had 'party parents'.

The country averages hide variation among parties. The old 'movement parties' are prone to family recruitment. In Denmark as well as in Norway, the social democrats and the liberals (the old agrarians) score high on family membership. Especially high scores are found among members in the (old) Norwegian Christian and the

Table 3.11. Denmark. Family, friends or colleagues member of your party before you entered? 2012

	Left Socialist		Social Dem.	Other	Christ. Dem.	Liberal	Conservative	Radical Right	All*
	Unity EL	SPPSF	SD	RV	KD	V	KF	DF	
Family, friends or colleagues	42	33	49	25	62	45	36	24	41

*Weighted. N=21,623. Note: Data presented are expressed as percentage.

Table 3.12. Norway. Any social milieu particularly important for joining? 2017

	Left Socialist	Social Dem.	Green	Agrarian	Christ. Dem.	Liberal	Conservative	Radical Right	All*
	SV	Ap	MDG	Sp	KrF	V	H	FrP	
No	36	26	48	28	15	53	39	49	31
Family	13	26	10	24	28	14	18	13	22
Close friends	18	8	12	5	23	7	17	13	13
Work colleagues, schoolmates, etc.	14	13	8	7	5	8	8	5	9
Organizational attachments	8	22	9	21	23	8	11	10	17
Other	11	5	13	15	6	10	7	10	7
Total	100	100	100	100	100	100	100	100	100

* Weighted. N=2,471. Missing=5%. Note: Data presented are expressed as percentage.

Table 3.13. Has either parent been a party member?

	Left Socialist	Social Dem.	Green	Agrarian	Christ. Dem.	Other	Liberal	Conservative	Radical Right	All*
Denmark 2012	37/34**	41	–	–	48	35***	46/23****	36	21	39
Norway 2017	49	51	62	59	63	–	40	48	29	50

*Weighted; **Enhedslisten/Socialistisk Folkeparti; ***Radikale Venstre; ****Venstre/Liberal Alliance. Note: Data presented are expressed as percentage yes answers.

(new) Danish Christian parties. Here, we may see the effect of religion as a part of family culture. The (old) conservative parties are different, with a lower family factor. On the other hand, not all new parties scored low on family background. For example, 62 per cent of the members in the Norwegian Green party report that their parents were also party members. This may reflect the 'old interest-group' recruitment profile noted earlier.

Politically active parents are likely to encourage and trigger political interest and engagement. Membership comes in part through the parental example and is in some measure 'socially inherited'. This perspective must, however, be balanced with the fact that many members (in Denmark the majority them) do not have this family background.

CONCLUSION

The Scandinavian party surveys all had questions on why members joined their party. Based on the literature, we expected political motives – ideological as well as issue interests – to dominate, and that scores for career or material rewards would be low. We also expected ideology to be strongest among members of the small, ideologically based parties. The 'movement parties', which still have a foot in the social cleavage structures, were expected to be more likely to recruit members on a social basis. We also expected family connections to be a strong force for party recruitments.

We found that parties recruit members from all age groups, although the 'under 30s' are most numerous. Still, a substantial group of members also enter the parties after turning 50. In other words, parties are not only attracting the young. We also found a balance in the periodic intake of new members. Today's members reflect that parties recruited members over different decades and that no particular period dominates. Naturally, the most recently recruited members are most strongly represented in the parties.

About one in seven party members has previously been a member of another party in Denmark and Norway. The most recently founded parties have – naturally – a higher share of party switchers, but it would be an exaggeration to say that member volatility is particularly high. The new recruits, however, dominate party membership – at least numerically. The post-2000 intake dominates, except within some movement parties such as the Christians and social democrats. About one in three members in Norway, and three in four in Denmark, had signed up during the last five to seven years.

We found only limited differences across the party generations; the decade of entrance is not decisive for type of motivations given. In Denmark and Norway, party cohorts varied to a limited extent, and in Sweden, the member generations were completely similar. The importance of ideology declined over time in Denmark and Norway, and the inclination to offer passive support increased. On the whole, parties seem to recruit their members on a stable motivational basis. If there is a generational conflict within the parties, this is not due to differences in motivation. It may of course look different when studying the policies proposed by the youth sections within the parties (Kosiara-Pedersen and Harre 2015).

Politics and ideology are the main motivations for roughly two-thirds of the party members. This finding clearly does not support the 'career-seeking' or 'materialist gain' picture sometimes painted of politicians. According to the members, they join both for idealist, expressive reasons as well as for the more instrumental goal of exercising their democratic rights and fighting for particular interests. Ideology is, as expected, most commonly expressed by recruits to the small ideological parties like the left socialists and the greens. All parties also recruit members who signal general support but have no intention to be active. Career building is hardly mentioned by Norwegian and Swedish members, but it is mentioned to some extent in Denmark. But again, this is probably easier to pick up through the Danish questionnaire. Social factors and occupational background do play a part in all countries, and particularly in old movement parties like the Social Democrats in Sweden and Norway and the Norwegian agrarians.

We also look at the importance of social milieus in more detail. Family and friends and the work milieu are considered particularly important by four out of ten members in Denmark and Norway. Memberships do run in families! Half of Norway's party members had parents who were also party members. As shown by Kosiara-Pedersen, parents were not necessarily members of the same party, but an activist political 'gene' was registered in Denmark (Kosiara-Pedersen 2017, ch. 4). Again, this gene is more noticeable in the old, social movement parties than in the more recently formed parties. The family factor appears particularly strong in the Christian parties.

The main message of this chapter is that party members join predominantly for political reasons. Some members join to offer general, non-participatory support. Material or careerist motives are barely registered. Ideology is an important factor for recruitment to the smaller niche parties. Some also join because it is a 'natural thing to do' within their social circles, and particularly within their family. We found that 'movement parties', like the social democrats, the agrarians and the Christians, mobilized members from their old, social and organizational cleavage milieus.

Returning to the question of party linkage (cf. chapter 1), the linkage to civil society through party organizations is primarily an interest-based linkage. But remember that 'interest' here sums up fighting for particular local or national issues as well as seeking to influence party policies. It is political interest that makes most members join, signalling a pragmatic political culture among prospective members. The motivations of party members also indicate a political (bottom-up) linkage, not a careerist (top-down) one. The member cultures emphasize politics, not careers. The members' motivations for enrolment show that linkage to civil society also operates through families and social networks. For the old movement parties (although not all), this linkage works through sectionalized, 'cleavage' milieus. In the next chapters, we discuss whether the motivation for joining parties actually results in better social or political representativity of party members compared to the party voters.

NOTES

1. We would like to thank Tor Gaute Syrstad (MA) for his efficient assistance in analysing the data used in this chapter.

2. See chapter 1, for more information on the surveys.

3. We do not go into the contextual factors that influence and interact with individual motivations to join, although these are – particularly in a broader comparative perspective covering a wider variety of countries – clearly important (Morales 2009).

BIBLIOGRAPHY

Allern, Elin H. 2012. 'Appointments to Public Administration in Norway: No Room for Political Parties'. In *Party Patronage and Party Government in European Democracies*, edited by Petr Kopecky, Peter Mair and Maria Spirova, 272–93. Oxford: Oxford University Press.

Barnes, Samuel H. 1967. *Party Democracy: Politics in an Italian Socialist Federation*. New Haven, CT: Yale University Press.

Bengtsson, Åsa, Kasper M. Hansen, Olafur Th. Hardarson, Hanne Marthe Narud and Henrik Oskarsson. 2013. *The Nordic Voter: Myth and Exceptionalism*. Milton Keynes, UK: ECPR Press.

Bennet, Lance W. and Alexandra Segerberg. 2011. 'Digital Media and the Personalization of Collective Action'. *Information, Communication & Society* 14 (6): 770–99.

Bischoff, Carina S. 2012. 'Party Patronage in Denmark: The Merit State with Politics "On the Side" '. In *Party Patronage and Party Government in European Democracies*, edited by Petr Kopecky, Peter Mair and Maria Spirova, 92–120. Oxford: Oxford University Press.

Bond, Robert M., Christopher J. Fariss, Jason J. Jones, Adam D.I. Kramer, Cameron Marlow, Jaime E. Settle and James H. Fowler. 2012. 'A 61-Million-Person Experiment in Social Influence and Political Mobilization'. *Nature* 489 (7415): 295–98.

Dahlgaard, Jens Olav. 2017. 'It Runs in the Family: How Social Relations within the Household and Family Shape the Decision to Vote'. PhD diss., University of Copenhagen.

Dalton, Russell J. 2014. *Citizen Politics: Public Opinion and Political Parties in Advanced Industrial Democracies*, 6th ed. Los Angeles, CA: SAGE.

den Ridder, Josje, Joop van Holsteyn and Ruud Koole. 2015. 'Party Membership in the Netherlands'. In *Party Members and Activists*, edited by Emilie van Haute and Anika Gauja, 134–50. London: Routledge.

Duverger, Maurice. (1954) 1972. *Political Parties: Their Organization and Activity in the Modern State*. London: Methuen.

Faucher, Florence. 2015. 'New Forms of Political Participation: Changing Demands or Changing Opportunities to Participate in Political Parties'. *Comparative European Politics* 13 (4): 409–59.

Gallagher, Michael and Michael Marsh. 2002. *Days of Blue Loyalty: The Politics of Membership of the Fine Gael Party*. Dublin: PSAI Press.

Gauja, Anika. 2015. 'The Individualization of Party Politics: The Impact of Changing Inter-nal Decision Making on Policy Development and Citizen Engagement'. *The British Journal of Politics & International Relations* 17 (1): 89–105.

Gibson, Rachel K. 2015. 'Party Change, Social Media and the Rise of "Citizen-Initiated" Campaigning'. *Party Politics* 2 (2): 181–97.

Graubard, Stephen Richards. 1986. *Norden: The Passion for Equality*. Oslo: Norwegian University Press.

Hansen, Bernhard. 2002. *Party Activism in Denmark: A Micro Level Approach to a Cross-Sectional Analysis of the Correlates of Party Activism*. Århus: Politica.

Hansen, Jonas Hedegaard. 2017. 'Social Influence, Voter Turnout and Mobilization'. PhD diss., University of Copenhagen.

Heidar, Knut. 2006. 'Party Membership and Participation'. In *The Handbook of Party Politics*, edited by Richard S. Katz and William Crotty, 301–15. London: SAGE.

———. 2015. 'Party Membership in Norway: Declining but Still Viable?' In *Party Members and Activists*, edited by Emilie van Haute and Anika Gauja, 151–68. London: Routledge.

Heidar, Knut and Jo Saglie. 2003. 'A Decline of Linkage? Intra-Party Participation in Norway 1991–2000'. *European Journal of Political Research* 42 (6): 761–86.

Karvonen, Lauri and Stein Kuhnle, eds. 2001. *Party Systems and Voter Alignments: Looking Back, Looking Forward*. London: Routledge.

Katz, Richard S. 1990. 'Party as Linkage: A Vestigial Function?' *European Journal of Political Research* 18: 143–61.

———. 2017. 'Afterword'. In *Organizing Political Parties. Representation, Participation, and Power,* edited by Susan E. Scarrow, Paul D. Webb and Thomas Poguntke, 321–36. Oxford: Oxford University Press.

Kosiara-Pedersen, Karina. 2017. *Demokratiets ildsjæle – Partimedlemmer i Danmark*. København: Djøf Forlag.

Kosiara-Pedersen, Karina and Asmus Harre. 2015. 'Politiske ungdomsorganisationers ild-sjæle'. In *Tag del i fremtiden – en antologi om unges deltagelse i den politiske offentlighed,* edited by J. N. Nielsen, C. Klauber, J. M. Olsen and M. D. Sørensen, 119–72. København: DUF – Dansk Ungdoms Fællesråd.

Kristinsson, Gunnar Helgi. 2012. 'Party Patronage in Iceland: Rewards and Control Appoint-ments'. In *Party Patronage and Party Government in European Democracies*, edited by Petr Kopecky, Peter Mair and Maria Spirova, 186–205. Oxford: Oxford University Press.

Krouwel, André. 2006. 'Party Models'. In *Handbook of Party Politics,* edited by Richard S. Katz and William Crotty, 249–69. London: SAGE.

Morales, Laura. 2009. *Joining Political Organizations: Institution, Mobilisation and Participa-tion in Western Democracies*. Colchester: ECPR Press.

Panebianco, Angelo. 1988. *Political Parties: Organization and Power*. Cambridge: Cambridge University Press.

Poguntke, Thomas. 1993. *Alternative Politics: The German Green Party*. Edinburgh: Edin-burgh University Press.

Rolfe, Meredith 2012. *Voter Turnout: A Social Theory of Political Participation*. Cambridge: Cambridge University Press.

Scarrow, Susan E. 1996. *Parties and their Members*. Oxford University Press.

Scarrow, Susan E. 2015. *Beyond Party Members: Changing Approaches to Partisanx Mobiliza-tion*. Oxford: Oxford University Press.

Seyd, Patrick and Paul Whiteley. 1992. *Labour's Grass Roots: The Politics of Party Membership*. Oxford: Clarendon Press.

Shehata, Adam and Erik Amnå. 2017. 'The Development of Political Interest among Adolescents: A Communication Mediation Approach Using Five Waves of Panel Data'. *Communication Research*, first published online 18 June 2017: 1–13. London: SAGE.

van Haute, Emilie and Anika Gauja, eds. 2015. *Party Members and Activists*. London: Routledge.

von Beyme, Klaus. 1985. *Political Parties in Western Democracies*. Aldershot: Gower.

Webb, Paul D, Thomas Poguntke and Susan E. Scarrow. 2017. 'Conclusion'. In *Organizing Political Parties: Representation, Participation, and Power*, edited by Susan E. Scarrow, Paul D. Webb and Thomas Poguntke, 307–20. Oxford: Oxford University Press.

Weber, Max. 1958. 'Politics as Vocation'. In *From Max Weber: Essays in Sociology*, edited by Hans H. Gerth and C. Wright Mills, 77–128. London: Routledge.

Whiteley, Paul and Patrick Seyd. 2002. *High-Intensity Participation: The Dynamics of Party Activism in Britain*. Ann Arbor: University of Michigan Press.

Wilson, James Q. 1973. *Political Organizations*. New York: Basic Books.

Appendix

Table A3.1. Operationalization of fixed answers for joining a political party.

	DENMARK	NORWAY	SWEDEN
Question:	Why did you enrol in the party (maximum of four reasons)?	Do you remember your most important reason for joining the party?	How important were the following reasons for becoming a member?
Political issues	– party's specific country policies – party's specific local policies – need for a stronger challenge to the other parties – desire for influence on party policies – in order to get more information about politics	– wanted to engage myself in work for certain political issues – to support a specific politician	– a better understanding of politics – meet others with same political preferences – influence party policies locally – influence party policy on a particular issue nationally
Ideology	– party ideology	– had clear ideological beliefs that made it natural for me to join the party	– a belief in what the party stands for
Org.occupation	– influence from trade unions	– active in organizations/ political action groups where party membership became natural	– continue other assignments (trade union, interest organization)

	DENMARK	NORWAY	SWEDEN
		– natural for a person with my occupation	
Social/family/ friends	– influence from work colleagues, from family, from friends – opportunity to participate in other events (culture, etc.)	– attracted by a good social milieu in the party – a family tradition – drawn into the party by close friends	– meet interesting people and broaden my social life – natural in my context – someone asked me (family, friend, colleague)
Political career opportunities	– desire to pursue a political career	– wanted to build a political career	– wanted to have a political career – would help my career
Express passive support	To support: – the party – democracy – the party's local leader/mayor – the party's leader	– just wanted to express (passive) support for the party	– admired the local party leader – admired the national party leader
Counting	The fixed alternative answers included options that did not match the categories used in the Norway and Sweden tables, such as 'information on politics', 'other parties need counter-balancing', 'the party leader', etc. These were excluded from the table. As the respondent could tick off up to four alternatives, these figures have been standardized to add up to 100.	Answers included under 'other': – to increase my political skills and understanding of politics – other	We included only the 'very important' answers in the percentage base. The sum of these percentages exceeded 100 as the respondent could tick off more than one 'very important' answer. These figures have been standardized to add up to 100.

II

REPRESENTATION

Social and Political

4

Who Are the Party Members and Are They Representative of the Party Voters?

Knut Heidar, Gunnar Helgi Kristinsson,
Arttu Saarinen, Aki Koivula and Teo Keipi

Do parties represent their voters? Do parties provide linkages to the electorate through their members? Alternatively, have they become venues dominated by narrow party elites and professional politicians who bear little resemblance to the voters they represent? In this chapter, we look at linkage through a socio-demographic composition of party members.

To study linkage through the party membership organization, we need to map degrees of 'mirroring' for two main reasons.

First, the literature on representation emphasizes that 'descriptive representation' (mirroring) is an important factor contributing to voters' sense of being represented, insofar as they can identify 'their group' in the party. Independent of whether 'their kind' actually pursues 'their policies', this mirroring sustains attachment and acceptance, thereby solidifying legitimacy.

Second, having 'our' experiences reflected among party members increases the likelihood of having 'our' policy interests represented and fought for through the party. In other words, it helps to create 'substantive representation'. Descriptive representation is neither a sufficient nor a necessary precondition for substantive policy representation, but it is likely to promote/enhance such representation.

These two mechanisms make mirroring an important element in representative party linkage, as described in chapter 1. Still, all four elements of linkage (reach, representation, activity, influence) must be studied before we can make conclusions about the extent to which party members provide a democratic linkage between voters and political elites.

This chapter has a dual purpose: first, to describe Nordic party members in terms of their socio-demographic background, and second, to study whether members mirror the voters they represent. We begin with some expectations based on existing studies in this area. We then present our data and methods before studying party profiles and member-voter congruence along several dimensions. First, we analyse the basic demographic profiles in terms of age and gender. Second, we turn to region and religion, cleavages which Lipset and Rokkan (1967) associated with the 'National Revolution' (their term for the emergence of the modern nation state). Third, we move on to assess factors more commonly associated with the socio-economic position as indicated by education and occupation. Finally, in light of the decline in party membership (see chapter 2), we discuss whether party member density (the membership per voter, or Party-Member/Electorate [PM/E] ratio) affects party representativeness, operationalized as member-voter congruence. Together, this should illustrate the socio-democratic linkage, or lack of linkage, provided by Nordic party members.

SOCIO-DEMOGRAPHIC PROFILES
AND REPRESENTATIVENESS

While *socio-demographic* representation is not necessarily the objective of all representation, the presence of specific groups among decision makers is seen as central in the literature. Hannah Pitkin (1967) describes this type of representation as 'reflecting without distortion' (60). Ann Phillips, in her book on the 'politics of presence' (1995), refers to descriptive representation as essential, especially in the case of groups that have traditionally been subjugated or that have lacked access to the system of power. Are parties mobilizing the working class also dominated by working-class members? Are women present proportionally among party members? The question of who party members are is significant for building party organizations that provide democratic linkage.

The democracy argument claims that the rule 'of the people and by the people' sustains legitimacy. However, there is also the question of how social representativeness may – or may not – affect *political representation* (e.g. Mansbridge 2015; Norris and Lovenduski 1995). Does social background lead to particular political preferences? Many deprived groups have been well represented by high-status, elite politicians. Still, the notion of a non-representative political advocacy is contested.

Socio-demographic political cleavages are upheld and reinforced by parties. Parties act as mobilizing agents at elections, and they direct member recruitment campaigns at particular groups. Some parties base their politics on promoting agrarian, religious or ethnic interests and seek to enlist members from these groups. Recruitment serves three purposes besides increasing membership in general. First, it increases the party's 'labour force'. Second, it enhances internal legitimacy by recruiting people on whose behalf they have fought. Third, it increases the party's external legitimacy by giving voters a sense of social and cultural representation. When a party pursues a 'people's party' strategy, however, the targeting of particular groups declines. 'Catch-all' strategies are widely seen as having replaced more narrowly targeted party strategies, at least among the main contenders for power.

Party members are central political actors in all Nordic democracies. Their role varies, but in most parties, members are at least formally involved in the internal decision-making processes (Bolin et al. 2017; Kosiara-Pedersen, Scarrow and van Haute 2017). The argument for descriptive representation is that members are in a better position to interpret the voters' policy interests than the political elites, as they are generally embedded in different social, economic and cultural milieus. The assumption of the 'descriptive representation literature' mentioned earlier is that when the social equivalence between members and voters declines, the organized party linkage through the members to civil society will be weakened.

Class voting in Nordic countries was among the highest in the world during the second half of the twentieth century (Knutsen 2005; Nieuwbeerta 1996), but there were also other cleavages, which influenced party systems to an important degree (cf. chapter 1). This included the urban-rural divide as well as religious, regional and, in some cases, linguistic differences (e.g. Westinen 2015). According to Bengtsson et al. (2013), class voting in the Nordic countries has declined dramatically over time, though it still remains relatively high by international standards in Sweden and, to a lesser extent, Finland and Denmark. Iceland, with an unusually homogeneous population, had a less complicated cleavage structure and it also experienced a relatively early trend towards declining class voting. Other features of voters' social situations are strongly related to voting, including occupation (e.g. public vs. private sector), region (degree of urbanization), gender and education (Bengtsson et al. 2013, 154–57; Piketty 2018).[1] Private sector employees are more likely to vote for parties on the right, and voters in less built-up areas are more right-wing than urban voters. We should expect the recruitment of party members to reflect these differences in the social profiles of party members.

More recent changes in political cleavage structures are associated with a number of social structure variables. The growth of public sector employment and the higher level of education among voters are associated with a rise of post-materialism, while globalization of regional economies and increased immigration have led to populist movements and parties on both the left and right. Our expectation is that the composition of party memberships reflects the social structure of the political support market. Our first expectation, based on the cleavage perspective, is consequently that *the social composition of party members is, to a large degree, similar to the social composition of party voters, reflecting the cleavage base of the parties*. These variables include, among others, place of residence, occupation and religion.

There is, of course, room for doubt as voter groups may vary in terms of the ease with which they can be mobilized. Based on the cartel party theory, party organizations have become increasingly professionalized and less reliant on input from ordinary party members (e.g. Katz and Mair 1995; Kirchheimer 1966). The professionalized party is likely to attract members who are substantially different in composition compared to the ordinary supporters with regard to social background. In these elite-professional parties, the social base of party members counts for less.

The literature on political participation tells us that it is the individuals with the most resources who sign up for party membership (Heidar 2006). This is in line with general research on political participation (Dalton 2014; Putnam 1976). Despite efforts by parties to recruit women and young people, these groups are likely to be under-represented. Males have traditionally had a head start on women in politics. This may not affect all parties to the same degree and may affect parties on the centre-left and parties with strong female support less than others. In the latter decades of the twentieth century, the integration of women was a major goal for many parties. Many left-wing parties and green parties took active organizational steps (like quotas) to include women in the parties, a legacy that may continue to influence their gender profiles. Some parties, like the Icelandic Women's Alliance established in the 1980s, were open to women only. In Denmark and Norway, female membership rose from roughly one-third to roughly one-half of total membership from the early 1970s to 1990 (Sundberg 1995).

Within the specific social, cultural or geographical segments mobilized by the parties, we expect that people with relatively high scores on education and income disproportionately join parties. This expectation does not contradict the cleavage thesis presented earlier, but rather supplements it. Despite the general tendency of party members to reflect the electoral bases of parties, there are likely to be systematic sources of bias. We expect *party members to be a more socially exclusive group than party voters, that is, disproportionately male, more middle-aged, more educated and employed in more high-income fields.*

The decline of party membership organizations may also make them less representative. Countries with a high membership density (PM/E ratio) could be expected to have more representative party members than low PM/E countries. In the old democracies, there has been a decline in traditional political participation (Dalton 2014). Declining party membership is not the only factor influencing party representativeness, however.

Well-established parties may rely on professional party workers, financed by generous state support, rather than by voluntary contributions from rank-and-file members. This may lead to a more elitist or professional organization where descriptive representation and organized linkage are less important (Katz and Mair 1995; Kirchheimer 1966). Declining membership and professionalized party organizations will change the member recruitment and make the membership less representative of party voters. The gap in socio-demographic profiles between members and voters will increase. This forms the basis of our third general expectation, namely that *declining PM/E ratios will make party members less representative of party voters.*

This proposition is central to the concern over declining party membership figures. Without data from different years, however, we have no means to test this directly. We will, however, ask if parties with a low PM/E density also have a weaker linkage in terms of socio-demographic member-voter congruence.

The Data and Method[2]

The data we use to study these expectations are generally collected through representative surveys of party members and voters in all countries except for Iceland. In some parties in Denmark, the questionnaire was sent to all members registered with e-mail addresses. In Finland, the surveys for the National Coalition Party and the Green League were carried out via e-mail only. For other parties, surveys were also mailed by traditional post. The Icelandic data on members as well as voters are from the election survey carried out in 2013. Here, the party members make up a sufficient subsample to enable specific analyses. The member and voter surveys are presented in more detail in chapter 1 (see table 1.3). We also use some data on membership numbers and ratios found in chapter 2.

While the data do not allow for rigorous statistical testing of our expectations, we maintain that our findings are suggestive. Some of the questions on which we base our analysis are not included in all of the country surveys, which means that the countries included in the tables will differ. Some question formulations will also vary between countries, making cross-country comparisons difficult.

Interpreting the data describing member-voter congruence can be challenging for two general reasons. First, excepting Iceland, the data on members and voters were not collected at the same point in time. However, the social variables, like education and occupational sector, tend to change slowly. A more serious problem is that variables such as occupation and education have not always been collected and coded in the same way. This makes cross-country comparisons challenging and sometimes impossible. When appropriate, we have discussed these problems explicitly when interpreting our figures. In general, we can have greater confidence in intra-country party results than in cross-country comparisons.

Our question here is, to what extent do party members mirror the voters on sociodemographic variables (i.e. to what degree is there member-voter congruence)? The expectations presented earlier are explicit in terms of which variables are relevant to consider. The expectations all suggest deviations from what one could expect from a random 'lottery' selection of members from the voter base. As an indicator of proportionality – or congruence – between party members and party voters, we use two different measures. First, in the case of dichotomous variables, we use percentage difference between members and voters. To standardize the congruence measure (C) and make it more similar to the Gallagher's Proportionality Index (GPI) below, we subtract the numerical difference from 100. The gender congruence score will be

$$C = 100 - \left| \% \text{ male members} - \% \text{ male voters} \right|$$

Second, most tables on congruence between members and voters have more than two values. In these cases, we use what we call the 'GPI' (Allern, Heidar and Karlsen 2016). The index changes the well-known Gallagher's *Dis*proportionality Index (GDI) by inverting it (GPI=100 – GDI). It is easier to relate to a high GPI being a high level of congruence. GDI (=LSq) takes the square root of half the sum of the squares of the difference between the group percentages and varies between 0 (perfect congruence) and 100 (no congruence):

$$LSq = \sqrt{\frac{1}{2}\sum_{i=1}^{n}\left(V_i - M_i\right)^2}$$
,

where V=percentage in the voters' group; M=percentage in the members' group (In Gallagher 1991, the M is a S=Seats).

The index is traditionally used to measure the impact of electoral systems, looking at the difference (i.e. distortion) between percentage of votes for a party (V) and percentage of parliamentary seats for the same party (S). In this chapter, we look at the difference between party voters (V) and party members (M). The inverted GPI varies between 100 (completely matching distribution between voters and members) and 0 (no match whatsoever). However, what is high and what is low congruence? Looking at the scores for proportionality of an electoral system, this would give the near perfect proportionality of the Netherlands with a 'high' GPI score of 99 (based on elections between 2000 and 2010), while the UK would get a 'low' score of 83. As a rule of thumb, we will *consider scores from 95 to 100 'high' congruence, 94–85 as 'medium', 84–75 as 'low' and below 75 as 'poor'*.

Gender and Age

Gender has been a major source of representative bias in all democratic systems. Despite trends towards greater gender equality, we expect men to be over-represented among party members. In table 4.1, we first present party profiles in terms of percentage of male members, then the congruence measure for members compared to voters. We measure the gender congruence by percentage of male members minus the percentage of male voters. As noted earlier, we subtract the numerical value of this difference from 100.[3]

Table 4.1A shows that there are majorities of men in all but three of the parties: the Finnish Greens, the Swedish Feminists and the Norwegian Left Socialist Party. The male dominance is particularly strong in the Nordic radical right parties, but the conservatives also stand out with a high proportion of males. The least male-dominated parties are the left socialist parties and the greens, while the Nordic social democrats and agrarians are slightly below the male averages.

In terms of congruence, Swedish parties are close to a complete match between party members and voters with a score of 98, which means a difference of two percentage points between male party members and voters. In Denmark, there is a wide gap between party members and their voters, resulting in a low score of 82. Five out of nine Danish parties actually have scores as low as 75 to 78.

In terms of age, our expectation is that middle-aged and older members dominate parties. We also expect that 'new' (post-1960) parties have the youngest members.[4] Table 4.2A shows that the average age of party members in all countries, except in Iceland, is over 53. In Finland, party members seem to be the oldest.

Table 4.1. Gender profiles and member-voter congruence.

A. Profile % (male members)

	Left Socialist	Social Dem.	Green	Agrarian	Other	Christ. Dem.	Liberal	Conservative	Radical Right	All*
Denmark 2012	55/51	66	–	–	65	68	75/84	78	71	68
Finland 2016	58	61	37	59	–	–	–	62	75	59
Iceland 2013	50	57	–	58	60	–	–	61	–	57
Norway 2017	42	62	54	66	–	69	61	71	81	65
Sweden 2015	53	60	52	–	21	65	64	68	–	52

B. Congruence (100 – [% male members minus % male voters])

	Left Socialist	Social Dem.	Green	Agrarian	Other	Christ. Dem.	Liberal	Conservative	Radical Right	All*
Denmark 2012	93/85	78	–	–	78	88	78/77	75	91	82
Finland 2016	86	88	98	93	–	–	–	93	83	92
Iceland 2013	86	90	–	97	93	–	–	97	–	95
Norway 2017	89	80	98	87	–	68	84	83	80	85
Sweden 2015	99	89	92	–	92	80	88	89	–	98

*Weighted figures.
Finland: N=12,273, Missing=154; Iceland: N=382, Missing=50; Norway: N=2,566, Missing=40; Sweden: N=10,199 Missing=193. Denmark=17,096.
'All': N=10,199 Missing=193. Denmark=193.
For party families, see chapter 1.

Table 4.2. Age of party members and member-voter age congruence.

A. Profile (averages)

	Left Socialist	Social Dem.	Green	Agrarian	Other	Christ. Dem.	Liberal	Conservative	Radical Right	All*
Denmark 2012	46/50	59	–	–	51	60	58/46	56	56	54
Finland 2016	56	62	43	60	–	–	–	56	54	58
Iceland 2013	42	48	–	48	–	–	–	48	–	48
Norway 2017	49	55	48	53	–	58	46	56	56	54
Sweden 2015	51	61	49	–	43	58	61	62	–	56

B. Congruence (GPI)

	Left Socialist	Social Dem.	Green	Agrarian	Other	Christ. Dem.	Liberal	Conservative	Radical Right	All*
Denmark 2012	89/87	80	–	–	84	76	77/78	86	93	81
Finland 2016	81	79	83	86	–	–	–	93	83	85
Iceland 2013	96	99	–	99	96	–	–	100	–	99
Norway 2017	88	84	75	96	–	85	96	80	86	85
Sweden 2015	91	82	88	–	93	94	83	72	–	93

*Weighted figures. Denmark/Norway/Sweden: GPIs are based on the following three age cohorts: 18–30 / 31–50 / 51+. Finland: Differences in six age cohorts.

For the different party families cross-nationally, there are no clear tendencies in the data. We find a slightly higher average age for the Christian democrats and a slightly lower one for the greens and left socialists, but both the Christian democrats and left socialists have scores close to the overall average. The main reason for the lower averages among party members in Iceland compared to the others is likely due to a slightly younger population. Older parties are likely to contain a broader age spectrum than newer ones given that they have had more time to establish loyalty among older generations. This is true of the social democrats, liberals and conservatives in some instances (although not in all cases). This, however, does not necessarily make them more representative of their voters. Parties with a strong post-materialist element (e.g. left socialists and greens) seem to be relatively younger, while the radical right is close to the average.

The age composition of party members is quite similar to that of the voters in Iceland and Sweden. For Denmark, Finland and Norway, the congruence is low to medium. From the background data, we know that a lack of congruence means that members are older than voters. Five parties in Denmark have a low congruence between party members and voters. The lowest level, however, is found in the Swedish Conservative party, with a score of 72. Among party families, the social democrats account for four out of five parties with a low congruence. In Finland especially, members of the Social Democrats are clearly older than their voters.

REGION AND RELIGION

To evaluate parties' social linkage to the structural cleavages, we start with some basic information about the regions in which the members live and whether the members reflect their voters in terms of religious affiliations or practice.

First, are the members mostly living in and around the country capital, close to the parliament, the government and the national media? Do they match their voters in the sense that the regions made up of the most party members are also those where we find most party voters? Are some party families stronger in peripheral or capital regions than others? Table 4.3 shows the regional party member profiles, and table 4.3B illustrates the degree of regional congruence between members and voters in Nordic countries. In table 4.3A on members' profiles, we look at the percentage of members found in the capital region; in table 4.3B we report the congruence (GPI), that is, the match between members and voters in a specified number of regions.

There is no basis for comparing country differences in table 4.3A, as the size of the regions vary. The fact that 60 per cent of Icelandic party members live in the capital only reflects that a great majority of Icelanders actually live in the capital, Reykjavik. In terms of party differences, we can note that conservative parties in all countries have their member strongholds in the capital region. Some of the new parties, notably the greens in Finland and Norway, are also particularly strong in the capital region, which may reflect a relatively high level of education (see table 4.5A).

Table 4.3. Regional profiles and member-voter congruence.

A. Profile (% party members in capital region)

	Left Socialist	Social Dem.	Green	Agrarian	Other	Christ. Dem.	Liberal	Conservative	Radical Right	All*
Denmark 2012	40/57	31	–	–	38	15	23/40	42	27	32
Finland 2016	33	29	52	10	–	–	–	35	22	21
Iceland 2013	65	71	–	25	87	–	–	65	–	60
Norway 2017	35	23	40	9	–	7	34	36	11	23
Sweden 2015	33	30	33	–	35	28	36	38	–	33

Capital regions – Denmark: Hovedstaden. Finland: Helsinki–Uusimaa. Iceland: Reykjavik area. Norway: Central (Oslo/Akershus). Sweden: Region Öst (1. Stockholms, 2. Södermanlands, 3. Östergötlands och, 4. Gotlands län).

B) Congruence (GPI. All regions**)

	Left Socialist	Social Dem.	Green	Agrarian	Other	Christ. Dem.	Liberal	Conservative	Radical Right	All*
Denmark 2012 (5)	87/83	92	–	–	74	–	94/93	94	85	98
Finland 2016 (5)	92	95	85	91	–	–	–	97	93	93
Iceland 2013 (2)	96	100	–	87	99	–	–	98	–	99
Norway 2017 (5)	94	94	88	95	–	90	93	90	96	98
Sweden 2015 (5)	92	91	96	–	95	92	94	97	–	96

* Weighted. ** Regions: Denmark: Hovedstaden, Sjælland, Midtjylland, Nordjylland, Syddanmark. Finland: Helsinki-Uusimaa, West Finland, South Finland and North & East Finland. Iceland: Reykjavik area, all others. Norway: Central, East, South-West, Mid-Norway, North. Sweden: North, Middle, East, West, South.

We also note that the radical right parties disproportionately have their membership outside the capital region. In Norway, only the agrarian and the Christian parties have fewer members in and around the capital.

In all Nordic parties, differences in the regional member bases tend to reflect the regional distribution of their voters rather well. Table 4.3B shows that the GPI generally has a high or medium degree of proportionality between members and voters, and all five countries have scores of 90 or more. The only parties with a low or poor score are the Danish Socialist People's Party and the Social Liberals along with the Finnish Greens. The overall picture indicates that Nordic party members reflect party voters well as far as region is concerned. This supports the linkage view of party memberships. In sparsely populated regions, and with relatively decentralized states, this constitutes an important dimension of representation.

Religious affiliation is another central variable in traditional debates on Nordic (and European) political cleavages. Religion has not, however, been a major cleavage in all of the Nordic countries. During the late nineteenth century, free churches and lay movements contributed to the growth of liberal parties, while conservative parties were more closely associated with the hierarchy of the Protestant state church. All of these countries later saw the rise of 'Nordic style' Christian parties – some earlier (Norway) and some later (Sweden, Denmark and Finland) – supporting Christian values and resisting secular trends. The relevant survey questions differ, however, making cross-country comparisons difficult. Some surveys ask about membership in religious organizations, while other surveys refer more to attachment to Christian values and practices.

Table 4.4A shows that the association with religious organizations or beliefs is strong in the case of Christian democratic parties, which is as expected. Conservative and agrarian party members are also highly attached to religious practice. On the other hand, we see the left socialist parties with a very low degree of religious affiliation. Table 4.4B on congruence shows figures for Finland, Iceland, Norway and Sweden. In Finland, parties are generally highly representative in terms of strong attachment with religious communities. This is especially true with the left socialists, the social democrats, the greens and the radical right. However, there was only medium congruence among the centre-right parties, namely the agrarians and conservatives, as their members are more likely to be highly associated with religious practices. The Swedish and Icelandic parties are highly congruent on this dimension. Members seem to mirror voters closely in all parties except for the Icelandic Left-Greens. In this party, members are less likely than voters to belong to religious organizations. In Norwegian parties, we find medium or low congruence in seven out of eight parties. We find low or poor congruence in the social democratic, green, liberal and radical right parties. The Christian party, on the other hand, has a complete match between members and voters on this dimension (GPI=100).

The old cleavages arising from centre-periphery and religion are still active among Nordic parties. The conservative parties are stronger in the central, capital area. The Christian parties, along with the agrarians and conservatives, are more attractive to

Table 4.4. Member of (or highly associated with) religious organization? Party profiles and member-voter congruence.

A. Profile (%)

	Left Socialist	Social Dem.	Green	Agrarian	Other	Christ. Dem.	Liberal	Conservative	Radical Right	All*
Denmark 2012	5/8	10	–	–	11	91	13/7	13	10	12
Finland 2016	6	–	9	40	–	–	–	23	16	21
Iceland 2013	60	76	–	95	73	–	–	94	–	89
Norway 2017	31	53	39	74	–	97	50	68	66	63
Sweden 2015	20	35	30	–	18	76	41	35	–	35

B. Congruence (GPI, Finland – see further)

	Left Socialist	Social Dem.	Green	Agrarian	Other	Christ. Dem.	Liberal	Conservative	Radical Right	All*
Finland 2016	98	99	99	89	–	–	–	90	98	94
Iceland 2013	86	97	–	97	99	–	–	99	–	96
Norway 2017	86	79	83	85	–	100	77	85	83	84
Sweden 2015	91	94	98	–	99	91	95	98	–	98

* Weighted.

Data and questions. Denmark: 'Are you a member of a religious or Christian organization?' No voter data available for Denmark. Finland: N=11,774, Missing=653. Initial question: 'How strongly do you feel that you are a part of Church or religious community?' Voter-based data: 'Everyday life and participation 2017.' Finnish congruence measured by percentage difference between members and voters who were strongly associated with religious organization. Iceland: includes all respondents reporting membership of religious organizations, including the state church. N=382, Missing=50. Norway: 'Are you a member of a religious organization?' N=2,509, Missing=97; Sweden: 'Do you have any "philosophy of life" (livsåskådning), faith, or religious attachment?' F! and L are not included in the weighting and are excluded from 'All'. N=9,446, Missing=946. Denmark: N=16,900.

members with a religious attachment. It seems that party members are representative of their voters in terms of where they live. The Swedish, Icelandic and Finnish parties, however, are more representative on the religious cleavage than Norwegian parties.

Education and Occupation

While we observe a relatively high degree of congruence between party members and voters with regard to many social indicators, we expect systematic sources of bias in member recruitment in terms of education and occupation. Our main expectation is that party members are a more socially exclusive group than party voters. As such, we expect that they will be more highly educated and work disproportionately in high-income occupations. The parties' positions on the left-right spectrum and their origins in the social and political cleavage structures as well as in time (old vs. new parties) would suggest systematic differences in recruitment from different occupational groups. Scholars debate whether sector employment should have the status of a cleavage, although the voting patterns of private and public sector employees clearly differ (Knutsen 2001, 2005). We expect to find public employees disproportionately represented among party members, particularly in left-leaning parties.

Table 4.5 shows, on the one hand, the percentage of party members with a college-level education (4.5A) and the member-voter congruence measured on the bases of two to five different educational categories (4.5B). The data have been challenging to present as the educational groups are coded differently for the different countries, which is a problem for cross-national comparisons. It has also been problematic to group 'equivalent' types of education. Therefore, we shall not comment on the cross-country differences in the tables below. Our main concern will be the differences between parties and party families within each country.

In table 4.5A, two party families, the agrarians and the radical right, are below average in college education. The left-socialist parties are generally above average (except in Finland), and so are the new parties, namely the greens and the Swedish Feminists. The liberal party family, excepting the old (partly agrarian) Danish liberal party, tends to be more highly educated than other parties. Comparing party families, the conservatives are, by and large, more educated than the social democrats. Notwithstanding, it is difficult to reconcile these figures with the traditional image of left-wing parties being the parties of the underprivileged (and not highly educated), while the right-wing parties are the natural parties for the highly educated (and consequently, high-income groups). In most cases, realities are far from clear-cut. However, in contrast, a traditional distinction between the left (the left socialists and the social democrats) and the right (the conservatives) was found in Finland. The new parties, like the greens, have a higher share of college-educated members than the old ones. However, this is not the case for the (fairly) new radical right parties. Part of this pattern may simply reflect generational differences. The older generations had less access to educational opportunities, and this may affect education levels in these parties.

Table 4.5. Educational profiles and member-voter congruence.

A. Profile (% college education or equivalent)

	Left Socialist	Social Dem.	Green	Agrarian	Other	Christ. Dem.	Liberal	Conservative	Radical Right	All*
Denmark 2012	72/76	56	–	–	87	61	66/80	75	42	65
Finland 2016	54	59	84	64	–	–	–	88	49	67
Iceland 2013	65	57	–	35	60	–	–	45	–	46
Norway 2017	82	61	87	59	–	64	83	71	36	64
Sweden 2015	72	46	78	–	79	65	80	69	–	69

B. Congruence (including number of educational categories; GPI)

	Left Socialist	Social Dem.	Green	Agrarian	Other	Christ. Dem.	Liberal	Conservative	Radical Right	All*
Denmark 2012 (2)	87/89	87	–	–	89	72	83/86	92	83	86
Finland 2016 (5)	84	85	80	90	–	–	–	91	84	90
Iceland 2013 (3)	94	96	–	98	84	–	–	98	–	98
Norway 2017 (3)	85	67	68	61	–	66	84	74	64	68
Sweden 2015 (3)	82	85	91	–	91	–	89	80	–	80

*Weighted.
Educational groups compared.
Denmark: College vs. non-collegiate. N=17,027, Missing=5,631;
Finland: Primary, Secondary, Tertiary, Bachelor's and Master's N=12,341, Missing=86;
Iceland: N=382, Missing=50; Norway: classified in low, medium and high. N=2,586, Missing=20;
Iceland: Low=Compulsory or less; Medium: Secondary school; High: University.
Sweden: F1 and L are not included in the weighting and are excluded from 'All'. N=10,256, Missing=136.

Given the large size of the Nordic welfare states, the public sector accounts for a significant proportion of the electorate in all five countries. The level of public sector employment varies between 21 per cent (Finland) and 30 per cent (Norway).[5] Our expectation is that public sector employees are more engaged in parties than their share in the public sector employment suggests, in particular, in the case of left-leaning parties. If this is correct, the congruence levels for member-voter sector employment congruence should be low. Table 4.6 presents data on the share of members employed in the public sector and the congruence between members and voters. Table 4.6A shows the percentage of participants employed in the public sector, while table 4.6B displays the congruence measure for members compared to voters.

Table 4.6A shows – as expected – that members of the left parties have higher than average membership of those occupied in the public sector, while parties on the right are below average in this respect. However, this was not the case in Finland, where the left and right parties have a relatively equal share of public sector employees. In Norway, the share of public employees in the centre-left parties was particularly high. Three out of four members of the Socialist Left Party worked in the public sector, compared to one in four in the conservative and radical right parties. The Norwegian social democrats, the greens and the Christian democrats had a majority of public employees as members.

The general left-right pattern in public sector employment holds for party voters as well, creating a high level of congruence in all parties, even if the sector employment of their members differs greatly. The exception is Norway, where public sector employees are more strongly represented among party members on the centre-left than among party voters. In Norway, congruence is poor for most parties, and only the liberals, conservatives and the radical right gained a medium level of congruence. In Denmark, Finland and Iceland, parties generally had a higher match between members and the voters. Representativeness in the Danish left-wing parties is high in terms of sector employment. In Finland, the members of the left socialists and the radical right were the most highly matched with voters. Interestingly, the members of radical right parties matched their voters very well (GPIs 91–92) in all three countries.

A similar analysis was performed with regard to white-collar vs. blue-collar occupations for those countries where data were available (i.e. Finland, Iceland and Norway). For reasons of space, we do not present the results here. Differences between parties were, on the whole, small and irregular. We found a tendency for agrarian parties to have a below-average proportion of white-collar members, while conservative parties are above average in this regard. Congruence between party members and party voters, on the other hand, was medium to high.

In sum, we found that party members of the left were not less educated than members of parties on the right, but when comparing the conservative and the social democratic members, we found the latter to be less educated. We also found the agrarians and the radical right members to be less educated than average, while the greens and the new parties had more highly educated members. In general, the left

Table 4.6. Occupational sector profiles (public-private) and member-voter congruence.*

A. Profile (% in the public sector)

	Left Socialist	Social Dem.	Green	Agrarian	Other	Christ. Dem.	Liberal	Conservative	Radical Right	All**
Denmark 2012	55/61	46	–	–	49	40	20/13	23	27	35
Finland 2016	40	42	–	41	–	–	–	39	30	40
Iceland 2013	47	54	–	33	40	–	–	30	–	37
Norway 2017	76	59	56	41	–	53	41	27	24	48

B. Congruence (GPI)

	Left Socialist	Social Dem.	Green	Agrarian	Other	Christ. Dem.	Liberal	Conservative	Radical Right	All**
Denmark 2012	93/97	96	–	–	95	–	78/89	84	92	90
Finland 2016***	92	84	–	85	–	–	–	84	91	89
Iceland 2013	75	97	–	96	98	–	–	97	–	98
Norway 2017	65	66	71	84	–	77	88	88	92	74

* Pensioners, students and unemployed are excluded. Denmark: N=9,858;
Finland: N=9,252, Missing=1,546 (The Greens are completely missing);
Iceland: N=382, Missing=50;
Norway: N=1,455, Missing=1,151. GPIs are calculated based on the following classification: (1) Employees in the private sector, (2) employees in the public sector and (3) employees in various organizations. Pensioners, students and homeworkers are excluded.
** Weighted figures.
*** Voter data: Finnish National Election Study 2015.

parties had more members with occupations in the public sector than the right parties. This was particularly the case in Norway, while in Finland there was virtually no difference. Congruence levels were medium to high in all countries except Norway, where members had a poor match with voters.

PM/E RATIOS AND MEMBER/VOTER CONGRUENCE

In chapter 1, the argument was that democratic linkage operated through two channels: elections and membership parties. If that is the case, declining party membership represents a problem for 'two-pillar' democracies. Fewer members weaken the citizen-state linkage. Earlier, we suggested that low PM/E ratios would make party members less representative of party voters than high ratios. Country differences seem to indicate support for this, as shown in table 4.7.

The highest degree of congruence – or proportionality – is found in Iceland, which also has the highest PM/E ratio by far. The pattern holds, broadly speaking, for Finland, Denmark and Norway as well. Finland has a relatively high number of party members and high mean proportionality, while Denmark and Norway are low on both member density and congruence. Sweden, on the other hand, does not fit the expected picture. Its PM/E ratio is the lowest among the Nordic countries, while member-voter congruence is second only to Iceland, which is partly the result of a high gender congruence score. In addition, Sweden also scores relatively high on the other indicators compared to Denmark and Norway.

There is reason to suspect that Iceland constitutes a deviant case, given the generally high levels of PM/E ratios compared to the other countries. High PM/E ratios in Iceland are the result of relatively inclusive nomination processes, which have tended to boost the membership profiles of the parties. Although fully open primaries have become rare, the nomination processes of the parties are highly inclusive and tend to attract new members to a far greater degree than in the other countries (Kristinsson 2010). In the Icelandic case, this seems to result in a higher level of member-voter

Table 4.7.   Member/electorate (M/E) ratios and member-voter congruence indicators for the Nordic countries.

	PM/E ratio*	GPI for Age	Gender Congruence	GPI for Education	Mean Congruence (age, gender, education)
Denmark	0.04	81	82	89	84
Finland	0.09	85	92	90	89
Iceland	0.15	99	95	98	97
Norway	0.05	85	85	80	83
Sweden	0.03	93	98	88	93

* Data from chapter 2 and the relevant tables given earlier.

congruence. For a partial test of this idea, we matched mean congruence per party in terms of age, gender and education to the party-members-to-votes ratio (i.e. PM/V) in the election closest to 2013 in each country. With Iceland included, the correlation (Pearson's r) was 0.57 (significant at the 0.01 level), but without Iceland the correlation all but disappeared (0.12 and non-significant).[6]

Our data are too limited to provide a conclusive method of analysing what lies behind the differences observed between Iceland and the other countries. A plausible interpretation, however, might be that while membership in all five countries is fairly representative of voters, the method of inclusive primaries has the potential to reach sections of the voting population that are not normally reached by party efforts. This might account for both the higher levels of PM/E ratios and the greater congruence. This interpretation seems to be in line with the findings of Achury et al. (2018), who suggest more broadly that greater benefits from membership, for example, in the form of having a direct say over party decisions, lead to smaller disparities between members and supporters.[7] The more political influence that parties grant to members, the more membership will be in line – or congruent – with party voters both socially and politically: quality involvement leads to quality linkage.

CONCLUSION

Our main concern in this chapter has been to present members' socio-demographic profiles in Nordic parties and to discuss whether members mirror the characteristics of party voters. We expected that the social profiles of party members would reflect the cleavage base of parties, that members are more resourceful than party voters and that low member density would make member-voter congruence low. The empirical focus has been on politically relevant background variables, including region, religious affiliation, education, sector employment, gender and age.

Party members differed markedly in terms of religious affiliation. Not surprisingly, the affiliation is most prominent in the Christian parties, but a large share of agrarian party members were also attached to religious organizations. Men dominate among party members, particularly in Denmark and Norway, where close to two out of three members are men. Even though men dominate in nearly all parties, there is a left-right impact, with the right parties being more male dominated than the left. In terms of members' age, Icelandic members are younger than the rest, most likely due to a younger population in general. As for education, the green parties have more college-educated members than the other parties, particularly compared to the radical right parties. Finally, we find a clear left-right pattern in occupational sectors, with the left-leaning parties having a larger part of their membership working in the public sector.

Given the traditional emphasis on membership organizations as linkage mechanisms in Nordic countries, we expected the representativeness of the party organizations to remain strong despite declining memberships. We found that on all indicators, most country scores reflected high or medium congruence. Party members resemble party voters to a high degree – even with considerable differences in membership profiles across parties. In other words, Nordic parties have maintained a high level of representativeness when looking at the social composition of their membership. Only six out of twenty-five scores fell into the 'low' or 'poor' categories. Interestingly, the Icelandic scores were always in the high group, while four of the six low/poor scores were Norwegian. For Iceland, this may be an effect of the inclusive nomination process found in Icelandic parties.

On the other hand, the data give some qualified support for our expectations that members differ from voters on some background variables. We found disproportionalities (low congruence) in the educational and gender composition of members compared to voters. However, we did not find an overall bias with regard to age, although the higher age cohorts are more prominent in the old parties than in the new ones. These differences in congruence measures are still relatively small. In Sweden and Iceland, there are hardly any gender differences in the composition of members and voters, although imbalances can be found in certain parties. The expectations regarding biased recruitment patterns are therefore only partly verified, or at least verified to a smaller extent than expected. Our main conclusion is that education, gender and age biases in the Nordic parties are relatively small.

The decline in party membership may also make parties less representative. The possibility exists that a shrinking of membership is associated with a qualitative change in the nature of membership, as parties change from linkage organizations to more elitist and professional ones. Our data offer only limited ways of testing this idea, as we do not present any time-series data. We might still expect that low party-member density will go together with low member-voter congruence. We do find that member-voter congruence levels vary according to PM/E ratios. Sweden is the exception, with the lowest member density of the five countries, but with the second-highest congruence level. This was surpassed only by Iceland. Iceland, on the other hand, has both the highest PM/E ratio and the highest average congruence level. If we eliminate Iceland from the analysis, however, and compare PM/E ratios and party congruence, the expected pattern all but disappears. The special case of Iceland is most likely accounted for by some third factor, such as the inclusive method of nominations, which affects both PM/E ratios and member/voter congruence.

Hence, we conclude that there is no straightforward relationship between the size of party membership and its representativeness. This is certainly no great surprise as – in 'two-pillar democracies' – the party elites also have other means of staying in line with their electorate than through the member linkage.

The findings indicate that the traditional 'linkage' model of party organization in the Nordic countries remains viable with regard to social representativeness, despite the decline in membership in both absolute and relative terms. Party members are, by and large, ordinary people who resemble the voters of their respective parties in most respects. Level of education, however, makes them somewhat less 'ordinary' in most parties.

NOTES

1. Piketty argues that European social democracy has increasingly recruited highly educated middle-class voters at the expense of low-educated workers.

2. Thanks to Tor Gaute Syrstad for efficient research assistance with the Danish, Norwegian and Swedish data, and to Lára Hrönn Hlynsdóttir for assistance with the Icelandic data.

3. Had we not used numerical values, we would have obtained figures above 100 in the case of the Finnish Greens and the Swedish Feminists.

4. On 'new' (post-1960) and 'old' (pre-1960) parties, see chapter 1.

5. OECD, *Government at a Glance*, figures from 2015. Iceland is not included. See https://www.statista.com/chart/10346/scandinavia-first-for-public-sector-employment/.

6. *N* was 26 with Iceland included, but 22 without it. In the Icelandic case, we used self-reported membership according to the national election study of 2013 rather than the MAPP figures on account of large fluctuations in party support that year. Generally, PM/E is a more reliable indicator of party membership than PM/V on account of the latter's sensitivity to vote fluctuations. In the present case, however, this was not applicable.

7. Their research is based on party organizational data from the Political Party Database (see Poguntke et al. 2016) and from the European Social Survey's population survey in ten countries in 2008 and 2010.

BIBLIOGRAPHY

Achury, Susan, Susan Scarrow, Karina Kosiara-Pedersen and Emilie van Haute. 2018. 'The Consequences of Membership Incentives: Do Greater Political Benefits Attract Different Kinds of Members?' *Party Politics*. doi: 10.177/1354068818754603.

Allern, Elin Haugsgjerd, Knut Heidar and Rune Karlsen. 2016. *After the Mass Party: Continuity and Change in Political Parties and Representation in Norway*. New York: Lexington Books.

Bengtsson, Åsa, Kasper Møller Hansen, Olafur Hardarson, Hanne Marthe Narud and Henrik Oscarsson. 2013. *The Nordic Voter. Myths of Exceptionalism*. Colchester: ECPR Press.

Bolin, Niklas, Nicholas Aylott, Benjamin von dem Berge and Thomas Poguntke. 2017. 'Patterns of Intra-Party Democracy across the World'. In *Organizing Political Parties*, edited by Susan E. Scarrow, Paul D. Webb and Thomas Poguntke, 158–86. Oxford: Oxford University Press.

Dalton, Russell J. 2014. *Citizen Politics: Public Opinion and Political Parties in Advanced Industrial Democracies*, 6th ed. Los Angeles, CA: SAGE.

Gallagher, Michael. 1991. Proportionality, Disproportionality and Electoral Systems. *Electoral Studies* 10 (1): 33–51.

Heidar, Knut 2006: 'Party Membership and Participation'. In *The Handbook of Party Politics*, edited by Richard S. Katz and William Crotty, 301–15. London: SAGE.

Katz, Richard S. and Peter Mair. 1995. 'Changing Models of Party Organization and Party Democracy: The Emergence of the Cartel Party'. *Party Politics* 1: 5–28.

Kirchheimer, Otto. 1966. 'The Transformation of the Western European Party Systems'. In *Political Parties and Political Development*, edited by Joseph LaPalombara, and Myron Weiner, 177–200. Princeton, NJ: Princeton University Press.

Knutsen, Oddbjørn. 2001. 'Social Class, Sector Employment, and Gender as Party Cleavages in the Scandinavian Countries: A Comparative Longitudinal Study, 1970–95'. *Scandinavian Political Studies* 24 (4): 311–50.

———. 2005. 'The Impact of Sector Employment on Party Choice: A Comparative Study of 8 West European Countries'. *European Journal of Political Research* 44: 593–621.

Kosiara-Pedersen, Karina, Susan E. Scarrow and Emilie van Haute. 2017. 'Rules of Engagement? Party Membership Costs, New Forms of Party Affiliation, and Partisan Participation'. In *Organizing Political Parties*, edited by Susan E. Scarrow, Paul D. Webb and Thomas Poguntke, 234–58. Oxford: Oxford University Press.

Kristinsson, Gunnar Helgi. 2010. 'Fjölmennustu flokkar heims. Meðlimaskipulag íslenskra stjórnmálaflokka'. *Icelandic Review of Politics and Administration* 6 (2): 123–50.

Lipset, Seymor M. and Stein Rokkan. 1967. 'Cleavage Structures, Party Systems, and Voter Alignments: An Introduction'. In *Party Systems and Voter Alignments: Cross-National Perspectives*, edited by Seymor M. Lipset and Stein Rokkan, 1–64. New York: Thew Free Press.

Mansbridge, Jane 2015. 'Should Workers Represent Workers?' *Swiss Political Science Review* 21 (2): 261–70.

Nieuwbeerta, Paul. 1996. 'The Democratic Class Struggle in Postwar Societies: Class Voting in Twenty Countries, 1945–1990'. *Acta Sociologica* 19: 346–81.

Norris, Pippa and Joni Lovenduski 1995. *Political Recruitment: Gender, Race and Class in the British Parliament.* Cambridge: Cambridge University Press.

Phillips, Anne. 1995. *The Politics of Presence.* Oxford: Oxford University Press.

Piketty, Thomas. March 2018. *Brahmin Left vs Merchant Right: Rising Inequality and the Changing Structure of Political Conflict (Evidence from France, Britain and the US, 1948–2017).* Paris: EHESS and Paris School of Economics.

Pitkin, Hanna Fenichel. 1967. *The Concept of Representation.* Berkeley: University of California Press.

Poguntke, Thomas, Susan E. Scarrow, Paul D. Webb, Elin H. Allern, Nicholas Aylott, Ingrid van Biezen, Enrico Calossi, Marina Costa Lobo, William P. Cross, Kris Deschouwer et al. 2016. 'Party Rules, Party Resources and the Politics of Parliamentary Democracies: How Parties Organize in the 21st Century'. *Party Politics* 22 (6): 661–78.

Putnam, Robert. 1976. *The Comparative Study of Political Elites.* Englewood Cliffs, NJ: Prentice-Hall.

Sundberg, Jan. 1995. 'Women in Scandinavian Party Organizations'. In *Women in Nordic Politics: Closing the Gap*, edited by Lauri Karvonen and Per Selle, 83–114. Aldershot, UK: Dartmouth.

Westinen, Jussi. 2015. 'Cleavages – Dead and Gone? An Analysis of Cleavage Structure and Party Choice in Contemporary Finland'. *Scandinavian Political Studies* 38 (3): 277–300.

5

Parties' Ideological Representation in the Nordic Countries

Comparing Party Voters, Members and Candidates

Jonathan Polk and Ann-Kristin Kölln[1]

The introductory chapter of this book highlights four elements of party linkage between citizens and government: reach, representation, activity and influence. The preceding chapter (chapter 4) was concerned with the second of these linkages, representation. But representation is itself a multidimensional concept, composed of both social and ideological parts. Chapter 4 focused on the former by examining the socio-demographic representativeness of political party members compared to the broader population of voters. In this chapter, we look more closely at the *ideological* representativeness of party members through a systematic analysis of opinion structures within political parties in the Nordic countries.

Based on John May's (1973) famous law about intra-party opinion structures, one would expect to see that the mid-level elite, party members, are more extreme in their ideological positions than the party elite or party voters. However, there are two important reasons to suspect that this might not be the case. First, the empirical evidence for May's law has been mixed in multiparty-based systems so far (e.g. see Dahl 2011; Kitschelt 1989; Narud and Skare 1999; Norris 1995; van Haute and Carty 2012; van Holsteyn, den Ridder and Koole 2017; Widfeldt 1999). Second, May formulated his law during a very different time of party politics. Since then, scholars have documented not only the almost universal decline of party membership (Kölln 2016; van Biezen, Mair and Poguntke 2012) but also the increase in intra-party democracy that has empowered individual members at the expense of the candidates or activists within the party (e.g. see Bolin et al. 2017; Cross and Katz 2013; Hazan and Rahat 2010). Motivated by both aspects, we ask, what is the opinion structure within contemporary Nordic parties? And to what extent are party members more ideologically extreme than parliamentary candidates and party voters in the Nordic party systems? To be clear, our goal is not to settle the debate about the applicability of May's law but rather to provide another and more comprehensive test through systematic comparison of intra-party opinion structures within three levels of a party *and* across four similar countries.

To our knowledge, we are the first to combine national election studies, party membership surveys and party candidate surveys to investigate the ideological preferences of three levels or strata of a political party: the elite (candidates), the mid-level elite (members) and the non-elite (party voters) (see May 1973; Narud and Skare 1999). Investigating the ideological structure of the party at all three levels informs us about the degree to which the unitary actor assumption common in party politics research (see Polk and Kölln 2017) can be upheld. But more substantively, it also informs us about one of the important preconditions for the policy linkage between political parties and voters. If party voters, members and candidates are all in ideological agreement, even highly democratized parties are likely to provide a strong policy linkage with voters. In contrast, ideological disagreement between these three groups can have important ramifications for each of the groups and for the party as a whole: party voters likely feel less represented by their party (e.g. see Rohrschneider and Whitefield 2012), party members likely express their discontent through exit, voice and disloyal behaviour (e.g. see Kölln and Polk 2017), and party candidates likely get less electoral support. As a consequence, a party as a whole is substantially constrained or even weakened if it is internally divided (Greene and Haber 2015).

Within the framework of this book's overarching focus on party members, the goal of this chapter is to assess the political representativeness of party members in four Nordic countries with respect to both party voters and candidates for parliament. We do this on the most dominant and comparable dimension across the ten surveys we analyse: the general left-right dimension. Even in a time and age of multidimensional party competition, the left-right scale is still today considered a 'super issue' (Dalton, Farrell and McAllister 2011, 26), not least because most individuals know what researchers are talking about when they ask respondents to place themselves on the left-right scale. For reasons of pragmatism and substance, it makes sense to begin with general left-right ideology for any investigation into the political representativeness of Nordic party members compared to voters and candidates.

The next section lays out May's law and discusses the two reasons that speak against finding support for it in the Nordic parties. We then move on to present our analytical strategy and introduce the ten different data sets we draw on as well as our measure of ideology. The third section presents and discusses our empirical findings from our four Nordic countries: Denmark, Iceland, Norway and Sweden. A conclusion summarizes our findings.

MAY'S LAW:
Evidence for and Against

Party voters, members and candidates share their positive attitude towards the same party. However, what distinguishes them is the way they express their positive attitude. Party voters express it through their vote every four or five years. Party members go a step further and sign up to the party's membership list, which comes with rights and obligations. Finally, party candidates can be characterized as doing all of the things mentioned earlier, but they are additionally willing to be among the public faces of the party. They also promote and vote on the party's policy proposals. Given these differences in involvement in and for the party, it is not surprising that several studies provide empirical evidence that breaks up the unitary actor assumption of a political party (for recent work, see Aylott and Bolin 2017; Ceron 2017; Kölln and Polk 2017). In fact, it seems almost implausible that a party comprising such different groups with diverse incentive structures would be entirely united above and beyond a shared positive attitude towards the same party.

One of the most prominent examples of scholarship that breaks up the unitary actor assumption comes in the form of May's 'Law of Curvilinear Disparity' (1973). His proposition is straightforward as he argues that mid-level elites, such as party members, should hold more ideologically extreme policy preferences than the party leadership or a party's broader voter base. May (1973, 143–51) argues based on a number of suppositions that there are at least three clusters of reasons to observe such a pattern of opinion differences within parties: intra-party control, recruitment and political socialization. In brief, his idea is that the three different groups have different levels of control over each other, differ in their socioeconomic and geographical background characteristics and face different incentives and interactions within the party. All three reasons are not causally responsible for the proposed opinion structure but coincide with it. Yet May provides no empirical evidence for his law.

Subsequent research has taken up this task and so far has shown mixed support for May's hypothesis (Dahl 2011; Kitschelt 1989; Narud and Skare 1999; Norris 1995; van Haute and Carty 2012; van Holsteyn, den Ridder and Koole 2017; Widfeldt 1999). For example, while Kitschelt's (1989) analysis of Belgian parties shows some support for May's idea under specific conditions, Narud and Skare (1999) were unable to confirm the revisited theory based on Norwegian data. Across four policy issues and the general left-right scale, Narud and Skare (1999, 59) found most support for an opinion structure of 'a fan, in which the top elites hold the most radical opinions, the non-elites are the most moderate, and the sub-elites are in between'. This is echoed in other studies, which report, 'To be sure, voters are more moderate than party members and activists, but party elites are usually just as extreme as the activists, perhaps even more so' (Saglie and Heidar 2004, 387). Analysis of Sweden, another country we investigate in this chapter, reports 'some evidence that members and activists have become radicalized compared to the voters' (Widfeldt 1999, 307). This divergence in the empirical studies warrants renewed attention, not least because most of these studies were case studies from individual countries. What is lacking so far is systematic comparative evidence from a number of countries using the same methodology.

In addition to the mixed empirical evidence, another reason to reassess the relationship between ideological agreement and position in the chain of party-based representation is the fundamental change in the composition of party membership.

May's proposition was developed in a different era of party politics, and the past few decades have seen a large quantitative shift in party membership. Former mass parties characterized by a large body of members were forced to transform into smaller organizations without giving up their advantageous political position targeted at the median voter. And although party membership numbers are and have been in decline for many European parties (e.g. see van Biezen, Mair and Poguntke 2012), this is not uniformly the case. While most parties lost large numbers of members, new parties emerged and naturally registered a net gain in members (Kölln 2016). From the Feminist Initiative in Sweden (Blombäck and de Fine Licht 2017) to Podemos in Spain (Ramiro and Gomez 2016), new political parties continue to spring up across Europe, many of which have seen a rapid rise in membership. Membership sizes are also more evenly distributed now than before due to an increase in the number of parliamentary parties across European party systems. What is more, in many parties' remaining members have increased power to choose candidates and leaders as well as to shape policy (Bolin et al. 2017; Scarrow and Gezgor 2010). Translated into May's conceptual framework, it means that today's parties are characterized by a mid-level elite that is a lot smaller but potentially also more powerful. The smaller size of the mid-level elite and its weaker position might make it less likely to deviate from the ideological position held by the party elite or the party voters. Therefore, we would expect the political parties' internal opinion structure to be relatively homogeneous today. On the other hand, the increase in direct (formal and informal) power given to party members over the past decades might counteract this force. And so there is also reason to expect that we will find evidence for May's law in today's parties.

Any of these proposed patterns within Nordic political parties also yields more general and substantive interest for party politics strategists and researchers. We should care about intra-party opinion structures, and specifically about ideological disagreement between a party's voters, members and candidates for office, because they can exert an impact on important political decisions. A recent analysis of the class composition of the British Labour Party presents evidence that working-class members of parliament differed sharply from professional career politicians in their policy positions on the welfare reforms of the 1990s and 2000s (O'Grady 2018). Studies that focus on intra-party ideological, rather than class, heterogeneity come to similar conclusions. For example, more ideologically centrist social democratic voters in Germany, Sweden and the United Kingdom responded to these parties' left-right moderation in the latter part of the twentieth century in a substantially different way than did the more ideologically extreme, highly partisan voter group (Karreth, Polk and Allen 2013). Intra-party disagreement of members with either the entire party or only parts thereof can also easily have electoral consequences (Polk and Kölln 2018), and it is at the very least a potential broken link in the chain of representation in modern democracies.

In summary, this means that, while we have theoretical reason to believe that party voters, members and candidates differ in their ideological positions, with members being the most extreme, there is also ample reason to suspect that the opposite is more prevalent. In order to bring more information to this debate, we provide below the first systematic comparison of opinion structures in four multiparty countries and across a total of twenty-four political parties.

DATA AND MEASUREMENT

We provide the first cross-national comparisons of three levels of a party and compare party voters, members and candidates in Denmark, Iceland, Norway and Sweden.[2] We opt for the mean position of parties' candidates for elected office as an estimate of the position of the parties' leadership both because the central tendencies of candidates are increasingly used in congruence studies (e.g. Andreadis and Stavrakakis 2017; Costello, Thomassen and Rosema 2012; Leimgruber, Hangartner and Leemann 2010) and because it allows us to explicitly focus on the self-reported ideological orientations of the three levels of a party. In all four countries, we compare the average left-right positions of survey respondents who indicated they had voted for a particular party with the average self-reported left-right positions of that party's members. Each group, the candidates, members and voters, placed themselves on the same 0 (left) to 10 (right) scale. We did not create mutually exclusive groups for any of our analyses, which means that the group of voters may also comprise party members or even party candidates. Likewise, the group of party members may also include party candidates. We do not separate these three groups for conceptual and empirical reasons. As our discussion has already made clear, the three levels of the party coincide with different levels of involvement. A level further up in the hierarchy simply adds involvement and does not substitute involvement. Therefore, it would be conceptually incorrect to artificially separate party voters from party members and party candidates. In addition to that, we were also not always able to separate the groups empirically. For example, the national election studies, which form the basis for our measure of party voters, do not include a variable on party candidacy, sometimes not even on party membership or at least not on membership in individual parties. For these reasons, the three groups overlap conceptually and empirically, and any separation would have been artificial and not clear-cut.

For all four countries, we aimed at analysing surveys for all three levels conducted in close succession to one another. We therefore use for the candidate surveys Wave I (2005–2013) and Wave II (2013–2018) from the Comparative Candidate Survey (CCS 2016, 2018) project. Unfortunately, the CCS does not include Iceland, and so our analyses in this country are limited to mid-level elite (members) and the non-elite (voters). For voters and members, we obtained data from individual national survey projects.

In Denmark, mean party voter placements are derived from the 2011 Danish National Election Study, and those of the party members are from the most proximate member study, which was administered in 2012 (Kosiara-Pedersen and Hansen 2012). Iceland does not have a study of party members, so the positions of party voters and party members are each calculated from the 2013 national election study. The data on Norwegian voters and members were both collected in 2009 in separate studies (Jupskås and Heidar 2009). Finally, the information for party voters is taken from the 2014 Swedish National Election Study (SNES), and the estimates for the aggregate position of Swedish party members are derived from the 2015 Swedish Party Membership Survey (SPMS) (Kölln and Polk 2017). While the timing of these various surveys is not identical, the surveys were conducted rather close to one another within each country and across all countries, providing a useful snapshot of the contemporary political preferences of party members and voters across the Nordic region.

We choose to focus on left-right ideology for substantive and practical reasons. Although we recognize the multidimensional nature of contemporary European politics (Bakker, Jolly and Polk 2012), party politics in the Nordic democracies in particular have been shaped by and according to the left-right dimension (Rovny and Polk 2019). In Sweden, for instance, left-right ideology has been so dominant that analysts have referred to it as one of the most unidimensional political systems in the world (Oscarsson and Holmberg 2016). The specific content, measurement and validity of the left-right dimension often varies from country to country (e.g. see Bauer et al. 2017; Benoit and Laver 2006; Däubler and Benoit 2017; Gabel and Huber 2000), but few would dispute that left-right ideology has served as a dominant organizing structure to political competition in Western Europe in the era of mass participation (for recent discussions, see Dalton and McAllister 2015; Somer-Topcu 2015, 846). This makes left-right ideology one of the most important means of investigating the functioning of party-based representation. On a more practical level, with a total of ten data sets under scrutiny, it was difficult to find other measures of ideological preferences that existed across all levels and countries.

RESULTS

To investigate our research question, we inspect the placement of candidates, members and voters across parties and countries on the left-right scale. In order to find support for May's hypothesis, two conditions need to be met: (1) members need to be ideologically more extreme than candidates and (2) members need to be ideologically more extreme than voters. Figures 5.1 through 5.4 allow us to assess these conditions because they show mean positions for candidates (squares), members (circles) and voters (triangles) per country per party within the same graph. For Iceland, we do not have information on candidates' positions. Several noteworthy patterns appear in the figures.

The first observation to make is that we do not see a coherent pattern in support of May's law with respect to the first condition. On the whole, the pattern within Swedish parties is generally supportive of the first condition of May's law because only members of the Social Democrats report themselves as more moderate than the party's candidates. In all other Swedish parties, candidates hold the more moderate

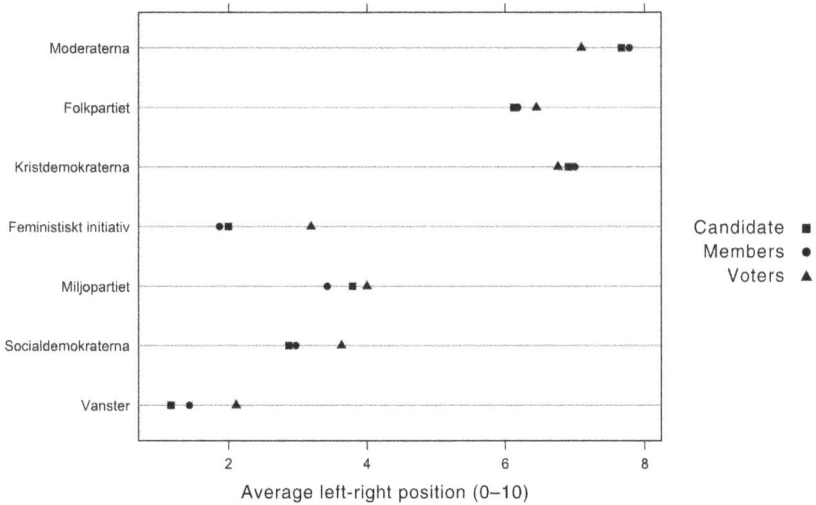

Figure 5.1. Mean left-right ideology positions party voters, members and candidates in Sweden 2014/2015.

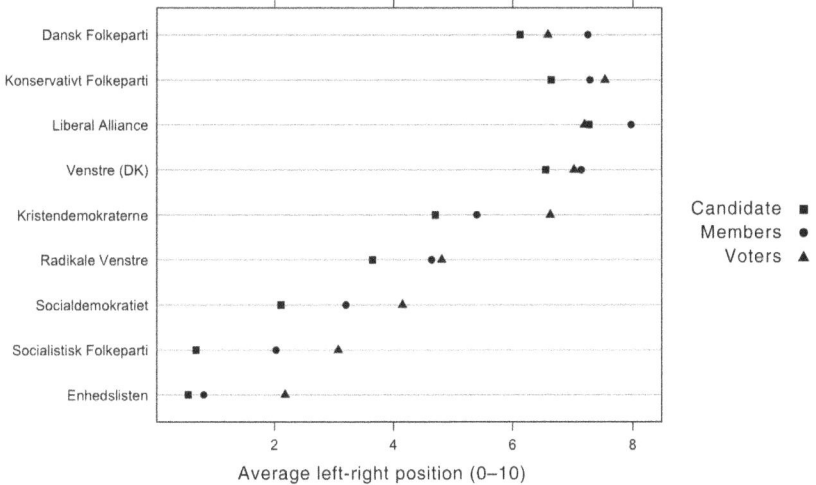

Figure 5.2. Mean left-right ideology positions party voters, members and candidates in Denmark 2011/2012.

ideological position. Yet, the differences between candidates and members in the Swedish parties are all quite small (figure 5.1), particularly in comparison to differences in the other countries. Among Danish and Norwegian parties (figures 5.2 and 5.4), candidates seem to be consistently more left-leaning than their own members – irrespective of the general political leaning of the party. The right-leaning parties in Norway do show members as more ideologically extreme than candidates, but if May's law were supported more generally, we should see that members are more right leaning among the conservative parties, and also that they are more left leaning than their own candidates among the left-leaning parties. However, this is not the case here. Candidates belonging to all Norwegian and Danish parties included in the data set place themselves further to the left on the left-right scale than their own members. This is a very curious pattern, and it thus only supports the first condition of May's hypothesis for parties on the right but not on the left.

It is interesting to observe that within countries, party-level differences are relatively coherent. All Danish, Norwegian and Swedish parties cluster around similar country-level distances between candidates' and members' average left-right placements. This suggests that unmeasured country-level factors might be playing a more prominent role.

With respect to condition two, figures 5.1 through 5.4 also make apparent that the voters and members of political parties place themselves on the left-right ideological spectrum more or less where we would expect them to be based on the party families to which they belong (see chapter 1). Looking at Sweden in figure 5.1, for example, voters and members of the Left Party (Vänster), Feminist Initiative (Feministiskt initiativ), Greens (Miljöpartiet) and Social Democrats (Socialdemokraterna) are all to the left of the mid-point, with the Left Party furthest to the left. The same is true for the other ideological bloc in Sweden. Voters and members of the Moderates (Moderaterna), Liberals (Folkpartiet) and Christian Democrats (Kristdemokraterna) are all to the right of the mid-point, with the Moderates the most right-leaning party in the system, though not by much. We also see a substantial gap between the left- and the right-leaning parties, which reinforces Swedish politics' reputation as being structured by ideological blocs (e.g. see Allern and Aylott 2009; Hinnfors 2015), but of course these data precede the 2018 general election, the results of which

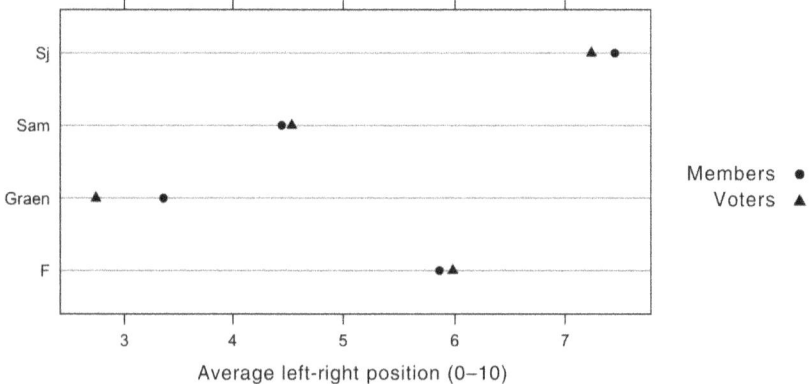

Figure 5.3.   Mean left-right ideology positions party voters and members in Iceland 2013.

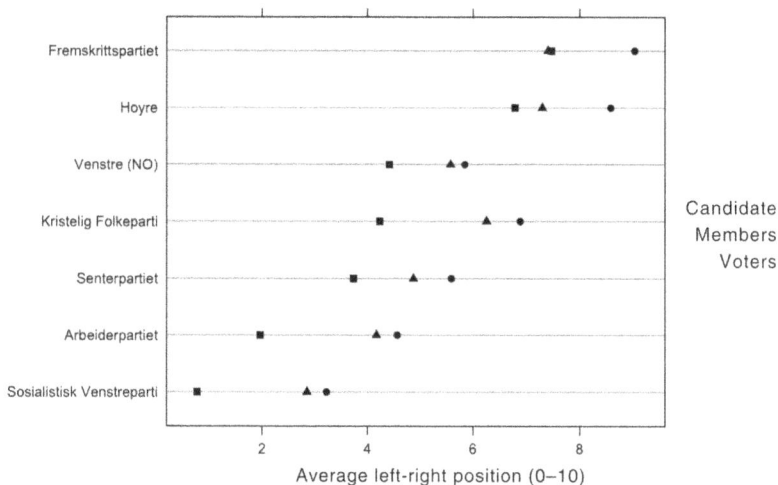

Figure 5.4. Mean left-right ideology positions party voters, members and candidates in Norway 2009.

place increasing strain on bloc politics in Sweden. Looking at the three other Nordic democracies displayed in the figure reveals similar patterns, with, for example, voters and members of the Norwegian Socialist and Labour parties to the left and the Conservative and Progress Party to the right of the ideological divide. This provides both some face validity on data quality and preliminary evidence that voters and party members can meaningfully sort themselves according to left-right ideology.

An additional pattern apparent throughout all four figures is the rather high level of agreement between the average position of party voters and party members on the general left-right dimension, although there is interesting variation here as well. For most parties, particularly in Iceland, the two groups are rather closely aligned in their left-right preferences. Although there is never perfect overlap between the voters and the members, for parties such as the Danish (Venstre) and Swedish Liberals or Swedish Christian Democrats (Kristdemokraterna), differences are nearly impossible to detect. This pattern speaks in favour of the ideological representativeness of political parties when it comes to the comparability of the left-right position of members and the wider group of party voters.

Finally, and as the most straightforward test of the second condition of May's law, we would expect voters of all parties to be more moderate and members to be more extreme in their ideological positions. However, this is not what we always find. In Sweden, voters of the Liberal Party (Folkpartiet) are the most extreme in their ideological placement rather than the most moderate. In Denmark (figure 5.2), another three parties do not fit the party-voter pattern hypothesized by May and formalized in our second condition: voters of the Danish People's Party (Dansk Folkeparti), the Conservative People's Party (Konservativt Folkeparti) and the Liberals (Venstre) are all more extreme than these parties' members. Within the Icelandic Left Green Movement (Graen), members are again less extreme than voters, and in Norway, party voters of almost all parties see themselves, on average, as more extreme in their ideological placements than members' own self-placements. The notable exceptions here are the Progress Party (Fremskrittspartiet) and the Conservatives (Høyre). These opinion structures within our twenty-four political parties in the Nordic countries suggest that (a) the second condition of May's law is regularly not supported by our data, (b) often, particularly members of right-leaning parties are more extreme than their parties' voters, and (c) the ideological representativeness of members is still relatively high, or at least higher than that of candidates.

The finding that the members of some right-leaning Scandinavian parties appear to be more ideologically extreme than the voters and candidates of that same party is interesting given that recent studies provide little support for the hypothesis in the context of other Northern European democracies, such as the Netherlands (van Holsteyn, den Ridder and Koole 2017). Of course, we must reiterate that for some parties, such as the Christian Democrats (Kristdemokraterna) in Sweden, these distances are not large, and we also find much less support for the ideological extremity of members relative to party voters or candidates among the parties of the left. While there does appear to be a clear trend towards more ideological extremity in party members compared to the voters for these parties in Denmark and Sweden, this is not the case in Norway.[3] A big part of the reason we do not find support for May's law on the left is the overall more left-leaning orientation of the candidates in Denmark and Norway compared to the voters. Concerning the possibility of a 'fan-like' opinion structure in which the elites are the most extreme, followed by members and then voters as the most moderate group (Narud and Skare 1999), we only see this pattern among the parties of the ideological left in Denmark. On the whole, the variation we report across the countries of our sample and ideological blocs could at most be read as mixed support for 'May's law' in Nordic democracies (e.g. Narud and Skare 1999; Nielsen 2003; Widfeldt 1999), but these qualifications call into question the law-like nature of May's central hypothesis in this region.

DISCUSSION AND OUTLOOK

In this chapter, we make three interrelated contributions to our understanding of the relationship between party members, candidates and voters in Nordic democracies and the ability of political parties to serve as organizations that link members of society to the state through political representation. First, taken on the whole, the members, candidates for parliament and voters of political parties place themselves on the left-right scale in a position that makes sense given the parties that they support. Candidates, members and voters of social democratic parties place themselves on the centre-left portion of the scale, the members and voters of the parties further to the left of social democrats also place themselves further to the left than social democrats, and so on. Second, while the distance between candidates and other parts of a party can be larger for parties of the left in Denmark and Norway, the absolute distance between party members and voters in the Nordic democracies is not that large. Third, we find some qualified support for the idea that party members are more ideologically extreme than party voters and candidates, but this pattern is not uniform across countries or parties and must be understood in light of the relatively small absolute distances between members and party voters in the region. Overall, the chapter reports rather high agreement or representativeness in the Nordic democracies when it comes to party member and party voter ideological preferences as measured by the general left-right dimension. When it comes to representativeness of candidates and members, there seems to be more variation. A curious pattern that emerged from our analysis in this respect is that candidates of all parties in Denmark and in Norway place themselves further to the left than their own members.

This chapter has provided an overview of the ideological representativeness of political parties in Denmark, Iceland, Norway and Sweden by examining the relative agreement of party voters, party members and party candidates on the general left-right dimension. This is a key concept to party systems in Western European, party-based democracy. In general, our findings point in a normatively desirable direction. The voters and members of political parties are rather similar to each other in their ideological preferences. Nevertheless, there is interesting variation beneath this top-level story that is worthy of additional exploration, and there are other areas that we were not able to explore because of data limitations. Among the latter, one of the most important would be the level of member-voter agreement on the socio-cultural dimension or issues closely related to it, such as immigration.

A number of researchers highlight the relevance of the socio-cultural dimension to contemporary European politics (e.g. Bornschier 2010; Hobolt and de Vries 2015; Hooghe and Marks 2009; Hooghe, Marks and Wilson 2002; Kriesi et al. 2006), and it is widely discussed in the Nordic countries in light of the influx of refugees between 2015 and 2016. What is more, other scholars emphasize that while there are relatively substantial numbers of citizens with left-leaning economic preferences and more authoritarian cultural attitudes, this particular package of policy preferences is offered by few, if any, Western European parties (Lefkofridi, Wagner and Willmann 2014; Thomassen 2012; van der Brug and van Spanje 2009). The tensions involved in attempting to simultaneously represent multiple groups of voters on multiple dimensions give rise to what Rohrschneider and Whitefield (2012) describe as 'the strain of representation'. We lacked comparable data on second-dimension politics to examine party candidates, members and voters across the Nordic countries here, but we hope that future data collection efforts will advance this cause, and in chapter 11, we turn to a fuller examination of ideological representativeness between members and parliamentary candidates that begins to tackle some of the questions surrounding multidimensionality. We report a rather rosy picture of representation in this chapter, but even in the famously unidimensional politics of Sweden, second-dimension contestation is increasingly present.

NOTES

1. Both authors contributed equally to this chapter. The authors received funding from the Swedish Research Council project 2016-01810. We thank Gunnar Helgi Kristinsson for advice and assistance with the Icelandic data.

2. (Some of) the data applied in the analysis in this publication are based on Norway's 'Election Survey 2009'. The data are provided by Statistics Norway (SSB) and prepared and made available by the Norwegian Social Science Data Services (NSD). Professor Bernt Aardal and the Institute of Social Research (ISF) were responsible for the original study, and Statistics Norway collected the data. Neither Bernt Aardal, ISF andSSB nor NSD are responsible for the analyses/interpretation of the data presented here.

3. Recall that the Norwegian data are from 2009, which opens the possibility that analysis of more recent data for members and voters could follow the trends present in the Danish and Swedish data.

BIBLIOGRAPHY

Allern, Elin Haugsgjerd and Nicholas Aylott. 2009. 'Overcoming the Fear of Commitment: Pre-Electoral Coalitions in Norway and Sweden'. *Acta Politica* 44 (3): 259–85.

Andreadis, Ioannis and Yannis Stavrakakis. 2017. 'European Populist Parties in Government: How Well Are Voters Represented? Evidence from Greece'. *Swiss Political Science Review* 23 (4): 485–508.

Aylott, Nicholas and Niklas Bolin. 2017. 'Managed Intra-Party Democracy: Precursory Delegation and Party Leader Selection'. *Party Politics* 23 (1): 55–65.

Bakker, Ryan, Seth Jolly and Jonathan Polk. 2012. 'Complexity in the European Party Space: Exploring Dimensionality with Experts'. *European Union Politics* 13 (2): 219–45.

Bauer, Paul C., Pablo Barberá, Kathrin Ackermann and Aaron Venetz. 2017. 'Is the Left-Right Scale a Valid Measure of Ideology?' *Political Behavior* 39 (3): 553–83.

Benoit, Kenneth and Michael Laver. 2006. *Party Policy in Modern Democracies*. Oxon: Routledge.

Blombäck, Sofie and Jenny de Fine Licht. 2017. 'Same Considerations, Different Decisions: Motivations for Split-Ticket Voting among Swedish Feminist Initiative Supporters'. *Scandinavian Political Studies* 40 (1): 61–81.

Bolin, Niklas, Nicholas Aylott, Benjamin von dem Berge and Thomas Poguntke. 2017. 'Patterns of Intra-Party Democracy across the World'. In *Organizing Political Parties: Representation, Participation, and Power*, edited by Susan E. Scarrow, Paul Webb and Thomas Poguntke, 158–86. Oxford: Oxford University Press.

Bornschier, Simon. 2010. 'The New Cultural Divide and the Two-Dimensional Political Space in Western Europe'. *West European Politics* 33 (3): 419–44.

CCS. 2016. Comparative Candidates Survey Module I – 2005–2013 [Dataset – cumulative file]. Distributed by FORS, Lausanne, 2016.

CCS. 2018. Comparative Candidates Survey Module II – 2013-2016 [Dataset – cumulative file]. Distributed by FORS, Lausanne, 2018.

Ceron, Andrea. 2017. 'Intra-Party Politics in 140 Characters'. *Party Politics* 23 (1): 7–17.

Costello, Rory, Jacques Thomassen and Martin Rosema. 2012. 'European Parliament Elections and Political Representation: Policy Congruence between Voters and Parties'. *West European Politics* 35 (6): 1226–48.

Cross, William P. and Richard S. Katz. 2013. *The Challenges of Intra-Party Democracy*. Oxford: Oxford University Press.

Dahl, Svend. 2011. 'Efter Folkrörelsepartiet'. PhD diss., Stockholm University.

Dalton, Russell J. and Ian McAllister. 2015. 'Random Walk or Planned Excursion? Continuity and Change in the Left-Right Positions of Political Parties'. *Comparative Political Studies* 48 (6): 759–87.

Dalton, Russell J., David M. Farrell and Ian McAllister. 2011. 'The Dynamics of Political Representation'. In *How Democracy Works: Political Representation and Policy Congruence in Modern Societies*, edited by Martin Rosema, Bas Denters and Kees Aarts, 21–38. Amsterdam: Pallas Publications.

Däubler, Thomas and Kenneth Benoit. 2017. 'Estimating Better Left-Right Positions through Statistical Scaling of Manual Content Analysis'. University of Mannheim Working Paper.

Gabel, Matthew J. and John D. Huber. 2000. 'Putting Parties in Their Place: Inferring Party Left-Right Ideological Positions from Party Manifestos Data'. *American Journal of Political Science* 44 (1): 94–103.

Greene, Zachary David and Matthias Haber. 2015. 'The Consequences of Appearing Divided: An Analysis of Party Evaluations and Vote Choice'. *Electoral Studies* 37: 15–27.

Hazan, Reuven Y. and Gideon Rahat. 2010. *Democracy within Parties: Candidate Selection Methods and Their Political Consequences.* Oxford: Oxford University Press.

Hinnfors, Jonas. 2015. 'Socialdemokraterna: Från klar vaghet till vag klarhet'. *Statsvetenskapliga tidskrift* 117 (2): 137–52.

Hobolt, Sara B. and Catherine E. de Vries. 2015. 'Issue Entrepreneurship and Multiparty Competition'. *Comparative Political Studies* 48 (9): 1159–85.

Hooghe, Liesbet and Gary Marks. 2009. 'A Postfunctionalist Theory of European Integration: From Permissive Consensus to Constraining Dissensus'. *British Journal of Political Science* 39 (1): 1–23.

Hooghe, Liesbet, Gary Marks and Carole J. Wilson. 2002. 'Does Left/Right Structure Party Positions on European Integration?' *Comparative Political Studies* 35 (8): 965–89.

Jupskås, Anders and Knut Heidar. 2009. Norwegian Party Member Survey 2009. Department of Political Science, University of Oslo.

Karreth, Johannes, Jonathan T. Polk and Christopher S. Allen. 2013. 'Catch All or Catch and Release? The Electoral Consequences of Social Democratic Parties' March to the Middle in Western Europe'. *Comparative Political Studies* 46 (7): 791–822.

Kitschelt, Herbert. 1989. 'The Internal Politics of Parties: The Law of Curvilinear Disparity Revisited'. *Political Studies* 37 (3): 400–21.

Kölln, Ann-Kristin. 2016. 'Party Membership in Europe: Testing Party-Level Explanations of Decline'. *Party Politics* 22 (4): 465–77.

Kölln, Ann-Kristin and Jonathan Polk. 2017. 'Emancipated Party Members: Examining Ideological Incongruence within Political Parties'. *Party Politics* 23 (1): 18–29.

Kosiara-Pedersen, Karina and Kasper Møller Hansen. 2012. *Danske partimedlemmer 2012: Dokumentationsrapport fra projektet Moderne Partimedlemskab.* Aarhus, Denmark: Center for Valg og Partier, Institut for Statskundskab, Københavns Universitet.

Kriesi, Hanspeter, Edgar Grande, Romain Lachat, Martin Dolezal, Simon Bornschier and Timotheos Frey. 2006. 'Globalization and the Transformation of the National Political Space: Six European Countries Compared'. *European Journal of Political Research* 45 (6): 921–56.

Lefkofridi, Zoe, Markus Wagner and Johanna E. Willmann. 2014. 'Left-Authoritarians and Policy Representation in Western Europe: Electoral Choice across Ideological Dimensions'. *West European Politics* 37 (1): 65–90.

Leimgruber, Philipp, Dominik Hangartner and Lucas Leemann. 2010. 'Comparing Candidates and Citizens in the Ideological Space'. *Swiss Political Science Review* 16 (3): 499–531.

May, John D. 1973. 'Opinion Structure of Political Parties: The Special Law of Curvilinear Disparity'. *Political Studies* 21 (2): 135–51.

Narud, Hanne Marthe and Audun Skare. 1999. 'Are Party Activists the Party Extremists? The Structure of Opinion in Political Parties'. *Scandinavian Political Studies* 22 (1): 45–65.

Nielsen, Hans Jørgen. 2003. 'Partierne som holdingsfælleskaber'. In *Partiernes medlemmer*, edited by Lars Bille and Jørgen Elklit, 132–57. Aarhus: Aarhus Universitetsforlag.

Norris, Pippa. 1995. 'May's Law of Curvilinear Disparity Revisited: Leaders, Officers, Members and Voters in British Political Parties'. *Party Politics* 1 (1): 29–47.

O'Grady, Tom. 2018. 'Careerists versus Coal-Miners: Welfare Reforms and the Substantive Representation of Social Groups in the British Labour Party'. *Comparative Political Studies*. doi: 0010414018784065.

Oscarsson, Henrik and Sören Holmberg. 2016. 'Issue Voting Structured by Left-Right Ideology'. In *The Oxford Handbook of Swedish Politics*, edited by Jon Pierre, 260–74. Oxford: Oxford University Press.

Polk, Jonathan and Ann-Kristin Kölln. 2017. 'The Lives of the Party: Contemporary Approaches to the Study of Intraparty Politics in Europe'. *Party Politics* 23 (1): 3–6.

———. 2018. 'Electoral Infidelity: Why Party Members Cast Defecting Votes'. *European Journal of Political Research* 57 (2): 539–60.

Ramiro, Luis and Raul Gomez. 2016. 'Radical-Left Populism during the Great Recession: Podemos and Its Competition with the Established Radical Left'. *Political Studies* 65 (1) (suppl.): 108–26.

Rohrschneider, Robert and Stephen Whitefield. 2012. *The Strain of Representation: How Parties Represent Diverse Voters in Western and Eastern Europe*. Oxford: Oxford University Press.

Rovny, Jan and Jonathan Polk. 2019. 'New Wine in Old Bottles: Explaining the Dimensional Structure of European Party Systems'. *Party Politics* 25 (1): 12–24.. doi: 10.1177/1354068817752518.

Saglie, Jo and Knut Heidar. 2004. 'Democracy within Norwegian Political Parties: Complacency or Pressure for Change?' *Party Politics* 10 (4): 385–405.

Scarrow, Susan E. and Burcu Gezgor. 2010. 'Declining Memberships, Changing Members? European Political Party Members in a New Era'. *Party Politics* 16 (6): 823–43.

Somer-Topcu, Zeynep. 2015. 'Everything to Everyone: The Electoral Consequences of the Broad-Appeal Strategy in Europe'. *American Journal of Political Science* 59 (4): 841–54.

Thomassen, Jacques. 2012. 'The Blind Corner of Political Representation'. *Representation* 48 (1): 13–27.

van Biezen, Ingrid, Peter Mair and Thomas Poguntke. 2012. 'Going, Going, . . . Gone? The Decline of Party Membership in Contemporary Europe'. *European Journal of Political Research* 51 (1): 24–56.

van der Brug, Wouter and Joost van Spanje. 2009. 'Immigration, Europe and the "New" Cultural Dimension'. *European Journal of Political Research* 48 (3): 309–34.

van Haute, Emilie and R. Kenneth Carty. 2012. 'Ideological Misfits: A Distinctive Class of Party Members'. *Party Politics* 18 (6): 885–95.

van Holsteyn, Joop J. M., Josje M. den Ridder and Ruud A. Koole. 2017. 'From May's Laws to May's Legacy: On the Opinion Structure within Political Parties'. *Party Politics* 23 (5): 471–86.

Widfeldt, Anders. 1999. 'Losing Touch? The Political Representativeness of Swedish Parties, 1985–1994'. *Scandinavian Political Studies* 22 (4): 307–26.

6

United or Divided?

Preferential Agreement among Party Members in Scandinavia

Sofie Blombäck, Anders Ravik Jupskås and Jonas Hinnfors

In most contemporary democracies, not least in 'party democracies' such as the Scandinavian countries (Demker and Svåsand 2005, 40), parties perform several crucial tasks. One of these tasks is to aggregate and articulate political interests (Almond and Powell 1966). By representing certain interests, parties provide a linkage between the citizens and the political system (Lawson 1980). However, if parties are internally divided, the processes of aggregating and articulating interests become far more difficult, which, in turn, might affect how parties function in the electoral, organizational and governing arenas. Party elites may have a hard time knowing which issues to prioritize and which positions to communicate. Members who disagree with the party's position might be less willing to participate.[1] And divided parties might be unreliable coalition partners or fail to enter government in the first place (Bäck 2008). Moreover, from the perspective of representative democracy, divided parties might be problematic because voters need not only *different* alternatives but also *clear* alternatives (den Ridder 2014). If party positions are blurry, contradictory or non-existent, voters simply do not know what they are voting for and it becomes difficult to hold elected representatives accountable in elections.

In contemporary Western democracies, party unity – and thus the character of citizen-party linkage – seems to be under pressure due to a more complex cleavage structure and a more fragmented party system. The Scandinavian countries are by no means an exception to this general trend towards a new political landscape (Aylott 2011; Jupskås 2018). In fact, from a comparative perspective, party system change and electoral volatility have been relatively high in the Scandinavian region – in Denmark and Norway since the 1970s and in Sweden since the late 1980s (Chiaramonte and Emanuele 2017, 378; Emanuele and Chiaramonte 2018). The emergence of new political issues and the rise of new parties mean that established parties may eventually have to deal with issues where they are less internally united. At the same time, it might be difficult for new parties to deal with issues that existed long before they were founded.

In this chapter, we study internal divisions of parties by looking at *preferential agreement* among ordinary party members in the three Scandinavian countries: Norway, Denmark and Sweden. Preferential agreement refers to the extent to which members agree on normative statements about different policy-related issues. It differs from cohesion, which often refers to behavioural aspects, such as voting in parliament. It also differs from *perceptual agreement*, which is concerned with the extent to which people agree on statements about how the reality *is* as opposed to how it *should be*.

The question of preferential agreement – or similar aspects – is far from new among party scholars (e.g. Janda 1980) but is rarely addressed by looking at ordinary members. Most research tends to look at the elite level, such as voting patterns in parliament (see Close and Gherghina [2017] for a comprehensive review). And although there are a few exceptions to this rule, they are all single-case studies (e.g. den Ridder 2014; Heidar and Saglie 2002, 128–34; Kosiara-Pedersen 2017). Our study is heavily inspired by den Ridder's (2014) analysis of Dutch members, but the comparative perspective allows us to gauge whether patterns of preferential agreement are similar or different across different contexts.

The chapter is structured as follows. First, we discuss some tentative expectations about why preferential agreement among members would be higher or lower. Second, we elaborate upon how we measure preferential agreement, including the issues we focus on, how they are operationalized, and the method we use to calculate levels of preferential agreement. As in other chapters in this edited volume, the data come from party membership surveys in Denmark (2012), Sweden (2015) and Norway (2017). Third, we present the empirical results – first within each country and then across countries, the old/new divide and party families. Towards the end, we summarize key findings and discuss some of the implications, including possible effects on party membership linkage.

DRIVERS OF PREFERENTIAL AGREEMENT:
Country-Specific Issue Competition, Party Age and Party Family

Why would we expect differences among the Scandinavian countries in terms of whether the various parties' members are more or less in agreement? Parties have been exposed to new inter-party competition logics (Chiaramonte and Emanuele 2017; Emanuele and Chiaramonte 2018), not least through the emergence and consolidation of populist radical right parties (Jupskås 2018). This change has exposed the established parties to tremendous pressures in terms of whether or not to adapt to a new issue agenda (Bale et al. 2010). However, the parties have reacted differently, in the sense that, while the Sweden Democrats are still a stigmatized and politically isolated party, the Norwegian Progress Party was invited to join a centre-right government in 2013. In Denmark, the Danish People's Party became accepted as a viable cooperation partner by the Conservative Party and the Liberals after the Social Liberals had left the previous non-socialist bloc and sided with the Social Democrats in the mid-1990s (Green-Pedersen and Krogstrup 2008). In comparison, the previous Swedish two-bloc format is about to be 'dismantled' into a centre-left, a centre-right and a populist right bloc (Aylott and Bolin 2015, 738). Further, the Swedish Green Party has been in parliament since the 1990s, two decades earlier than its Norwegian cousin. There, and in Denmark, where there was no green party in parliament until 2015, green issues were co-opted by other parties (Bjørklund and Hellevik 1988; Tonsgaard 1989).

Yet another potential reason why parties might encounter different levels of internal agreement is suggested by Önnudóttir (2014, 549): 'Party age can be expected to influence policy congruence as older parties would have a clearer policy position than younger and less established parties. Older parties have had a longer time to establish themselves and mobilize voters'. Although focusing on a slightly different aspect of agreement, Dahlberg (2009, 272) also suggests that 'party age should thus have a positive impact on' the degree of agreement between voters and their parties regarding policy positions. The main reason would be down to the propensity of younger parties to change (parts of) their policies and ideological profiles, which in the end will be confusing for the voters (van der Brug, Franklin and Tóka 2008) – and by inference, for the members. The more stable the party's overall policy positions, the more likely members are to know and agree with the full set of positions. A less ideologically clear party might instead attract members with more divergent policy preferences. In the following, we will expect older parties to display higher levels of preferential agreement among their members than younger parties do.[2]

Finally, the different ideological roots of political parties have always provided a mobilizing logic (Mair and Mudde 1998, 223). In general, some party families tend to be more ideologically homogeneous than others (social democratic parties more; liberal parties less; Carroll and Kubo 2017, 7ff.; Ennser 2012, 162, 167; Marks and Wilson 2000, 452). Prima facie, there is as yet little to indicate theoretically why the degree of preferential agreement among party members would change when we move from one party family to another. However, according to Blondel (1978, 142), parties belonging to 'extreme' party families often prefer to 'give unity precedence over size'. Moreover, some parties tend to present themselves to the voters via a more pronounced 'nicheness', that is, a narrower ideological frame (Meyer and Miller 2015, 265). While 'mainstream', 'extreme', or 'niche' are rather nebulous as concepts, we have reason to believe that, following Rokkan, parties do not present themselves de novo to their voters and members (Lipset and Rokkan 1967, 2). They have histories of prioritizing certain issues and certain ideological dimensions over others. Some party families share a historically defined logic rooted in clashes over traditional-class politics concerned with economic issues. Others are rooted in 'new' cultural politics concerned with identity, values and norms (Bakker et al. 2015;

Dalton 2009). In contemporary European politics, new parties have tended to focus on libertarian (e.g. green parties) and authoritarian (e.g. radical right parties) issues, whereas the established parties have tended to be more concerned with traditional economic left/right issues (Koedam 2017, 6ff.). Potentially, ideological dimensions can develop into 'first-' and 'second-order' status. Still, although parties belonging to the traditional 'five-party model' (see chapter 1) might historically focus on state/market issues, there are clear exceptions to this pattern. In Denmark, for example, liberal parties began to be concerned with libertarian issues decades ago (e.g. Knutsen 1990).

On the one hand, assuming that the historically rooted ideological profile of the party might impact upon the recruitment of members and the attitudes of those already in the party, members would be likely to hold relatively more cohesive views on certain issues. On the other hand, 'In competitive democracies, parties cannot simply focus only on their most favoured issues, as they do not control the political agenda'. Potentially, internally divided parties 'lose credibility and voters sooner rather than later' (Kitschelt 2007, 1182), which will therefore force the parties to manage the internal arena in such a way as to boost preferential agreement. Thus, whether different party families manage to develop more or less internal preferential agreement on different types of issues is an empirical question, but since the parties have different origins, some parties are probably going to be more successful than others.

To sum up, in the following, we will map the degree of party member preferential agreement among Scandinavian political parties in relation to potential explanations based on differences/similarities between (1) countries, (2) party ages and (3) party families.

HOW TO MEASURE PREFERENTIAL AGREEMENT:
Issues, Operationalization and Calculation

In this section, we discuss in detail the issues we focus upon in the study, including how important they are in contemporary Scandinavian politics and how we have operationalized them. We analyse levels of preferential agreement on five issues: economy, immigration, environment, the EU and law and order (see table 6.1).[3] With the exception of the law and order issue, which we included for reasons of comparability (see below), these issues 'have come to play an important role in shaping the party competition and voting behavior' in the Scandinavian region (Bengtsson et al. 2014, 33).[4] They also reflect both traditional (i.e. economy) and more recent (i.e. immigration, environment and the EU) political conflicts.

The economy has been important for almost a century and constitutes the key conflict dimension for the 'old parties', and it continues to be important to voters (Bergh and Karlsen 2017; Stubager and Hansen 2013; Oscarsson and Holmberg 2016, 177). Due to a limited number of comparable items across the three surveys, we cannot aim for a comprehensive and nuanced operationalization of 'the economy' in our study. In fact, there are no questions about the economy that are identical or even similar across all three surveys. Instead, we first compare Norwegian with Danish members by analysing whether members support or oppose progressive taxation. Then, we can compare Norwegian and Swedish members by focusing on attitudes towards economic redistribution. The Norwegian survey asks whether members agree or disagree that 'income and assets should be reallocated to the benefit of ordinary people', whereas the Swedish survey asks whether members agree or disagree that 'the state should take measures to reduce income disparities'. Although the exact wording in the Norwegian and Swedish surveys is not identical on this topic, the mean position of the members within each party suggests that the questions largely measure the same underlying concept, that is, of economic redistribution.

The other issues included in this study have emerged more recently. The environmental issue was brought into politics in the 1980s and advocated by new green parties (as in Sweden) or left-wing and liberal parties (as in Norway and Denmark). Again, the surveys have no question about the environment that is identical across all three countries. The Norwegian and Swedish surveys include a question on what we refer to as 'environmental protection', namely, whether stronger measures should be taken to protect the environment. The Danish survey, however, only includes a question which contrasts environmental efforts with business activity.[5] This seems to make a real difference, as the Danish survey indicates much larger inter-party conflict – and thus most likely, larger intraparty conflict – than the valence issue in the other surveys. Fortunately, a similar question tapping into what we call 'environmental priority' is also included in the Norwegian survey, though the greener policies are instead contrasted with lower personal consumption for the individual. Mean positions of the parties suggest that the two items are largely comparable.

The immigration issue became important for voters somewhat later, in the 1990s in Norway and Denmark and about a decade ago in Sweden, linked to the rise of a new party family, the radical right (Andersen and Bjørklund 1990; Green-Pedersen and Krogstrup 2008). As in the case of the two previous issues, we need to measure attitudes towards immigration using two different items. In the Norwegian and Swedish surveys, members are asked about their views on assimilation. More specifically, they are asked whether they agree or disagree that it is important for immigrants to adapt to Norwegian/Swedish customs and values. The Danish and Norwegian surveys include a more controversial topic, namely, whether immigration represents a serious threat to the national identity.

The EU is also a more recent political issue in Scandinavian politics, first appearing on the agenda in the 1970s when Norway and Denmark organized national referendums on whether or not to join the European Economic Community. While this issue is generally characterized by low salience in recent elections, voters do seem to care strongly about the issue when it is put on the agenda, which happened in both Norway and Sweden in the early 1990s due to national referendums. In the membership surveys, the questions about the EU are far from identical, partly because Norway is still not a member, whereas the two others are. Not surprisingly, the main question for Norwegian party members is whether Norway should join the union or not. This framing of the issue makes it more likely that members will choose an extreme position, which, in turn, might have an impact on levels of preferential (dis)agreement, compared with the Swedish question, namely, whether European integration should go further or if it has already gone too far. Not only does this capture a more general feeling about European integration, but it also allows for a more nuanced response compared to the Norwegian question. In Denmark, members are not given a general statement on which to agree or disagree. Instead, the members need to choose between four scenarios. Although phrased differently (compared to Sweden), the distribution of views within each party suggests that this item also effectively captures attitudes towards European integration. The main challenge to keep in mind, however, is that levels of agreement tend to be higher when we have four response categories (in Denmark) compared to five categories (in Sweden and Norway).

The final issue we focus on is law and order. While this issue does not seem to play a major role in contemporary Scandinavian politics (Bergh and Karlsen 2017), it is often used as an indicator of the emerging libertarian-authoritarian cleavage (Aardal 2015, 56; Møller Hansen and Stubager 2017, 403; Oscarsson 2017, 421). Perhaps more importantly, this is the only issue for which we can make direct comparisons across the three membership surveys. All three surveys ask the respondents about the extent to which they believe that those who commit violent crimes (in Denmark) or people who break the law (in Norway and Sweden) should be punished more severely.

As in previous research on preferential agreement among party members (see den Ridder 2014), we measure levels of (dis)agreement by calculating Agreement scores – or A-scores (van der Eijk 2001).[6] We use this measurement for two reasons. First, and most importantly, this approach is able to cope with scales with a fixed number of categories, a skewed distribution and clear peaks. Other common measures are problematic because they are either unable to distinguish between those that (dis)agree somewhat and those that (dis)agree completely (e.g. opinion balance) or are heavily influenced by the extent to which the 'mean of a distribution is located near one of the end-poles of a rating scale' (e.g. standard deviation) (van der Eijk 2001, 327).

While some other measures are difficult to interpret and depend on the number of categories, A-scores have fixed upper and lower bounds (–1 and +1, respectively) and are intuitively easy to interpret. A score of –1 refers to a situation in which half of the members disagree completely and the other half agree completely, that is, a much polarized party. When the score is 0, members are not polarized but still quite divided: there is an equal share of members in each category (in our study based on five-point Likert scales, this means 20 per cent of the members). A score of +1 is the result of a distribution where all members hold the same position, regardless of which position this is. This is obviously a very united party.

Table 6.1. List of issues and items used to measure preferential agreement among party members in Scandinavia.

	NORWAY	SWEDEN	DENMARK
Progressive taxation	High income should be taxed more heavily than today.		High income should be taxed more heavily than today.
Redistribution	Income and assets should be reallocated to the benefit of ordinary people.	The state should take measures to reduce income disparities.	
Immigration assimilation	It is important for immigrants to adapt to Norwegian customs and values.	Immigrants should adapt to Swedish customs and traditions.	
Immigrant threat	Immigrant represents a serious threat to our national identity.		Immigrant represents a serious threat to our national identity.
Environmental protection	We should introduce stronger measures to take care of the environment.	Stronger measures should be taken to protect the environment.	
Environmental priority	Where would you place yourself on the scale, where 0 represents the view that environmental protection should not be taken so far that it affects our standard of living, and 10 represents the view that we should do more for environmental protection, even if it means considerably lower personal consumption for the individual?*		Efforts to improve the environment must not go so far as to damage business.

Table 6.1.   (Continued)

	NORWAY	SWEDEN	DENMARK
EU	Norway should become a full member of the EU.	Some think European integration should go further, others think it has already gone too far. What do you think?*	Which of the following four statements about EU cooperation do you agree with most? (1) The EU should eventually evolve into United States of Europe with a joint government; (2) individual EU countries should increasingly leave decisions to the EU and join the community; (3) in EU cooperation, individual member states should maintain full autonomy and have the right to veto EU decisions; or (4) Denmark should withdraw from the EU.
Law and order	People who break the law should be given tougher sentences than today.	People who break the law should be given stiffer sentences.	Violent crimes should be punished far more severely than they are today.

*Two items – environmental priority in Norway and EU in Sweden – have been recoded from an 11-point scale into a 5-point scale in order to be able to compare with other countries and other issues.

SCANDINAVIAN PARTY MEMBERS:
Often United But Sometimes Divided

The overall finding is that party members in Scandinavia are united. This is important to keep in mind when we highlight some of the differences within and across parties on different issues. Even if they are notable and, in some cases, may explain why some parties are struggling more than others in the public debate, no parties, with the single exception of the Liberal party in Norway on the EU issue, seem to be profoundly polarized on any of the issues we study.

Norwegian Members

The empirical results suggest that party members in Norwegian parties are quite united (A-score across all parties and issues is 0.60). All parties receive A-scores above zero with the single exception of the EU question for the Liberal Party. In fact, the A-scores are above 0.5 on a majority of the seven issues covered for all parties except for the Conservative Party (which receives an A-score above 0.5 on three of the seven items). However, if we zoom in on the different issues, there are important differences between parties regarding levels of agreement.

On economic issues, both progressive taxation and redistribution, centre-left parties tend to be more united than centre-right parties. In fact, the only exception is the Liberals, which are slightly more united than the agrarian Centre Party on the issue of redistribution. The Socialist Left Party is particularly united. However, with the exception of the Progress Party, the centre-right is also rather united. The rather low agreement score for the Progress Party is somewhat surprising given its origins as an anti-tax party (see table 6.2). However, over the years, the party has become proletarianized with increasing support among the working class, resulting in ideological tensions between 'authoritarian social democrats' and 'libertarians' (Jupskås 2016).

As regards new issues, levels of agreement depend very much on which issue we focus on. On the item measuring attitudes to immigration assimilation, Norwegian

Table 6.2. Summary of A-scores per party and issue for Norwegian party members, 2017.

	SV	AP	MDG	SP	KRF	V	H	FRP	Mean
Progressive taxation	0.84	0.65	0.66	0.55	0.42	0.40	0.47	0.19	0.52
Redistribution	0.80	0.56	0.58	0.43	0.36	0.50	0.31	0.07	0.45
immigrant assimilate	0.54	0.55	0.53	0.61	0.60	0.51	0.68	0.92	0.62
Immigration threat	0.78	0.55	0.59	0.26	0.48	0.56	0.26	0.68	0.52
Law and order	0.45	0.42	0.52	0.49	0.51	0.47	0.51	0.66	0.50
Environmental protection	0.89	0.54	0.96	0.51	0.53	0.77	0.52	0.41	0.64
Environmental priority	0.61	0.49	0.82	0.53	0.50	0.61	0.52	0.38	0.56
EU	0.75	0.13	0.35	0.92	0.67	-0.21	0.17	0.61	0.42
Mean	0.72	0.49	0.60	0.54	0.51	0.43	0.42	0.50	0.60

Source: Norwegian membership survey 2017. See table 1 for the exact wording of the questions for each issue.

members are – perhaps somewhat surprisingly – quite united. Although there are important differences as regards *the extent to which* they agree that immigrants should adapt to Norwegian culture, very few members in any party disagree with the statement. The item tapping into more xenophobic aspects of immigration policies produces more intra-party tension. While the Progress Party obviously remains united (in favour of the statement) and the Socialist Left Party is much more united (against the statement) than it was on assimilation, both the Conservatives and the agrarian Centre Party seem characterized by lower levels of agreement, probably reflecting a not entirely unknown division between national conservatives on the one hand and liberals (in the Conservatives) and left-leaning farmers (in the Centre Party) on the other hand. However, it is important to note that there are no signs of polarization (i.e. A-score below 0) in either of the two parties.

On environmentalism, parties with a green profile – the Socialists, the Liberals and the Greens – are more united than the others on both environmental protection and environmental priority. The difference between these three parties and the other parties is bigger for protection compared to priority for the simple reason that members in green parties agree completely with the need for stronger protection but are divided between those who agree completely and those who agree somewhat when they need to prioritize between the environment and other benefits such as the living standard. Among the parties, the Progress Party is most divided internally.

As noted previously, the EU issue is not particularly salient in contemporary Norwegian politics, but it tends to generate strong feelings whenever it emerges on the political agenda. This was evident both in 1972 and 1994, when Norway had referenda on EU membership. In both of these referenda, some parties suffered from profound internal disagreement. The Liberals actually split in 1972 due to the EU question, while Labour had organized factions both in favour of and against Norwegian membership in the EU. Today, the issue continues to be a challenge for these two parties, the Liberals in particular. In fact, on this issue, the Liberals, as the only party in this study, receive a negative A-score, suggesting a polarization tendency. In Labour, on the other hand, 29 per cent of the members oppose the dominant view, which is to remain outside of the EU. Somewhat surprisingly, given its previous profile as a pro-EU party, this is the case also with the Conservatives. In this party, too, 29 per cent of the members oppose the dominant view of being pro-EU.

Regarding the final issue in the Norwegian survey – law and order – there are, with the exception of the Progress Party, small differences between the parties. The A-score varies between 0.42 for the Labour Party and 0.52 for the Greens. In the Progress Party, which – at least in recent decades – is the only party that has explicitly campaigned on law and order, most members (81 per cent) support stricter sentences.

Swedish Members

Swedish members are also quite united (A-score across parties and issues is 0.50). Again, and this time without any exceptions, all parties receive A-scores above zero on all five issues included in this study. Furthermore, all parties have A-scores above 0.3 with the exception of the Social Democrats on immigrant assimilation. As in the case of Norway, however, there are a number of important differences regarding levels of agreement between parties when we look more closely at each issue (see table 6.3).

With few (but significant) exceptions, the issue of economic redistribution has been at the forefront of Swedish political debate. Among party members, we find a high degree of unity among the leftmost parties. Virtually all Left Party members and most Feminist Initiative members agree that redistribution is a very good proposal. The other centre-left parties are somewhat less united, but it should be noted that this is the issue where the Social Democrats are the most united. Echoing the Norwegian results, the parties on the centre-right are less united, with A-scores ranging from the Christian Democrat's 0.32 to the Moderate Party's 0.39. In all three parties, roughly a third of the members opted for the 'neither good nor bad' option. Both the Liberals and the Christian Democrats then split fairly equally among the two remaining non-extreme options, while the remaining Moderates mostly opted for the 'fairly bad' or 'very bad' options.

Immigration is the issue that most divides the Swedish parties, even though only the less controversial issue of assimilation was included.[7] This is especially true for the Social Democrats, but only the Moderates have an A-score of more than 0.5. When it comes to law and order, the parties on the left are somewhat less united than the parties on the right. Again the Social Democrats are the most divided, closely followed by the Greens. The issue that most unites the party members is by far environmental protection. Unsurprisingly, the Green Party is most strongly in favour of the proposal and is also the most united. Nine out of ten members are strongly in agreement with proposals to increase environmental protection. For most of the other parties, members are split between the two most positive responses.

As was the case in Norway, the EU issue is not usually at the forefront of the political debates. Around the two EU-themed referenda, however, several parties experienced internal tensions (Jahn and Storsved 1995, 29). Looking at the party members today, the most united are the ones that are most in favour and most opposed to European integration; the Liberals and the Left Party respectively.

Table 6.3. Summary of A-scores per party and issue for Swedish party members, 2015.

	V	FI	S	MP	FP	KD	M	Mean
Redistribution	0.91	0.73	0.68	0.67	0.37	0.32	0.39	0.58
Immigrant assimilation	0.31	0.41	0.28	0.31	0.40	0.50	0.52	0.39
Law and order	0.40	0.36	0.33	0.34	0.43	0.46	0.57	0.41
Environmental protection	0.83	0.87	0.60	0.92	0.60	0.54	0.53	0.70
EU	0.53	0.33	0.39	0.39	0.49	0.34	0.39	0.41
Mean	0.60	0.54	0.45	0.53	0.46	0.43	0.48	0.50

Source: Swedish membership survey 2015. See table 1 for the exact wording of the questions for each issue.

Danish Members

The empirical pattern of preferential agreement among members in Danish parties is similar to that in Norwegian and Swedish parties (A-score across all parties and issues is 0.53). All the A-scores are above zero, but unlike in Sweden, we find a handful of cases with A-scores below 0.3. This is displayed in table 6.4.

On the economic issue of progressive taxation, we see large differences in the degree of agreement. The Liberal Alliance and the Red-Green Alliance both have their highest A-score on this issue, albeit reflecting diametrically different policy preferences. The Liberal Alliance members are firmly against the proposal, while the Red-Green Alliance members are equally firmly in favour of it. This reflects these parties' position at the wings of the economic dimension of Danish politics. The Danish People's Party, on the other hand, has the lowest A-score by far, reflecting the fact that economic issues are not the priority of the party and not the primary reason for joining it, and that they have moved along the economic dimension towards the centre.

This impression is reinforced when we look at the first of the newer issues, immigration. Here, most Danish People's Party members agree that immigration is a threat, giving a high A-score of 0.82. Again, the Red-Green Alliance members are also in agreement with each other, but in their case, it is because they disagree with the statement. The Red-Green Alliance and the Danish People's Party occupy either end of the new politics/value dimension of Danish politics, which is made up of immigration, law and order and environment policies. The Liberal Alliance, on the other hand, has its lowest A-score for this issue, as do the two other more established right-wing parties, the Liberal Party and the Conservative Party.

When it comes to law and order, the Danish People's Party is by far the most united. The lowest level of agreement is found among the Social Democrats, closely followed by the Socialist People's Party (SF). In the final two issues, there are smaller differences in the level of agreement between the parties. On the environmental issue, the parties' A-scores range from 0.42 (Christian Democrats) to 0.69 (Red-Green Alliance). The issue with the highest overall preferential agreement among Danish party members is the EU, where all parties have A-scores well above 0.5. In all parties except for the Social Liberals, the plurality of members support the same option – all countries retaining their autonomy – suggesting that there is preferential agreement not only within each party but also within the society at large.

Table 6.4.   Summary of A-scores per party and issue for Danish party members, 2012.

	EL	SF	S	RV	KD	V	KF	LA	DF	Mean
Progressive taxation	0.86	0.64	0.56	0.37	0.40	0.51	0.66	0.90	0.16	0.56
Immigration threat	0.84	0.72	0.45	0.75	0.42	0.28	0.24	0.19	0.82	0.52
Law and order	0.38	0.30	0.27	0.38	0.48	0.50	0.53	0.45	0.83	0.46
Environmental priority	0.69	0.50	0.43	0.47	0.42	0.56	0.49	0.47	0.49	0.50
EU	0.60	0.56	0.56	0.57	0.70	0.58	0.60	0.58	0.69	0.60
Mean	0.67	0.54	0.45	0.51	0.48	0.49	0.50	0.52	0.60	0.53

Source: Danish membership survey 2012. See table 1 for the exact wording of the questions for each issue.

DIFFERENCES BETWEEN COUNTRIES,
OLD AND NEW PARTIES AND PARTY FAMILIES

Preferential Agreement – Country by Country

Are there any differences between the three countries if we look at the mean score of preferential agreement across all parties? Due to different items in the different surveys, we first compare Norway and Denmark and then Norway and Sweden. While we should emphasize that differences between the countries are small, some differences are worth noting. On average, Danish parties are slightly more united on taxation (0.04 higher A-score) and slightly less united on law and order (0.04 lower A-score) and the environment (0.06 lower A-score) compared to Norwegian parties (see table 6.5). This is partly related to the existence of a libertarian party in Denmark, the Liberal Alliance, which is extremely united in its opposition towards any kind of taxation. Without this party, there are no differences between the two countries. Similarly, the higher level of agreement on the environmental issue in Norway is (at least partly) due to the existence of a green party, which is obviously profoundly united on this particular issue.[8] With regard to law and order, centre-left parties in Denmark are systematically less united compared to the centre-left in Norway, whereas the radical right in Denmark is more united than in Norway. These observations might reflect the higher salience of the so-called value dimension in Danish politics in recent decades, on which right-wing parties tend to be more united than left-wing parties. On the EU question, Norwegian parties seem to be much more divided, although the difference might be due to a methodological effect (i.e. quite different wording of the question and different numbers of response categories). However, the difference might also reflect the fact that the question of membership for a non-member country (Norway) is more polarizing than the question of various forms of commitment for a member country (Denmark).

Table 6.5. Preferential agreement across the Scandinavian countries.

	NORWAY	DENMARK	SWEDEN*
Progressive taxation	0.52	0.56	–
Redistribution	0.45	–	0.58
Immigration threat	0.52	0.52	–
Immigrant assimilation	0.62	–	0.39
Law and order	0.50	0.46	0.41
Environmental protection	0.64	–	0.70
Environmental priority	0.56	0.50	–
EU	0.42	0.60	0.43

*The Centre Party and the Sweden Democrats are not included. The A-scores are largely the same if we exclude the Feminist Initiative, which is not in parliament, from the Swedish figures, but Swedish parties become somewhat less united on redistribution (–0.02) and environmental protection (–0.03).

If we compare Norwegian and Swedish parties, there is virtually no difference on the EU question, but it seems as if the Swedish parties are somewhat more united on redistribution and the environment and more divided on immigrant assimilation and law and order. This might be due to the relative importance of different cleavages. Compared to Norway (and also Denmark), Swedish politics was dominated by the traditional class cleavage much longer and, since the 1980s, by the green dimension, while immigration and law and order have emerged more recently (Bengtsson et al. 2014, 33; Oscarsson and Holmberg 2016, 372). However, we should keep in mind that a direct comparison between two countries is problematic. After all, the Swedish survey does not include two parties – the radical right Sweden Democrats and the liberal (bur former agrarian) Centre Party – which would have significantly affected the average scores of preferential agreement.[9] Yet, if we exclude Norwegian parties for which there are no Swedish equivalents, the pattern is quite similar, although less clear. In fact, the only exception is the EU question, on which there is less agreement in Norway when the agrarians are not included.

Preferential Agreement – Old versus New Parties

Turning to differences between types of parties, we begin by looking at the average preferential agreement within old and new parties, respectively, on the different issues. We expected older parties to have higher overall levels of preferential agreement than newer parties, since they will have had a longer time to become ideologically stable and members can thus have a better idea of where their party stands, even before joining. The scores are displayed in table 6.6.

This turns out not to be the case, however. For all the issues we study, average preferential agreement is higher among the new parties than among the old parties. On the economic issues, the differences between the old and new parties are modest. This is particularly surprising since all of the old parties were formed when economic

Table 6.6. Preferential agreement in 'old' and 'new' parties.

	Old	New*	Countries included
Progressive taxation	0.52	0.57	NO and DK
Redistribution	0.50	0.53	NO and SE
Immigration threat	0.46	0.61	NO and DK
Immigrant assimilation	0.50	0.53	NO and SE
Law and order	0.44	0.49	All
Environmental protection	0.60	0.77	NO and SE
Environmental priority	0.51	0.55	NO and DK
EU	0.45	0.54	All

*SF is, as suggested in the introductory chapter, counted as an old party. Excluding the Feminist Initiative, which is not in parliament, from the calculation does not change the general pattern, but new parties become more divided on the environment (–0.13) and redistribution (–0.04) and somewhat more united on assimilation (+0.03), law and order (+0.02) and EU (+0.01).

issues dominated all the Scandinavian party systems, while several of the new parties were formed around newer issues, such as environment and immigration. This has not translated into the newer parties' members being less in agreement on economic issues. It seems that they have united in their views on both economic and other types of questions.

Among the newer issues, we find some larger differences between old and new, most clearly for the environmental protection issue (0.17 difference in A-score). As we have previously seen, the green parties have exceptionally high levels of agreement when it comes to the environment, which partially explains this difference. There is no corresponding gap between old and new parties on the other, more controversial, issue of environmental priority (0.04 difference). For our two immigration issues, we find the opposite pattern. The more controversial issue of immigration as a threat divides members in both new and old parties, and the average degree of agreement does not differ much between the two groups (0.03 difference). The average level of agreement among the new parties for the less controversial question about assimilation is substantially larger than among old parties, however (0.15 A-score difference).

Preferential Agreement for Different Party Families

Finally, we look at differences in average preferential agreement among different party families (see table 6.7). Here, we tentatively expected party families ideologically rooted in the traditional class cleavage to be more united on economic issues and less united on newer issues such as immigration, the environment and the EU. Conversely, we expected parties rooted in the (more recent) libertarian-authoritarian cleavage to be more united on new issues and less united on old issues such the economy.

Starting with the families on the left, we see that left socialist parties tend to have high levels of internal agreement, with the exceptions of law and order and assimilation of immigrants. The high level of internal unity is particularly pronounced on the economic issues, in line with our expectations. The social democrats have lower overall average A-scores, but these parties also conform to our expectation that they agree most on economic issues. We only have one agrarian party in our sample, the Norwegian one, which does not conform to the expectations. It has high levels of agreement on several newer issues, including assimilation and in particular the EU. Green parties, unsurprisingly, have high levels of preferential agreement on both of the environmental issues that we study, most pronounced on the environmental protection issue.

Among the families on the right, the radical right stands out due to their low average level of preferential agreement on economic issues and their high levels on law and order and immigration-related issues. This is in line with the expectations, but also a clear indication that not all of the newer issues are the same; the radical right is not particularly in agreement on environmental issues.

Table 6.7. Preferential agreement across party families.

	Left Socialist*	Social Democrat	Green	Agrarian	Countries
Progressive taxation	0.78	0.60	0.66	0.55	NO & DK
Redistribution	0.81	0.62	0.62	0.43	NO & SE
Immigration threat	0.78	0.50	0.59	0.26	NO & DK
Immigrant assimilation	0.42	0.42	0.42	0.61	NO & SE
Law and order	0.38	0.34	0.43	0.49	All
Environmental protection	0.86	0.57	0.94	0.51	NO & SE
Environmental priority	0.60	0.46	0.82	0.53	NO & DK
EU	0.57	0.37	0.39	0.92	All
Countries	All	All	NO & SE	Only NO	
Parties	SV, SF, EL, FI, V (SE)	AP, S, S	MDG, MP	SP	

	Chris. Dem.	Liberal**	Conservative***	Radical Right	Countries
Progressive taxation	0.41	0.39	0.55	0.17	NO & DK
Redistribution	0.34	0.44	0.35	0.07	NO & SE
Immigration threat	0.45	0.66	0.26	0.75	NO & DK
Immigrant assimilation	0.55	0.45	0.60	0.92	NO & SE
Law and order	0.48	0.43	0.53	0.74	All
Environmental protection	0.53	0.69	0.52	0.41	NO & SE
Environmental priority	0.46	0.54	0.52	0.44	NO & DK
EU	0.57	0.27	0.43	0.65	All
Countries	All	All	All	NO & DK	
Parties	KrF, KD, KD	V (NO), RV, FP	H, KF, M, V (DK)	FrP, DF	

*We include two Danish parties in the left socialist party family even if the Unity List is perhaps best seen as a far left party, being more radical on the economic dimension as well as on other issues. Excluding the Feminist Initiative from the left socialist party family has very little impact on the A-scores, though this party family becomes slightly more united on redistribution (+0.05) and more divided on the environment (−0.14) and the EU (−0.04).

**In Denmark, we classify the Social Liberals as liberals but not the libertarian Liberal Alliance or the liberal-conservative Liberals. The latter is included as part of the conservative party family.

***V (DK) is classified as conservative.

Conservative parties seem to have much higher levels of agreement on the immigrant assimilation issue than on the immigration as threat issue, possibly an indication that the latter is more controversial. The comparisons need to be made with care, however, since the two measures do not include the same set of parties. It should also be noted that while Christian democrats, liberals and conservatives all have higher levels of preferential agreement on economic issues than the radical right, they are still substantially lower than among party families on the centre-left, and in many cases lower than for one or several of the newer issues. In fact, the only case of average A-scores of more than 0.5 is conservatives on progressive taxation. The most agreed-upon issue for Christian democrats is the EU (A-score 0.57); for Liberals, environmental protection (0.69) and for Conservatives, assimilation (0.60).

OLD AND NEW ISSUES AS A POTENTIAL THREAT TO PARTY UNITY AND LINKAGE

We have studied the extent to which Scandinavian party members are in agreement on a range of issues, comparing levels of preferential agreement across countries, parties of different ages and different party families. Overall, most parties have relatively high levels of agreement on most issues, and there is only one party on one issue that can be considered polarized (i.e. the Liberals in Norway on the EU issue).

On average, there are small differences between the three Scandinavian countries, and our ability to draw strong conclusions is somewhat limited by the lack of comparable items in all three surveys. However, it seems like Swedish parties are slightly more divided on immigration and law and order, but slightly more united on environmental and economic issues compared to Norwegian and Danish parties. This might reflect the extent to which these various issues have been salient in the political discourse of the three countries in recent decades. Indeed, immigration and law and order have been part of the Danish and Norwegian political debate since the late 1980s (partly due to the presence of successful radical right parties), whereas environmental issues have been more important in Sweden (partly due to the existence of a successful green party). Given that the party system differences between the three countries seem to decrease, levels of preferential agreement on each issue may converge in the coming years.

Overall, there are also small differences between new and old parties. However, in contrast to our expectation, new parties are actually somewhat more united than old parties on both newer issues (in particular, immigration and the environment) and older issues. Part of the explanation is that several new parties in Scandinavia are actually rooted in an 'old issue' (i.e. the economy), including the neoliberal Liberal Alliance and left-socialists in Denmark (EL) and Norway (SV). But part of the explanation is also that other new parties – most notably the greens – have developed a quite united stance on the historically dominant left-right dimension, which they were initially less interested in.

As regards differences between party families, we argued that parties are likely to be more in agreement on issues that they care about, that is, those in which they are ideologically rooted. We find ample support for this argument, though with the exception of the conservatives. Left socialists and to some extent the social democrats are united on economic issues and more divided on immigration, law and order and the EU. The radical right and the greens are extremely united on their key issues – immigration and the environment, respectively – and less so on other issues. This is particularly the case with economic issues for the radical right. The only agrarian party – the Norwegian Centre Party – is extremely united on an issue (the EU) that reflects its position as a party consistently defending the interests of the periphery.

Among the other centrist parties, the pattern is less clear. However, the Christian democrats are, as expected, a bit more united on non-economic issues compared to economic issues. Furthermore, the social liberals are – in line with this party family's increasing emphasis on new issues – most united on environmental protection and immigration, particularly against xenophobia. The only party family that does not follow the general pattern of high levels of agreement on core issues is the conservative party family. Although strongly associated with right-wing economics, they are actually more divided on these issues than most other non-economic issues with the notable exception of xenophobia, which is also somewhat divisive. The lack of consensus on economic issues among conservative members may reflect the position of the social democrats in the Scandinavian region, which gradually pushed (parts of) the conservative parties towards accepting most of the Scandinavian welfare state.

CONCLUDING REMARKS

We offer some tentative conclusions. First, the newer issues, immigration and the EU in particular, are a potential source of trouble for the dominant party families in Scandinavia: social democrats and conservatives. Members do not hold (as) unified views on these issues, which, in turn, could mean that they are a latent source of intra-party conflicts and will pose a challenge to the parties regarding the nature of the link between parties and their core electorate. Thus far, these two party families have responded to the increased saliency of the immigration issue by co-opting parts of the radical right agenda (Bale et al. 2010; Jupskås 2018). However, as shown in this chapter, moving further in that direction would most likely be organizationally costly and strategically difficult. Given that the two dominant parties are divided on (different aspects of) the immigration issue, adopting a (even more) restrictive position (for the social democrats) or campaigning on xenophobia (for the conservatives) might very well upset a significant part of the membership.

Second, our findings shed light on the parties' possibilities of representing their members' opinions and hence also on the character of party membership linkage. The good news is that, overall, the Scandinavian party members do not display anything that could be called extreme disunity, even taking into account that most parties are more internally united on some issues than on others. Moreover, new parties are actually more united than old parties – not only on new issues but also on old issues. In other words, by having a more fragmented party system, the voters are actually offered more distinct policy positions on several issues. This bodes well for representativeness, since it is easier to be a good representative if those represented agree on what they want. However, in itself, members' ideological agreement is not a guarantee of well-functioning representation by the party leadership, since the leadership must also take the party voters' wishes into account – which might be somewhat different (e.g. May 1973). In addition, it could be argued that it also bodes well for a party linkage that members are not marching in line to such an extent that there is no room for disagreement.

NOTES

1. However, this does not seem to be case in Scandinavia (see chapter 9).
2. Blondel (1978, 142) suggests that 'the size of the party affects its unity and dynamism. Members of large parties are unlikely to agree on all aspects'. However, party size does not seem to co-vary with the degree of ideological cohesiveness among elected party representatives (Carroll and Kubo 2017, 7). We take this as a strong indicator that the relationship between party size and levels of member preference agreement is rather weak as well.
3. For an overview of how important these issues are to voters, see appendix 6.1.
4. Bengtsson et al. (2014) also include moral issues in their list of important dimensions in Scandinavian and Nordic politics, but there is a lack of suitable and comparative items tapping into this dimension in the membership surveys.
5. There is also one question asking about whether members want green policies or not. However, this question is not comparable to any questions in the Norwegian and Swedish surveys.
6. The actual calculation of A-scores is somewhat technical (see van der Eijk 2001). The principle is to give numeric expression to the patterns of similarity in the individual answers to policy questions within the group of party members. First, we decompose the empirical distribution of observations in the five categories into layers. Second, these layers can then be represented by (ordered) patterns consisting of 0s (if there are no observations in this category) and 1s (if there are observations in this category) with associated weights (the share of observations constituting this layer). These patterns in each layer correspond to specific measures of agreement (i.e. the number of 1s in each layer) and unimodality (i.e. the distance between those 1s). Third, we multiply these two measurements in order to calculate the agreement for each layer. Finally, the degree of overall agreement (on the item) can be described as the weighted average of these (layer-specific) agreement scores.
7. It should be noted that the Sweden Democrats are not included in the survey, and it is likely that their members are more united on this issue compared to other parties.
8. While the Red-Green Alliance (EL) in Denmark also has a green profile, it is primarily a Left Socialist party, and we treat it as such here and in the subsequent analyses.
9. Most likely, these parties would have significantly affected the mean score of agreement on almost all the issues: SD being united in favour of assimilation of immigrants and opposed to further EU integration and somewhat divided on economic redistribution (see Jylhä, Rydgren and Strimling [2018] for a summary of the position of the voters). The Centre Party, on the

other hand, would likely have less preferential agreement on the EU issue, which has traditionally been problematic for the party but more in agreement on environmental and economic issues (see Sundström and Sundström [2010] for an overview of the party's ideological development).

BIBLIOGRAPHY

Aardal, Bernt. 2015. 'Offentlig opinion-folkets vilje eller tilfeldige ytringer?' In *Valg og velgere. En studie av stortingsvalget 2013*, edited by Bernt Aardal and Johannes Bergh, 49–75. Oslo: Cappelen Damm.

Almond, Gabriel and Bingham Powell. 1966. *Comparative Politics: A Developmental Approach.* Boston, MA: Little Brown.

Andersen, Jørgen Goul and Tor Bjørklund. 1990. 'Structural Changes and New Cleavages: The Progress Parties in Denmark and Norway'. *Acta Sociologica* 33 (3): 195–217.

Aylott, Nicholas. 2011. 'Parties and Party Systems in the North' In *The Madisonian Turn: Political Parties and Parliamentary Democracy in Nordic Europe*, edited by Torbjörn Bergman and Kaare Strøm, 297–328. Ann Arbor: The University of Michigan Press.

Aylott, Nicholas and Niklas Bolin. 2015. 'Polarising Pluralism: The Swedish Parliamentary Election of September 2014'. *West European Politics* 38 (3): 730–40.

Bäck, Hanna. 2008. 'Intra-Party Politics and Coalition Formation: Evidence from Swedish Local Government'. *Party Politics* 14 (1): 71–89.

Bakker, Ryan, Catherine de Vries, Erica Edwards, Liesbet Hooghe, Seth Jolly, Gary Marks, Jonathan Polk, Jan Rovny, Marco Steenbergen, and Milada Anna Vachudova. 2015. 'Measuring Party Positions in Europe: The Chapel Hill Expert Survey Trend File, 1999–2010'. *Party Politics* 21 (1): 143–52.

Bale, Tim, Christoffer Green-Pedersen, André A. Krouwel, Kurt R. Luther and Nick Sitter. 2010. 'If You Can't Beat Them, Join Them? Explaining Social Democratic Responses to the Challenge from the Populist Radical Right in Western Europe'. *Political Studies* 58 (3): 410–26.

Bengtsson, Åsa, Kasper Hansen, Ólafur Þ. Harðarson, Hanne Marthe Narud and Henrik Oscarsson. 2014. *The Nordic Voter: Myths of Exceptionalism.* Colchester: ECPR Press.

Bergh, Johannes and Rune Karlsen. 2017. 'Politisk dagsorden og sakseierskap ved stortingsvalget i 2017'. Institutt for samfunnsforskning. https://www.sv.uio.no/isv/forskning/prosjek ter/valgforskning/aktuelle-saker/politisk-dagsorden-og-best-politikk-ssb.pdf.

Bjørklund, Tor and Ottar Hellevik. 1988. 'De grønne stridsspørsmål i norsk politikk'. *Politica* 20 (4): 414–31.

Blondel, Jean. 1978. *Political Parties: A Genuine Case for Discontent?* London: Wildwood House, Limited.

Carroll, Royce and Hiroki Kubo. 2017. 'Measuring and Comparing Party Ideology and Heterogeneity'. *Party Politics*. doi: 1354068817710222.

Chiaramonte, Alessandro and Vincenzo Emanuele. 2017. 'Party System Volatility, Regeneration and De-Institutionalization in Western Europe (1945–2015)'. *Party Politics* 23 (4): 376–88.

Close, Caroline and Sergiu Gherghina. 2017. 'Rethinking Intra-Party Cohesion: Towards a Conceptual and Analytical Framework'. ECPR Joint Sessions of Workshops, 25–29 April 2017, Nottingham.

Dahlberg, Stefan. 2009. 'Political Parties and Perceptual Agreement: The Influence of Party Related Factors on Voters' Perceptions in Proportional Electoral Systems'. *Electoral Studies* 28 (2): 270–78.

Dalton, Russell J. 2009. 'Economics, Environmentalism and Party Alignments: A Note on Partisan Change in Advanced Industrial Democracies'. *European Journal of Political Research* 48 (2): 161–75.

Demker, Marie and Lars Svåsand. 2005. *Partiernas århundrade: fempartimodellens uppgång och fall i Norge och Sverige.* Stockholm: Santérus.

den Ridder, Jozefina Maria Josje. 2014. *Schakels of obstakels? Nederlandse politieke partijen en de eensgezindheid, verdeeldheid en representativiteit van partijleden.* Leiden, the Netherlands: Institute of Political Science, Faculty of Social and Behavioural Sciences, Leiden University.

Emanuele, Vincenzo and Alessandro Chiaramonte. 2018. 'A Growing Impact of New Parties: Myth or Reality? Party System Innovation in Western Europe after 1945'. *Party Politics* 24 (5): 475–87.

Ennser, Laurenz. 2012. 'The Homogeneity of West European Party Families: The Radical Right in Comparative Perspective'. *Party Politics* 18 (2): 151–71.

Green-Pedersen, Christoffer, and Jesper Krogstrup. 2008. 'Immigration as a Political Issue in Denmark and Sweden'. *European Journal of Political Research* 47 (5): 610–34.

Heidar, Knut and Jo Saglie. 2002. *Hva skjer med partiene?* Oslo: Gyldendal Akademisk.

Jahn, Detlef and Ann-Sofie Storsved. 1995. 'Legitimacy through Referendum? The Nearly Successful Domino-Strategy of the EU-Referendums in Austria, Finland, Sweden and Norway'. *West European Politics* 18 (4): 18–37.

Janda, Kenneth. 1980. *Political Parties: A Cross-National Survey.* New York: Free Press; London: Collier Macmillan.

Jupskås, Anders Ravik. 2016. 'The Norwegian Progress Party: Between a Business Firm and a Mass Party', In *Understanding Populist Party Organization. The Radical Right in Western Europe,* edited by Reinhard Heinisch and Oscar Mazzoleni, 159–88. London: Palgrave Macmillan.

———. 2018. 'Shaken, but Not Stirred: How Right-Wing Populist Parties Have Changed Party Systems in Scandinavia', In *Absorbing the Blow: Populist Parties and Their Impact on Parties and Party Systems,* edited by Steven B. Wolinetz and Andrej Zaslove, 103–44. Colchester: ECPR Press.

Jylhä, Kirsti M., Jens Rydgren and Pontus Strimling. 2018. *Sverigedemokraternas väljare. Vilka är de, var kommer de ifrån och vart är de på väg? Forskningsrapport 2018/2.* Stockholm: Institutet för framtidsstudier.

Kitschelt, Herbert. 2007. 'Growth and Persistence of the Radical Right in Postindustrial Democracies: Advances and Challenges in Comparative Research'. *West European Politics* 30 (5): 1176–1206.

Knutsen, Oddbjørn. 1990. 'The Materialist/Post-Materialist Value Dimension as a Party Cleavage in the Nordic Countries'. *West European Politics* 13 (2): 258–74.

Koedam, Jelle. 2017. 'Change of Heart? Analyzing Stability and Change in European Party Systems'. Paper presented at the Party Research Seminar, University of Gothenburg, 14 November 2017.

Kosiara-Pedersen, Karina. 2017. *Demokratiets ildsjæle; Partimedlemmer i Danmark.* Copenhagen: DJØF Publishing.

Lawson, Kay, ed. 1980. *Political Parties and Linkage: A Comparative Perspective.* New Haven, CT/London: Yale University Press.

Lipset, Seymour M. and Stein Rokkan. 1967. 'Cleavage Structures, Party Systems and Voter Alignments: An Introduction'. In *Party Systems and Voter Alignments: Cross-National Perspectives,* edited by Seymour M. Lipset and Stein Rokkan, 1–63. New York: The Free Press.

Mair, Peter and Cas Mudde. 1998. 'The Party Family and Its Study'. *Annual Review of Political Science* 1 (1): 211–29.

Marks, Gary and Carole J. Wilson. 2000. 'The Past in the Present: A Cleavage Theory of Party Response to European Integration'. *British Journal of Political Science* 30 (3): 433–59.

May, John D. 1973. 'Opinion Structure of Political Parties: The Special Law of Curvilinear Disparity' *Political Studies* 21 (2): 135–51.

Meyer, Thomas M. and Bernhard Miller. 2015. 'The Niche Party Concept and Its Measurement'. *Party Politics* 21 (2): 259–71.

Møller Hansen, Kasper and Rune Stubager. 2017. 'Konklusion – en samlet vælgeradfærdsmodel'. In *Oprør fra udkanten*, edited by Kasper Møller Hansen and Rune Stubager, 385–414. Copenhagen: Juris- og Økonomiforbundets Forlag.

Önnudóttir, Eva H. 2014. 'Policy Congruence and Style of Representation: Party Voters and Political Parties'. *West European Politics* 37 (3): 538–63.

Oscarsson, Henrik. 2017. 'Det svenska partisystemet i förändring'. In *Larmar och gör sig till*, edited by Ulrika Andersson, Jonas Ohlsson, Henrik Oscarsson and Maria Oskarson, 411–27. Göteborg: SOM-institutet vid Göteborgs universitet.

Oscarsson, Henrik and Sören Holmberg. 2016. *Svenska väljare*. Wolters Kluwer.

Stubager, Rune and Kasper Møller Hansen. 2013. 'It's the Economy, Stupid!' In *Krisevalg. Økonomien og Folketingsvalget 2011*, edited by Rune Stubager, Kasper Møller Hansen and Jørgen Goul Andersen, 17–44. Copenhagen: Jurist-og Økonomforbundets Forlag.

Sundström, Malena Rosén and Mikael Sundström. 2010. 'Ett smalare men vassare Centerparti?' *Statsvetenskaplig tidskrift* 112 (2): 189–202.

Tonsgaard, O. 1989. 'Miljøpolitisk enighed?' In *To folketingsvalg. Vælgerholdninger og vælgeradfærd i 1987 og 1988*, edited by Jørgen Elklit and Ole Tonsgaard. Århus: Politica.

van der Brug, Wouter, Mark Franklin and Gábor Tóka. 2008. 'One Electorate or Many? Differences in Party Preference Formation between New and Established European Democracies'. *Electoral Studies* 27 (4): 589–600.

van der Eijk, Cees. 2001. 'Measuring Agreement in Ordered Rating Scales'. *Quality and Quantity* 35 (3): 325–41.

Appendix

Table A6.1. Share of voters mentioning the issues as important for their vote choice at the time of the membership surveys.

	Norway (2017)	Denmark (2011)	Sweden (–2014)
Economy (%)*	23	26	26
Immigration (%)	28	6	23
Environment (%)	20	6	20
EU (%)	–	3	1
Law and order (%)	–	–	0

* Economy in Denmark and Sweden includes two categories, namely taxation and 'economy', but not employment. In Norway, the economy only includes taxation. Sources: Møller Hansen and Stubager (2017, 25), Oscarsson and Holmberg (2016, 177) and Bergh and Karlsen (2017).

III

ACTIVITY

Participation and Types of Party Members

7

The Degree, Type and Quality of Participation

Dimensions in Participation

Knut Heidar and Karina Kosiara-Pedersen

The general trend across Western Europe, including the Nordic countries, is that membership figures are declining – even though trends vary both within and among countries (Katz et al. 1992; Mair and van Biezen 2001; Scarrow 2000; van Biezen, Mair and Poguntke 2012; van Haute, Paulis and Sierens 2018). While the older class-based mass parties and their 'catch-all' contemporaries are in decline, some of the newer and smaller parties are steadily increasing their membership, or to different degrees experiencing ups and downs. In light of the decreasing membership trends, some established parties are changing the ways in which they enable affiliation (Scarrow 2015; Gauja 2015a; Faucher 2015), with consequences for how many and who affiliates with the parties (Achury et al. 2018; Kosiara-Pedersen, Scarrow and van Haute 2017; Scarrow 2015). Some of the new parties also experiment with other forms of affiliation (Gomez and Ramiro 2017; Kosiara-Pedersen and Kristiansen 2016). While both members and other party supporters may participate in the same party activities (Scarrow 2015), most parties still place more emphasis on traditional party members and consider dues-paying members the relevant internal demos when implementing intra-party democracy (Kosiara-Pedersen, Scarrow and van Haute 2017; von dem Berge and Poguntke 2017).

In this chapter, we analyse variation in participation of formal party members in the Scandinavian countries. Through this descriptive analysis, we aim to contribute to the discussion on whether party members contribute to linkage and hence to the role of parties within representative democracy. Party members vary in the degree and type of activities they engage in (Barnes 1966, 351; Duverger 1964, 116; Heidar 1994; Panebianco 1988, 26; Whiteley, Seyd and Richardson 1994, 101). Party membership, like other forms of political participation, has 'a polymorphic nature' (Heidar 1994), and the manner with which party members contribute to party life, inter-party competition and ultimately to democracy varies (Allern and Pedersen

2007). If we are to understand how parties provide participatory linkage, we need to go beyond mere membership figures and dig into how party members are actually participating.

The analysis of how party member participation contributes to party linkage is divided into two parts. First, we analyse the extent to which party members participate in various types of activities on the basis of the most recent party member surveys in Denmark, Norway and Sweden. Second, we analyse changes in the levels and types of participation in Denmark (from 2000 to 2012) and Norway (from 1991 to 2017); these are the only Scandinavian countries with time series data on members. As in the other chapters in this book, we look at participation across parties, party families and countries. These analyses form the basis for the discussion in chapter 8 of whether some of the party member 'activity types' are more crucial in providing linkage than others.

PARTY MEMBER PARTICIPATION AND LINKAGE

Party members are defined as formally enrolled, dues-paying individuals (den Ridder, Holsteyn and Koole 2015; Heidar 2015; Kosiara-Pedersen 2015; Spier and Klein 2015). Membership entails rights and obligations, but there are no obligatory activities apart from paying dues. The broad definition of party activism is to 'participate in and for a political party'. This means that not only party members but also other supporters and hired staff can engage in party activism. Even if the party members provide a substantial part of party activism, they are not the sole actors (Scarrow 2015; Webb, Poletti and Bale 2017). Here we focus on how traditional party members participate, and the member surveys provide the basis for exploring parties' participatory linkage.

Party activities vary on a number of dimensions, such as timing, venue and commitment. Activities can take place at the Christmas Eve of party politics, that is, at elections, or between elections. The rise of permanent campaigning has blurred this distinction, so that activities aimed at convincing voters to vote for the party take place both at and between elections, but they are much more intensive at elections. In regard to venue, campaigning is not limited to handing out leaflets or participating in rallies. New technologies have added another distinction, namely, between offline and online activities. Offline activities require a physical presence somewhere, whereas online participation may take place anywhere and with any kind of communication device at hand. Party activities also vary in the required degree of commitment and in how time-consuming they are. Some activities, such as encouraging voters to support the party, promoting party policies on an online blog or delivering leaflets at the town hall square on a Saturday afternoon, require little commitment. These activities are not necessarily very time-consuming. Other activities require commitment far beyond that, in particular for individuals who are elected or appointed to public offices. Strong commitment is also required by those who take up internal party offices such as local chair or treasurer.

In this chapter, we distinguish between internal and external party activities. Party member linkage requires both external party work among the electorate and intra-party activities involving both members and party leaders. Participation in internal meetings is one thing, canvassing voters is another. Internal activities aim at sustaining and developing the party organization and preparing the organizational basis for external activities. The balance between internal and external party activities tells us something about the extent to which parties are, respectively, primarily membership organizations or campaign machines.

Focusing first on the internal activities, party meetings are essential. Within the old mass parties, important decisions, like local policy programmes and proposals for national policies, are taken at the annual meeting in the branch organizations. The party's election programme and the election of party leaders are decided at the (bi-)annual national party meeting or congress, which for many parties is the highest authority in the party organization. While social and cultural arrangements may not be important for parties' decision-making, they seem essential to party culture and are often well attended.

Party members enrol in support of party policies and ideology (see chapter 3; den Ridder, Holsteyn and Koole 2015; Heidar 2015, Kosiara-Pedersen 2015; Spier and Klein 2015). They participate to gain influence. In order to gain influence in classic mass party organizations, party members have to be present at party meetings. If members want to influence the party manifesto, they must come to agreement with fellow party members at the branch level or gain access to relevant meetings and networks at higher party levels. When nominating candidates, this means listening to nomination speeches and voting. Recent organizational changes have tended to individualize party members' influence (Katz and Mair 1995) both in general (e.g. Bille 2001; Cross and Blais 2012b; Cross and Katz 2013; Hazan and Rahat 2010) and in regard to party leader selection (Cross and Blais 2012a; Cross and Pilet 2015; Pilet and Cross 2014, Scarrow 2015), candidate selection (Pilet, van Haute and Kelbel 2015) and decisions on the political programme (Gauja 2013, 2015b; Scarrow 2015). This limits the need for meeting attendance.

Intra-party offices all the way from the local board member to the party leader are important in sustaining party member organizations. Previously, local party chairs were essential in organizing local campaigns, even though some parties today have left this task to 'campaign leaders'. These tasks require more time and commitment than simply ad hoc participation in the local annual meeting would. Party members provide a recruitment pool from which the party may recruit these intra-party office-holders (Scarrow 1996, 45).

The external activities are oriented towards the public sphere. The classic left-of-centre mass party members provide the many hands and feet needed at campaign time to compensate for the lesser capital resources of these parties, and probably also to support the 'mass' image of these parties. Hence, there has traditionally been a number of party activities of this sort. Even though campaigns have become more capital intensive and new campaign techniques allow parties to campaign without members, the latter may still contribute to parties' national campaigns, particularly to local and candidate campaigns. At election time, for example, party members distribute leaflets, staff party stalls and arrange meetings. Between elections, members may engage in campaigns for political issues, recruit members and arrange and participate in political and social events. Party members provide labour resources to handle different tasks – both at and between elections (Katz 1990, 152; Scarrow 1996, 44).

Party members promote their party among the voters not only when they engage in traditional campaign activities but also when they act as ambassadors and interact with ordinary people in their local communities, workplaces and online. Members are parties' 'ambassadors to the community' (Scarrow 1996, 43). This informal campaign mode based on personal relations is advantageous since people are less conscious of the 'propaganda' aspect when information is shared this way. The new technology has led to the emergence of online ambassadors, who promote the party on social media platforms. To some members, this is not a traditional party activity, since these outreach activities take place outside the normal party sphere.

While being an ambassador for the party may be among the least demanding party activities, elected office may easily be the most demanding. The defining purpose of parties is candidate nomination (Sartori 1976, 64). Since nomination is a central feature of political parties, party members potentially play an important role in the recruitment process. They not only decide on the candidates but also form a pool for recruitment of party nominees (Scarrow 1996, 45). Party members are 'warm bodies' (Mair 1997, 147). Hence, we also regard 'recruitment potential' as a way in which party members, in a sense, participate. Although this does not entail any activism in itself, the willingness to stand for election is of great value to the party.

Table 7.1 sums up the main types of activities to be analysed here, according to the internal-external dimension. We want to show the extent to which party members engage in these activities across the three Scandinavian countries since party linkage is dependent on both internal and external party member participation.

Table 7.1. Types of party member activities.

INTERNAL	EXTERNAL
– party meetings	– ambassador (online and offline)
– influence nominations	– campaigning (at and between elections)
– influence policies	– current or previous public office
– participate in party debate	– recruitment potential for public office
– current or previous party office	
– recruitment potential for internal office	

MEMBER PARTICIPATION IN SCANDINAVIA

The purpose of this section is to analyse the extent to which party members participate in various types of activities on the basis of the most recent party member surveys in Denmark (2012), Norway (2017) and Sweden (2015) (see chapter 1). All surveys include questions on most, but not all, activities presented in table 7.1. The standard challenge in comparative research applies: Not all questions are similarly phrased, and they are not all coded in the same way. These differences are discussed in the text when relevant. The analysis is structured along the distinction, highlighted earlier, between internal and external party activities.

Internal Activities

In tables 7.2 through 7.4, we present internal participation for all members in the three Scandinavian countries, broken down by party. The percentage figures for 'all' are weighted according to the relative size of the parties' membership. We first present 'general' participation and then distinguish between meeting attendance, influence seeking and intra-party office.

A rough estimate on general participation is the number of hours in an average month spent on party activities. In both Denmark and Sweden, party members on an average spend around four hours a month on party activities, slightly more in Denmark (4.1) than in Sweden (3.8). The variation is large within the parties; some members hold demanding offices, others are fairly passive (Kosiara-Pedersen 2017, 123). There is no objective standard for high versus low levels of participation. However, considering that most members participate in their leisure time, about one hour per week (four hours per month) seems high. The average is roughly similar in Denmark and Sweden, but while there is no variation across the Swedish parties (except for the Feminists), the variation is more marked across the Danish parties. Here some parties to both left and right (the Red-Green Alliance [EL], the Social Democrats [SD] Socialist People's Party [SF], and Danish People's Party [DF]) have a high level of activity (4.4–4.2 hours), whereas the members of the Social Liberal Party (RV) and the Christian Democrats (KF) are at a lower level (2.9).

The number of hours spent, however, is not a very precise measurement of participatory linkage. To some members, reading the party member magazine is considered a party activity, to others it is not. To some, encouraging others to vote for the party is a party activity, to others it is not. An analysis of the Danish members shows that even those who say they spend no time on party activities in an average month still engage in different types of activities; many participate in party meetings or social events, and many are 'ambassadors' for their party (Kosiara-Pedersen 2017, 123–24).

We now turn to the most traditional of all party activities, namely, attending meetings. About two out of three members attended at least one party meeting previous year; in Denmark, it was four out of five (80 per cent). Considering that some members

Table 7.2. Denmark. Internal member participation.

| | Left Socialist | | Social Dem. | Other | Christ. Dem. | Liberal | | Conservative | Radical Right | |
	EL	SF	SD	RV	KD	V	LA	KF	DF	All*
A. General activity										
– average hours in party work in average month	4.4	4.2	4.4	2.9	2.9	3.9	3.8	3.8	4.2	4.1
B. Meeting										
– local annual meeting	44	53	69	50	63	69	38	71	50	62
– meeting attendance within past year	81	73	79	73	66	82	85	80	88	80
– annual congress within 5 years	28	31	29	33	49	35	38	44	34	33
– social and leisure activities within 5 years	61	59	69	49	55	64	38	67	47	62
C. Influence										
– write political proposals within 5 years	32	36	42	34	34	39	22	39	22	37
– participate in the nomination of candidate for national election	28	39	50	26	37	39	12	39	24	39
D. Intra-party office										
– current party office	11	15	18	18	23	21	17	21	19	19
– previously held party office	16	28	34	25	36	35	10	39	13	30

Note: * Weighted.

Table 7.3. Norway. Internal member participation.

	Left Socialist	Social Dem.	Green	Agrarian	Christ. Dem.	Liberal	Conservative	Radical Right	All*
B. Meeting									
– participated in party event past year	53	65	49	70	65	63	67	57	63
C. Influence									
– participated in developing programme	50	55	43	67	61	60	61	42	56
– participated in party debates on policies/nominations	46	52	38	62	43	52	54	43	50
D. Intra-party office									
– current office	29	37	27	45	39	40	40	39	38
– previously held office	53	52	23	56	58	48	47	37	50

* Weighted.

Table 7.4. Sweden. Internal member participation.

	Left Socialist	Social Dem.	Green	Other F!	Christ. Dem.	Liberal	Conservative	All*
A. General								
– average hours in party work on average month	3.8	3.7	3.9	2.7	3.7	3.8	3.8	3.8
B. Meeting								
– participated at party meeting(s) past year	65	67	66	43	63	74	68	66
C. Influence								
– participated in developing national party programme	11	11	25	7	11	14	8	13
D. Office								
– current or previous intra-party or elected office	52	64	53	28	63	65	61	58
recruitment potential for party office	79	70	80	74	74	77	74	76

* Weighted.

who do not attend meetings may still be active in other party affairs, for example, as ambassadors, this is a high figure. Participation may also go in cycles with periodic activities (e.g. during elections). Attending meetings, however, is generally the way to influence decisions, and this – on the other side – means that about one in every three to five members does not contribute fully to linkage between voters and party elites. The most active party participants are to be found in the Danish People's Party, the Norwegian Centre Party and the Swedish Liberals. There are only modest party differences, however, and we do not find any distinctive party family patterns in meeting attendance.

There is no common question to cover participation directed at influencing party decisions across the three surveys. The Danes were asked about writing policy proposals and suggesting nominations for national public office, the Norwegians about programme proposal and nominations locally and nationally and the Swedes about the national party programme. In Denmark, about one-third of the members have been active in developing policies and deciding nominations. Here the Social Democrats are more active, and the Liberal Alliance and Danish People's Party members score low. More than half the Norwegian members have taken part in policy and nomination processes. The overall picture is that the more national-level and distant from the local branch the task is, the fewer participate. Broadly, this is more the situation in centre-right parties than in left parties and the radical right. Developing the national party programme in Sweden included just over a tenth of the party members. Here the Greens were the most inclusive party. The process of writing national party programmes is not very close to the branch affairs. We do not know, however, whether the low figure is due to members' lack of interest or the way the process is organized within the parties.

Finally, we see that a considerable part of the membership hold, or have previously held, internal party office. In Denmark, a fifth of the members currently hold office, while less than a third have done so previously. In Norway, this is more widespread, with 38 per cent in office now and 50 per cent having been in office in the past. There is most likely an overlap between those in office now and those who have been in the past, but still more than half the membership have been involved in office-holding. The differences between Norwegian parties are not large, but the members of the agrarian party seem to have some more experience in office-holding. For Sweden, we only have one question on office, namely, whether members are currently holding or have previously held party or public office. This question blends both the time dimension and the internal/external difference. However, the Swedes' experience with office nevertheless appears to be at the higher Norwegian level rather than the lower Danish one. The most striking party difference is that the Swedish Feminists score so low compared to all other parties, which is easily explained by the party's newness (it was founded in 2005) and limited electoral success. The willingness to take on an office is, however, just as high among Feminist Party members as in the other parties, about 75 per cent.

External Activities

While internal activities mainly take place inside parties, external activities are those that party members engage in among the electorate. These are the activities related to campaigning at and between elections. Tables 7.5 through 7.7 describe the extent to which party members participate in external activities on behalf of their party, that is, outreach activities, election campaign activities and holding public office. These vary in terms of how demanding they are, from the least demanding 'discuss party policies with non-members' to the most demanding, holding public elected office. External activities may take place both in private among friends, family and colleagues, and in public, when campaigning and holding elected office.

All surveys show that most members engage in political discussions with non-members. In Denmark, 87 per cent say that they have done so, and that is the practice in all Danish parties. It seems to be part of the self-image among party members to engage in discussions with non-members, advocating and defending party policies. This is also the case in Norway and Sweden, where three of four members promote their party externally, and this goes for all parties. In addition, a substantial part of the membership is online ambassadors. A third of the Danes had been active in online discussions during the past five years. This activity was particularly frequent within the small parties, the Red-Green Alliance (EL) and Liberal Alliance (LA). In Norway, 38 per cent of the members had been active in social media in the past year, and here the most active were in the radical right party. In the month prior to the Swedish parliamentary election in 2014, about half the party members had been active in social media. The most active members were in the left socialist and the Feminist (F!) parties. In all three countries, the largest share of active members could be found in the new parties, that is, in parties that are either small or are challenging the old party establishment in public debates (or both). We may also note that all these parties – apart from the Norwegian radical right – have a younger membership compared to the other parties (see chapter 4, table 4.5).

There are different levels of current or former public office in Danish and Norwegian parties. In Denmark, 5 per cent of members are currently holding public office, while 9 per cent have previously held office. Norwegian figures are much higher. Here, 32 per cent are currently in office and 44 per cent have previously been. The differences may, in part, be explained by the number of offices available at the local level: at the time of the survey, Norway had more than 400 local municipalities, while Denmark had 98. In Denmark, the old parties had a larger share of members with public office experience. This is to some degree also the case for the Norwegian parties, but in Norway, the Social Democrats score low. This may be due to the high membership number, that is, a higher percentage base. In Sweden, as noted earlier, the question included experience from any office. The figures indicate that the Swedes are at the higher Norwegian level.

We can also compare the recruitment potential of Danish and Swedish party members. About three out of four Swedish members state that they are willing to

Table 7.5. Denmark. External member participation.

	Left Socialist		Social Dem.	Other	Christ Dem.	Liberal		Conservative	Radical Right	All*
	EL	SF	SD	RV	KD	V	LA	KF	DF	
A. Ambassador										
– discuss party policies with non-members within 5 years	90	88	88	86	85	85	88	86	84	87
– discuss party policies online within 5 years	43	35	32	33	22	28	56	30	35	33
– encourage voters to vote for the party at election	72	60	71	59	71	60	70	59	66	65
B. Campaign										
– delivering campaign leaflets at national election	48	46	52	34	43	37	23	42	34	43
C. Office										
– potential local, regional or national, yes and would consider	50	49	42	56	32	47	61	52	51	47
– elected representative for the party	1	6	5	2	2	5	1	5	7	5
previously elected representative for the party	3	6	12	5	7	11	2	11	4	9

Note: * Weighted.

Table 7.6. Norway. External member participation.

	Left Socialist	Social Dem.	Green	Agrarian	Christ. Dem.	Liberal	Conservative	Radical Right	All*
A. Ambassador									
– discuss politics with non-members	75	73	71	80	62	79	73	77	73
– active in social media	44	40	41	35	24	39	37	52	38
B. Campaign									
– handed out leaflets in election campaign	42	46	33	55	46	53	49	39	46
– recruiting new members	20	35	21	34	23	28	32	37	31
– party promotion (in high street, etc.)	38	40	25	45	32	43	45	36	39
– demonstrations (etc.)	37	37	23	19	12	21	17	13	25
– active printed media	14	23	15	25	13	24	20	25	20
C. Office									
– public office now	21	30	21	46	29	31	39	32	32
– public office previously	41	45	6	52	52	35	45	30	44
– recruitment potential (asked and yes-share of those asked)	73	74	62	71	64	68	69	74	71

Note: * Weighted.

Table 7.7. Sweden. External member participation.

	Left Socialist	Social Dem.	Green	Other	Christ. Dem.	Liberal	Conservative	Radical Right	All*
A/B. Ambassador at campaign (in the month before the last national election in 2014, did you. . .)									
– convince voters to support party	81	80	72	83	68	71	76	–	76
– promote party in social media	63	44	55	69	44	41	45	–	52
– hand out campaign leaflets	54	55	51	43	53	62	54	–	54
C. Office									
– current or previous intra-party or elected office	52	64	53	28	63	65	61	–	58
– recruitment potential (yes and yes, maybe)	83	75	84	77	80	81	80	–	81
– recruitment potential for public office	71	62	75	67	70	71	72	–	71

Note: * Weighted.

become candidates for public office, while the figure is much lower in Denmark (close to half the membership). Hence, the recruitment pool of party members has far from dried out, even if parties in some districts may lack candidates with the particular profiles desired. When it comes to potential candidates, there is an important difference in the survey questions. Table 7.6 shows the share of Norwegian party members *asked* to be a candidate who responded 'yes'. Hence, this percentage is within a subset of the total membership. Those *not* asked are not included. Both the Danish and Swedish questions ask whether the party member would be positive, if asked by their party. In other words, the Norwegian figures should be higher compared to Sweden's. However, this is not the case. Among the members *actually approached* by their parties, the percentage willing to serve was the same as the percentage among *all* Swedish members.

HAS PARTY MEMBER ACTIVISM CHANGED IN DENMARK AND NORWAY?

Declining membership figures challenge parties' linkage between civil society and the political institutions. Parties with few members relative to their voters cannot rely on (and trust) members' information about voters' interests. This is amplified if people are less motivated to become members out of political conviction (van Biezen and Poguntke 2014, 214). In the 'cartel party', the party work becomes more capital intensive, the power structure stratarchial and the importance of members is reduced compared to non-members (Katz and Mair 1995, 18). In other words, the value of being an ordinary party member is less than it used to be. However, if a member has ambitions to rise into the office-holding segment of the party, for personal gain or political reasons, it will still be worthwhile to engage in party work. Katz and Mair stress the decoupling of parties from civil society and the vegetative party-state relationship (Katz and Mair 2009). The implication for parties is that their links to the old cleavage segments are waning.

In recent research on parties, party elites are expected to discourage a very active membership (e.g. Katz and Mair 2009). Some work still has to be done at the grassroots level, particularly the outreach work of canvassing and social media promotion. Developing party policies, on the other hand, should be left to the party elites, making internal activism, apart from filling the necessary party offices, less prominent among rank-and-file members. Members are expected to be less active in decision-making within the party, particularly in developing new party policies.

Although there are not many empirical studies looking at changing patterns of member participation (Allern et al. 2016, 23), some research challenges the gloomy picture of party members as no longer providing linkage to the voters. In a study of Danish and Norwegian parties (Heidar Kosiara-Pedersen and Saglie 2012), we found that there had been an increase in online activities for the party members during the 2000s, but otherwise there were no significant changes in the patterns of member activism. Allern, Heidar and Karlsen looked at Norwegian party member and voter surveys from 1991 to 2009. They found no change in the overall representative capacity of party members as measured by changes in party activities and members' social and political representativity compared to voters (Allern et al. 2016).

Turning to the empirical analyses of change, we must first note that the time spans covered by the surveys in Denmark and Norway are different. In Norway, the earliest member survey is from 1991, and in Denmark, from 2000. The data still tell us about the *changes* among party members who are relevant to the discussions on party change. First, the overall membership numbers declined over the entire period from about 1970 to 2015 in both countries (cf. chapter 2). This means that if membership decline is a causal factor behind changing activity levels, these changes should be visible for both countries in the given periods. Second, the cartel model was based on organizational changes noted for the years up till the early 1990s when Mair and Katz published their seminal article (1995). Given that this model summarizes central changes in the parties' modus operandi, this means that cartel parties were already in operation at the start of the period. However, changes in membership participation are unlikely to take place at the same time as organizational changes are unfolding. At least we would expect a lag in the habits and activities of party members. It is therefore unlikely that the organizational and contextual changes that were premised for the cartel model would not also have consequences for member activities in the following years, and therefore in the periods covered by the data. The expected changes in member activities within cartel parties would be that activity in general declined, that internal activities became less central than external activities and that decision-making involvement and office holding became less prominent among the members.

Internal Activism

We do not have identical questions in all four surveys and have selected the indicators that are most alike. In table 7.8, we see that, generally, there are increases in party member activism over the period. The number of hours an average Danish member spends on party work in a month has increased slightly from 3.6 to 4.1 hours. Norwegian members have also become more active in party work. In 1991, 47 per cent had attended a party event during the past year, while this had increased to 63 per cent in 2017. The Danes also increased their attendance at party meetings, and they have become more active in social events within the party. Participation in party decision-making has increased in the period. The questions are (again) not identical, but in both Denmark and Norway, members are today more actively engaged in influencing party policy than previously. Figures for the parties (not shown in table) show that in Denmark, this increase is most notable in the centre-right parties, less so on the left. In Norway, the increase is notable in all parties.

Table 7.8.   Changing member participation in Denmark and Norway.

| | DENMARK | | | NORWAY | | |
	2000	*2012*	*Difference*	*1991*	*2017*	*Difference*
Internal activity						
– average hours	3.6	4.1	*+0.5*	–	–	–
– attended a party event/meeting	53	62[1+2]	*+9*	47	63	*+16*
– annual congress	65	33[2]	*–32*	–	–	–
– internal policy proposal	26	37[2]	*+11*	9/37[3]	50	–
– social events	44	62[2]	*+18*	–	–	–
– current office	21	19	*–2*	31	38	*+7*
External activity						
– discuss with non-members	74	87[2]	*+13*	–	–	–
– recruiting	–	–	–	17	31	*+14*
– party promotion	–	–	–	28	39	*+11*
– demonstrations	–	–	–	15	25	*+10*
– active printed	–	–	–	7	20	*+13*
– encourage voters to vote	67	65	*–2*	–	–	–
– delivering campaign leaflets	28	43	*+15*	–	–	–
– public office now	7	5	*–2*	26	33	*+7*
– public office previously	10	9	*–1*	37	44	*+7*
recruitment potential	37	45	*+8*	48	71	*+23*

[1]Local annual meeting.
[2]Within five years.
[3]Developing programme/party debate in general.

Are there any changes in the degrees to which members hold party office? In Denmark, we see a small decline from 2000 to 2012, while Norwegian members increased their party office figures by seven percentage points. There were not necessarily more offices to fill in the period, but fewer members to fill them, thereby increasing the share of members holding office. The general picture of changes in internal member activities is that a higher share of members engage in such activities over the years. For the individual parties, there is no clear left-right pattern in the most recent data, but in the first surveys in 1991 and 2000, there is a tendency for the centre-left parties to have a higher share of active members than the centre-right parties. Hence, membership decline seems to have washed out the older ideology-based organizational differences.

External or 'Outreach' Activities

The Internet and the social media today constitute an important arena for members' outreach activities. In the 2012 Danish data, one-fifth of party members had discussed party policies online during the last five years, and in the Norwegian 2017 data, we find that 30 per cent of the members had defended/promoted their party's policies in the social media during the past year. Undoubtedly social media are important today and naturally are more important than in 1991 and 2000. We return to this in chapter 9; however, these were not central in 2000 or earlier so we do not include these activities here. Hence, the bottom part of table 7.8 shows 'traditional' member activities which promote the party and its policies in the public sphere.

The external activities are, according to the cartel party theory, expected to be more central to parties than internal activities as they change from policy workshops to elite instruments for voter mobilization. However, the tendency towards capital-intensive campaigns may restrain party member campaigning. All figures on Norwegian members in table 7.8 show an increase in the share of members involved in these activities in 2017 compared to 1991. In Norway, there is an increased share engaged in recruitment activities, general party promotion and political demonstrations, and in the printed media. In Denmark, the results are somewhat more mixed. A higher share of Danish members discuss policies with non-members, and there is also a substantial increase in the percentage of members handing out campaign leaflets – from 28 to 43 per cent. Encouraging voters to support their party remains at a high level.

Again, we see that the activist profile of the membership has increased over the past two to three decades in Denmark and Norway. We also see that centre-left party members tended to be more active in the past, while the current pattern is more random. As is the case with internal activities, we again see a tendency towards a levelling of differences across parties.

CONCLUSION

In this chapter, we move behind the membership figures and ask what kind of participatory input members provide to political parties. We show that Scandinavian party members are not merely numerical expressions of party strength. They participate in a range of diverse activities within the parties and for the parties. Of course, there is the question of what are considered to be 'high' and 'low' levels of participation. Some members clearly do not participate much. About one in five do not participate at all or only marginally. One may wonder why 20 to 30 percent of the members are not active. Two possible answers come to mind. First, they may have been active at an earlier stage, but due to illness, old age, children, work situation or just a sense of having done their duty, they have become inactive. But they remain members because they want to support their party! Another explanation may be that some people enlist as members because they feel pressured to do so by social networks and family (cf. chapter 3), but they are not interested in active engagement.

Although party membership figures have been in decline (see chapter 2), the surveys show that Scandinavian party members – in general – are active in party affairs. About eight out of ten are active as party members. They do party work and participate both internally and externally. A majority turn up at meetings now and then. They engage as ambassadors for their party vis-à-vis voters, both face-to-face and online. The differences we find between countries are not easy to interpret, however. There is a tendency for new parties, parties with relatively few members and in a position to challenge the hegemony of the old parties, to have a more active membership, although this is not without exceptions. Comparing the countries, we do not find major differences. Members work inside the organization to do the necessary organizational work and to influence party policies. They are also active as campaign activists and party ambassadors to promote their party externally.

Looking at changes in the activity profiles of party members in Denmark and Norway, we find several notable trends. First, members are – relatively speaking – more engaged in internal party activities now than in the 1990s. Second, campaign activities on behalf of their party have also increased. Finally, the percentage taking part in internal party decision-making has increased. The main picture is one of stability, although stability on a shrinking base. The party members are a distilled variant of former members. More 'dead-weight members' than active members have left, or not enrolled, in the parties, leaving a slightly more active membership. Behind the reduced membership numbers, we find a quantitative more than a qualitative change. Membership decline is like a sauce reduction.

Using the big brush, we find in all countries a group of party members with broad, comprehensive participation. Members' activities link the electorate to internal policy formation. Overall, there is definitely a basis for a party linkage, considering member participation in the Scandinavian countries. Is that all there is to it? The answer of course is no. A reduction in numbers has consequences. Parties' links to civil society weaken as numbers shrink. Even passive members are members in the sense that they signal attachment and ties in civil society (Heidar and Wauters 2019). This may have consequences for parties' ability both to represent and to lead in democracies.

In this chapter, we have studied members as atomized individuals. We do not know if there is a division of labour among the party members, with one group being externally active and another looking after the party organization. Are the members doing a generalist job for the party, canvassing in the morning and attending to policy development in the evening? Or are they divided into segments, making the linkage from voters to party policies more specialized? That is the theme for the next chapter.

BIBLIOGRAPHY

Achury, Susan, Susan E. Scarrow, Karina Kosiara-Pedersen and Emilie van Haute. 2018. 'The Consequences of Membership Incentives: Do Greater Political Benefits Attract Different Kinds of Members?' *Party Politics*. doi: 10.1177/1354068818754603.

Allern, Elin and Karina Pedersen. 2007. 'The Impact of Party Organizational Changes on Democracy'. *West European Politics* 30 (1): 68–92.

Allern, Elin Haugsgjerd, Knut Heidar and Rune Karlsen. 2016. *After the Mass Party Continuity and Change in Political Parties and Representation in Norway*. Lanham, MD: Lexington Books.

Barnes, Samuel H. 1966. 'Participation, Education, and Political Competence: Evidence from a Sample of Italian Socialists'. *The American Political Science Review* 60 (2): 348–53.

Bille, Lars. 2001. 'Democratizing a Democratic Procedure: Myth or Reality? Candidate Selection in Western European Parties, 1960–1990'. *Party Politics* 7 (3): 363–80.

Cross, William P. and André Blais. 2012a. *Politics at the Centre: The Selection and Removal of Party Leaders in the Anglo Parliamentary Democracies*. Oxford: Oxford University Press.

———. 2012b. 'Who Selects the Party Leader?' *Party Politics* 18 (2): 127–50. doi: 10.1177/1354068810382935.

Cross, William P. and Jean-Benoit Pilet, eds. 2015. *The Politics of Party Leadership: A Cross-National Perspective*. Oxford: Oxford University Press.

Cross, William P. and Richard S. Katz, eds. 2013. *The Challenges of Intra-Party Democracy*. Oxford: Oxford University Press.

den Ridder, Josje, Joop van Holsteyn and Ruud Koole. 2015. 'Party Membership in the Netherlands'. In *Party Members and Activists*, edited by Emilie van Haute and Anika Gauja, 134–50. London: Routledge.

Duverger, Maurice. 1964. *Political Parties*. London: Methuen & Co. Ltd.

Faucher, Florence. 2015. 'New Forms of Political Participation: Changing Demands or Changing Opportunities to Participate in Political Parties?' *Comparative European Politics* 13: 409–59.

Gauja, Anika. 2013. 'Policy Development and Intra-Party Democracy'. In *The Challenges of Intra-Party Democracy*, edited by William P. Cross and Richard S. Katz, 116–35. Oxford: Oxford University Press.

———. 2015a. 'The Construction of Party Membership'. *European Journal of Political Research* 54 (2): 232–48.

———. 2015b. 'The Individualisation of Party Politics: The Impact of Changing Internal Decision-Making Processes on Policy Development and Citizen Engagement'. *The British Journal of Politics and International Relations* 17 (1): 89–105. doi: 10.1111/1467–856x.12035.

Gomez, Raul and Luis Ramiro. 2017. 'The Limits of Organizational Innovation and Multi-Speed Membership: Podemos and Its New Forms of Party Membership'. *Party Politics*. Online first. doi: 10.1177/1354068817742844.

Hazan, Reuven Y. and Gideon Rahat. 2010. *Democracy within Parties: Candidate Selection Methods and Their Consequences*. Oxford: Oxford University Press.

Heidar, Knut. 1994. 'The Polymorphic Nature of Party Membership'. *European Journal of Political Research* 25: 61–86.

———. 2015. 'Party Membership in Norway: Declining but Still Viable?' In *Party Members and Activists*, edited by Emilie van Haute and Anika Gauja, 151–68. London: Routledge.

Heidar, Knut and Bram Wauters, eds. Forthcoming. *Do Parties Still Represent?* London: Routledge.

Heidar, Knut, Karina Kosiara-Pedersen and Jo Saglie. 2012. 'Party Change and Party Member Participation in Denmark and Norway'. In *Democracy, Elections and Political Parties: Essays in Honor of Jørgen Elklit*, edited by Jens Blom-Hansen, Christoffer Green-Pedersen, and Svend-Erik Skaaning, 155–63. Aarhus: Politica.

Heidar, Knut and Bram Wauters, eds. 2019. *Do Parties Still Represent?* London: Routledge.

Katz, Richard S. 1990. 'Party as Linkage: A Vestigial Function?' *European Journal of Political Research* 18 (1): 143–61.

Katz, Richard S. and Peter Mair. 1995. 'Changing Models of Party Organizations and Party Democracy: The Emergence of the Cartel Party'. *Party Politics* 1 (1): 5–28.

———. 2009. 'The Cartel Party Thesis: A Restatement'. *Perspectives on Politics* 7 (4), 753–66.

Katz, Richard S., Peter Mair, Luciano Bardi, Lars Bille, Kris Deschouwer, David Farrell, Ruud Koole, Leonardo Morlino, Wolfgang Müller, Jon Pierre et al. 1992. 'The Membership of Political Parties in European Democracies, 1960–1990'. *European Journal of Political Research* 22 (3): 329–45.

Kosiara-Pedersen, Karina. 2015. 'Party Membership in Denmark: Fluctuating Membership Figures and Organizational Stability'. In *Party Members and Activists*, edited by Emilie van Haute and Anika Gauja, 66–83. London: Routledge.

———. 2017. *Demokratiets ildsjæle. Partimedlemmer i Danmark.* København: DJØF Forlag.

Kosiara-Pedersen, Karina and Amalie Munkner Kristiansen. 2016. 'Alternativt partimedlemskab'. In *Statskundskab i praksis: Klassiske teorier og moderne problemer*, edited by Karina Kosiara-Pedersen, Gustav Nedergaard and Emil Lobe Suenson, 33–49. København: Karnov Group.

Kosiara-Pedersen, K., Susan E. Scarrow and Emilie van Haute. 2017. 'Rules of Engagement? Party Membership Costs, New Forms of Party Affiliation, and Partisan Participation'. In *Organizing Representation: Political Parties, Participation, and Power*, edited by Susan E. Scarrow, Paul D. Webb and Thomas Poguntke, 234–58. Oxford: Oxford University Press.

Mair, Peter. 1997. *Party System Change: Approaches and Interpretations.* Oxford: Oxford University Press.

Mair, Peter and Ingrid van Biezen. 2001. 'Party Membership in Twenty European Democracies, 1980–2000'. *Party Politics* 7 (1): 5–21.

Panebianco, Angelo. 1988. *Political Parties: Organization and Power.* Cambridge: Cambridge University Press.

Pilet, Jean-Benoit and William P. Cross. 2014. 'The Selection of Party Leaders in Comparative Perspective'. In *The Selection of Political Party Leaders in Contemporary Parliamentary Democracies: A Comparative Study*, edited by Jean-Benoit Pilet and William P. Cross, 222–39. New York: Routledge.

Pilet, Jean-Benoit, Emilie van Haute and Camille Kelbel. 2015. *Candidate Selection Procedures for the European Elections.* Brussels: Study for the European Parliament, Directorate General for Internal Policies – Directorate C: Citizens' Rights and Constitutional Affairs.

Sartori, Giovanni. 1976. *Parties and Party Systems: A Framework for Analysis.* Cambridge: Cambridge University Press.

Scarrow, Susan E. 1996. *Parties and Their Members: Organizing for Victory in Britain and Germany.* Oxford: Oxford University Press.

———. 2000. 'Parties without Members? Party Organization in a Changing Electoral Environment'. In *Parties without Partisans: Political Change in Advanced Industrial Democracies*, edited by Russell J. Dalton and Martin P. Wattenberg, 79–101. Oxford: Oxford University Press.

———. 2015. *Beyond Party Members: Changing Approaches to Partisan Mobilization*. Oxford: Oxford University Press.

Spier, Tim and Markus Klein. 2015. 'Party Membership in Germany: Rather Formal, Therefore Uncool?' In *Party Members and Activists*, edited by Emilie van Haute and Anika Gauja, 84–99. London: Routledge.

van Biezen, Ingrid and Thomas Poguntke. 2014. 'The Decline of Membership-Based Politics'. *Party Politics* 20 (2): 205–16.

van Biezen, Ingrid, Peter Mair and Thomas Poguntke. 2012. 'Going, Going, . . . Gone? The Decline of Party Membership in Contemporary Europe'. *European Journal of Political Research* 51: 24–56.

von dem Berge, Benjamin and Thomas Poguntke. 2017. 'Varieties of Intra-Party Democracy: Conceptualization and Index Construction'. In *Organizing Political Parties: Representation, Participation, and Power*, edited by Susan E. Scarrow, Paul D. Webb and Thomas Poguntke, 128–84. Oxford: Oxford University Press.

van Haute, Emilie, Emilien Paulis, and Vivien Sierens. 2018. 'Assessing Party Membership Figures: The MAPP Dataset'. *European Political Science*, 17 (3): 366–77.

Webb, Paul, Monica Poletti and Tim Bale. 2017. 'So Who Really Does the Donkey Work in "Multi-Speed Membership Parties"? Comparing the Election Campaign Activity of Party Members and Party Supporters'. *Electoral Studies*, 46: 64–74.

Whiteley, Paul, Patrick Seyd and Jeremy Richardson. 1994. *True Blues: The Politics of Conservative Party Membership*. Oxford: Clarendon Press.

8

Party Workers, Ambassadors, Veterans and All the Other Party Members

Knut Heidar and Karina Kosiara-Pedersen[1]

In chapter 7, we studied the party activities of members as individuals, both inside the party organization and outside as party ambassadors in the public domain. We found that the members were more active than expected and more so than fifteen to twenty years earlier. The increase in the share of active members was not in spite of a declining membership but because of it: the activists stayed on, while the passive member-supporters had left. In this chapter, we focus on how and to what extent it is possible to identify dimensions in party member participation. In other words, do party members practise a division of labour where some are mainly outreach ambassadors, others are mainly rank-and-file workers inside the party organization and still others are primarily party leaders. We study the different dimensions based on their participatory profiles within Scandinavian parties. We also look for changes in member types over time in Denmark and Norway. This leads to a discussion of whether some of these dimensions of participation are more crucial in providing linkage than others.

We operate solely at the country level. First, we want to know whether there are different dimensions of party member activism, distinguished by how party members participate, in the three Scandinavian countries. Second, based on time-series data from Denmark and Norway, we ask if such dimensions change over time. Provided we find such dimensions, what kinds of participation define these, and are they country-specific or similar across the Scandinavian countries? Do these dimensions contribute to parties' participatory linkages from voters to party elites through their membership organizations in different ways? Before turning to these questions, we start out with some remarks on previous studies and our general approach.

PARTICIPATORY TYPES OF PARTY MEMBERS

There is no reason to believe that party member participation is completely random. For example, it is likely that members holding intra-party office also attend meetings and (try to) influence the election manifesto. The traditional approach to the variation among party members, however, has been to distinguish between passive and active members or to place them on a 'participation continuum' (Panebianco 1988, 26; Kosiara-Pedersen 2017, 118). This is helpful, but insufficient in order to understand parties' participatory linkage.

A number of scholars have discussed how party members impute costs as well as benefits on electorally motivated political parties when they enrol and participate (Elklit 1991; Katz 1990; Scarrow 1994, 1996, 41–46; Seyd and Whiteley 1992; Whiteley, Seyd and Richardson 1994). Scarrow argues that party members may provide the advantages of legitimacy, votes, finances, outreach, labour, linkage, innovation and recruitment (1996, 41–46). These dimensions allow for a distinction between various types of activities in which party members may participate and hence may form the basis for distinguishing between different types of members. Party members contribute a measure of democratic legitimacy merely by enrolling in a party. The number of members serves as a reflection of the party's appeal to society, or its 'reach' (cf. chapter 1), as do the characteristics of the members (Katz 1990, 152; Scarrow 1996, 42). Party members allow parties 'to maintain at least the *image* of a mass party' (Mair 1997, 148; original emphasis). Tendencies in the number of members also matter, as increasing numbers may be taken as a signal of progress, vitality or increasing electoral support (Scarrow 1996, 176). In addition, the characteristics of party members may influence the degree of legitimacy that party members provide parties. This provision of legitimacy rests on the collective of the party members.

Party activism enables contacts between voters, members, party representatives and the party leadership and the members may act as a channel of communication between the party leadership and society at large (Scarrow 1996, 44). Members may contribute to 'the complex interaction between political voters about the issues which emerge on the political scene' (Seyd and Whiteley 1992, 3), thus serving as the eyes and ears of the parties (Whiteley, Seyd and Richardson 1994, 4). Communication is a two-way process, involving both bottom-up communication, where members provide the party leadership with information about voters' concerns and top-down communication, where members explain and justify the party's policies to voters. Party members provide linkage through their membership organizations when they take on internal party office, attend meetings, attend the national annual meeting or congress and participate in social and cultural arrangements within their party.

However, party members also provide linkage between their party and the voters when they campaign for their party. Campaigning takes place at election time, when party members may contribute labour resources by handing out election leaflets, putting up election posters and canvassing (Katz 1990, 152). While election time is the most important time for parties' promotion of their candidates and policies, party members may also provide linkage between elections, when they, through their presence in neighbourhoods, local communities and workplaces, promote the party and party policies. Members are 'ambassadors to the community' (Scarrow 1996, 43). Party members provide 'a base for proselytizing in the wider community; and it helps to publicize the existence of ideology among potential believers' (Ware 1996, 63). Since this kind of 'outreach' participation is less demanding, some members who are not active within the party member organization as such, for example, by attending meetings, may nevertheless engage in these kinds of activities and hence provide this looser kind of linkage.

Questions and Data

Previous studies have identified groups of members on the basis of their activism. Whiteley, Seyd and Richardson identified two groups, the activists and the supporters, among British Conservative party members (1994, 103). The activist group's activities include canvassing, standing for party office, attending meetings, delivering leaflets, helping at party functions and standing for public election, while the supporter group's activities include signing petitions, displaying election posters and donating money (Whiteley, Seyd and Richardson 1994, 103). Similar analyses, but identifying different groups, have been conducted on Norway (Heidar 1994a) and Denmark (Kosiara-Pedersen 2017). Hence, our first question of analysis in this chapter is, simply, which dimensions may be identified within party member activism in Scandinavian parties?

Political parties have undergone important changes in recent years. Most have become heavily professionalized organizations with capital-intensive election campaigns, centralized decision-making and an increasing number of party staff (Scarrow et al. 2017). Hence, they have less need for the labour or manpower that party members may provide. Furthermore, Scarrow (1996) shows that the German and British parties through the 1980s increasingly emphasized party members' outreach or ambassadorial role. Due to the advent of new information and communication technologies, it is now even easier for members to be ambassadors for their party by discussing party policies online. This leads to the second question of analysis, namely, whether the dimensions identified within party member activism change over time. In particular, is it possible to detect a lesser emphasis on labour and larger emphasis on outreach?

We use principal-components factor analyses to identify the patterns in party member activism. This is similar to the previous studies based on data from party member surveys (Heidar 1994b; Kosiara-Pedersen 2017; Whiteley, Seyd and Richardson 1994). We limit the detailed analysis to the most recent surveys in the Scandinavian countries – in Denmark (2012), Sweden (2015) and Norway (2017). The data are presented in detail in chapter 1. We shall also report findings from previous studies to look for changes and to make our findings more robust. Cross-time comparison is possible in Norway with previous surveys in 1991, 2000 and 2009, and in Denmark with a survey from 2000.[2]

HOW DO PARTY MEMBERS
IN SCANDINAVIA PARTICIPATE?

We seek out patterns in aggregate party member activism based on a wide range of party activities, some already discussed in chapter 7. These activities vary on a number of dimensions (see appendix, table A8.1). Hence, we have sought to include activities which vary in terms of how demanding they are, how big a share of members participate and how they contribute to parties' participatory linkage. Unfortunately, we are not able to include identical activity measures across countries and over time. Hence, the activities included in the factor analyses vary, which calls for caution in the comparative conclusions. Further sections focus on each country in turn.

Dimensions in Danish Party Member Participation

In the Danish case, the 2012 survey identified four clusters of members, namely 'party worker', 'ambassador', 'candidate' and 'veteran' (table 8.1). While the *party workers* are identified by traditional party activities at and between campaigns, as well as financial contributions, the *candidates* come out as a separate group based on recruitment potential, incumbency and online ambassador activities. The (offline) *ambassadors* encourage voters to vote for their party in election campaigns and also discuss party policies with non-members in between elections. The *veterans* previously held party or public office.

Table 8.1.   Denmark. Factor loadings for Danish party member activism, 2012.

FACTOR	1 Party Worker	2 Ambassador	3 Candidate	4 Veteran
– delivering campaign leaflets	0.71	0.25	–	–
– write political proposals	0.71	–	–	0.23
– participate in the nomination of candidates for the national election	0.70	–	–	–
– put up election posters	0.68	–	–	−0.21
– annual congress	0.68	–	0.17	0.18
– social and leisure activities	0.67	–	–	0.23
– party office	0.62	–	–	−0.45
– recruit members	0.61	–	0.19	–
– write letters to the editor	0.57	–	0.37	0.24
– meeting attendance	0.57	–	−0.16	0.30
– canvassing	0.49	–	–	−0.19
– financial contributions	0.34	0.20	–	–
– discuss party policies with non-members during election campaign	0.25	0.74	–	–
– encourage voters to vote for the party	0.43	0.63	–	–

FACTOR	1 Party Worker	2 Ambassador	3 Candidate	4 Veteran
– discuss party policies with non-members	0.28	0.53	–	0.16
– online discussion	0.18	0.36	0.71	–
– discuss party policies online during campaign	0.20	0.45	0.64	–
– recruitment potential	0.28	−0.18	0.57	–
– elected representative for the party	0.35	−0.25	0.41	–
– previously held party office	0.20	–	–	0.80
– previously elected representative for the party	0.20	–	–	0.53
– eigenvalue	5.33	1.82	1.70	1.59
% of variance	25	9	8	8

Note: Principal-components factor analysis. Oblimin Rotation. Kaiser Normalization. Only dimensions with eigenvalues > 1 and factor loadings > 0.15 are included.

In the 2000 survey analysis (see table 8.4) we identify three similar groups – the party worker, the light party worker/ambassador and the veteran (Kosiara-Pedersen 2017, 153). The party worker dimension encompasses traditional party activities such as writing letters to the editor, attending the annual meeting or congress and drafting political proposals. However, this also includes holding office, both in and for the party, and recruitment potential. Hence, compared to 2012, the activist and candidate dimensions are combined. In the 2000 analysis, the light party worker/ ambassador dimension includes discussing party policies with non-members, making financial contributions and putting up election posters. These are traditional and (previously) labour-intensive campaign activities. The veteran dimension identified in the 2000 analysis encompasses having held party or public office.

The differences from 2000 to 2012 are small, with the exception of the impact of the Internet. The candidate dimension in 2012 includes a mix of online activity and candidacy, while the online ambassador activities are not included in the Danish 2000 survey. Two general conclusions seem warranted. First, parties' core task is to generate a recruitment pool for nominations to public office. This seems well provided for by Danish party membership organizations. They do have potential candidates, including among their otherwise inactive members whom they may mobilize if needed. This finding supports a previous British study (Seyd and Whiteley 2002, 77). Second, the more subtle campaigning of party members who discuss party policies with non-members and encourage voters to vote for the party seems to make up a separate dimension of participation. This fits with other findings on what parties want from their members. As noted earlier, British and German parties had earlier increased their emphasis on members' contributions to the ambassadorial activities.

Dimensions in Norwegian Party Member Participation

The analysis of the Norwegian 2017 data (table 8.2) identifies four dimensions in party member activism: the party worker, veteran, party elite and online ambassador dimensions. The party worker dimension includes election campaign activities, holding branch and public office for the party and attending party meetings. The veteran dimension includes previously holding office and participation in selecting party leaders and candidates at all levels. The party elite dimension includes holding regional or national party office, participation in the selection of the regional or national leaders, participating in decision-making on the regional or national party manifestos, writing letters to the editor and making media appearances (TV/radio and newspapers) during election campaigns. The final dimension, party ambassador, is defined by online participation, that is, activities on social media during electoral campaigns as well as in between elections.

In the 1991 survey, three dimensions emerged: the party worker, the veteran and the opposition activist (Heidar 1994a). In both the 2000 and 2009 surveys, we found the party workers, the veterans and credit card members (table 7.4; also Heidar 2014). Just like in Denmark, the main picture is one of stability: there is a large and active group of members holding office and taking care of general party affairs. This dimension coexists with the veteran dimension, and those participating as veterans now probably did the same active party work in an earlier period. There are also some changes, however. The opposition activist dimension in 1991 and 2000 (internally active but not in office) disappears in later surveys. The credit card dimension, giving money, constituted a separate dimension in 2000 and 2009. New in 2017 are the dimensions of 'party elite' and 'online ambassador' activities. Some of this has historical explanations. The 1991 and 2000 surveys are from a turbulent period in Norwegian party politics, a period marked by internal opposition in some parties (e.g. Progress and Labour parties). The notable changes are that the online ambassadors stand out in 2017, and that we find both a 'rank-and-file' and an 'elite' party worker dimension.

Table 8.2.   Norway. Factor loadings for Norwegian party member activism, 2017.

FACTOR	1 Local party worker	2 Old guard /veteran	3 Informal party elite	4 Online ambassador
– campaign**	0.82	0.15	–	0.17
– deliver leaflets*	0.79	–	–	–
– local party office	0.75	–	0.16	–
– recruitment potential	0.74	–	–	–
– any meeting/event*	0.65	0.22	–	–

FACTOR	1 Local party worker	2 Old guard /veteran	3 Informal party elite	4 Online ambassador
– elected representative for the party	0.63	–	0.25	–
– recruit*	0.59	–	–	0.25
– demonstration*	0.40	–	–	0.31
– policy	0.37	–	0.36	0.15
– campaign canvassing**	0.37	–	–	–
– previously held party office	–	0.83	–	–
– previously elected representative for the party	–	0.76	–	–
– select local candidate	0.37	0.66	–	–
– select regional/national candidate	0.23	0.60	0.19	–
– select local leader	0.42	0.60	–	–
– decide on local manifesto	0.44	0.58	–	–
– select regional/national leader		0.50	0.50	–
– letters to the editor*	0.28	–	0.51	0.19
– campaign TV/radio**	–	–	0.68	–
– regional/national party office	–	0.21	0.61	–
– campaign newspaper**	0.27	–	0.60	–
– decide on regional/national manifesto	–	0.39	0.44	0.20
– online campaigning**	0.25	–	0.16	0.86
– online*	–	–	–	0.81
– discuss*	0.41	0.15	−0.26	0.45
– eigenvalue	9.03	2.40	1.66	1.20
– % of variance	23	15	11	9
– factor correlations	–	–	–	–
– 1	–	–	–	–
– 2	0.33	–	–	–
– 3	0.34	0.19	–	–
– 4	0.31	0.12	0.29	–

Note. Principal-components factor analysis, Oblimin Rotation, Kaiser Normalization. Only dimensions with eigenvalues > 1 and factor loadings > 0.15 are included.
* Within the past year; ** At the most recent local election.

Dimensions in Swedish Party Member Participation

In the Swedish factor analysis (table 8.3), four dimensions of party member activism turn up: the party worker, the online ambassador, the veteran and, finally, a new type, the election activist. Here the party worker factor loads on a range of party activities: organizing and attending party meetings, internal and external activism (on- and

Table 8.3. Sweden. Factor loadings for Swedish party member activism, 2015.

FACTOR	1 Party worker	2 Online ambassador	3 Veteran	4 Election activist
– general branch party meeting	0.85	–	–	–
– branch meetings preparing manifestos, electing party officers and candidates	0.81	–	–	–
– branch meeting for policy information	0.77	–	–	–
– discussions with regional/ national party officials	0.68	–	–	–
– electoral campaign: Handing out leaflets, etc.	0.64	–	–	0.23
– currently holding or previously held party or public office	0.61	–	–	0.20
– during past year: Contacted politician or public official, local/ national	0.59	–	–	–
– during past year: Debated with other parties	0.56	0.16	–	–
– participated in the nomination process 2014	0.54	–	–	0.43
– helped organize an election meeting 2014	0.53	–	–	0.32
– past year: Participated in activities directed at specific party groups	0.51	–	–	–
– distributed election posters 2014	0.46	–	–	0.30
– posted political comments in social media 2014	–	0.85	–	–
– past year: Friends or likes for politicians on social media	–	0.77	–	–
– shared campaign material with friends/family/colleagues with e-mail or on social media during 2014 campaign	–	0.71	–	0.18
– convinced others to vote for the party: 2014	0.18	0.41	–	0.17
– recruitment potential: Willing to take on party office?	0.28	0.33	0.22	−0.22
– nominated to or asked to be nominated for local/regional office?	–	–	0.76	–
– nominated to or asked to be nominated for national office?	–	–	0.73	0.18
– participated in developing the electoral manifest 2014	–	0.16	–	0.70

FACTOR	1 Party worker	2 Online ambassador	3 Veteran	4 Election activist
– voted at branch decisions on issues concerning 2014 election	0.30	–	–	0.55
	–	–	–	–
– eigenvalues	6.94	1.67	1.18	1.01
– % of total variance	33.06	7.94	5.62	4.79
– factor correlations	–	–	–	–
– 1	1.00	0.40	0.09	0.34
– 2	0.40	1.00	0.07	0.10
– 3	0.09	0.07	1.00	−0.02
– 4	0.34	0.10	−0.02	1.00

Note: Extraction Method: Principal Component Analysis. Rotation Method: Oblimin with Kaiser Normalization.

offline) and office holding. This is a more 'across the board' party worker than is found in the other countries. The online ambassador dimension is more familiar, with a focused use of social media. An obvious problem in interpreting the Swedish data is that the question about office merges current and former as well as party and public office holding. A veteran cluster is therefore only indirectly identified through the question of whether party members have been 'nominated to or asked to be nominated for' office. This differs from the questions in the Danish and Norwegian surveys, making comparisons difficult. The fourth dimension is difficult to interpret. This dimension is distinguished by activism at the 2014 election: preparing the national election manifesto and casting membership votes in preparation for the election but not considering nomination for office. This dimension seems to be mobilized by the election campaign, and in participatory terms, it may be termed an 'election activist' dimension.

Comparison across Countries and over Time

On the basis of the three country studies we now turn to the overall picture of variation in party members' patterns of participation. Table 8.4 sums up the dimensions identified in the seven available Scandinavian party member surveys; four in Norway (1991, 2000, 2009 and 2017), two in Denmark (2000 and 2012), and one in Sweden (2015). As the party member surveys do not include identical questions, we cannot conduct a rigorous comparative analysis. Hence, we paint with the broad brush here.

The party worker dimension is identified in all three Scandinavian countries today and in all analyses over time. This is similar to the activist dimension found among

Table 8.4. Types of Scandinavian party members.

	Party worker	Old guard /veterans	Offline ambassador	Online ambassador	Candidate	Opposition activist	Credit card	Party elite	Election activist
DK 2000	X	X	X*		X				
DK 2012	X	X	X		X				
N 1991	X	X							
N 2000	X	X				X	X		
N 2009	X	X				X	X		
N 2017	X	X		X				X	
S 2017	X	X		X					X

* Includes light campaign work.

British Conservative members (Whiteley, Seyd and Richardson 1994, 103). Party workers who participate in this way sustain the party organization and create linkage between the rank-and-file members and party leadership. Intra-party office (in Denmark and Sweden) also loads on this dimension. Party worker activism makes up the backbone of local party organization, including in the sense of forming the basis for external campaigning. While in Norway this dimension also included potential candidates, in Denmark and Sweden, this 'activity' makes a separate dimension. In Denmark and Sweden, potential candidates are active as online ambassadors. In Norway, parties stand a better chance of finding potential candidates among traditional activists, while in Denmark and Sweden, parties are also likely to find candidates among members who are not engaged in traditional party activities.

The old guard, or veteran, dimension is clearly identified in both Denmark and Norway, also over time. This dimension comprises members who have previously held elected or intra-party office. While this is a dimension on its own in Denmark, Norwegian veterans have also been active in policy and nomination decisions. They are still active in influencing party decisions. No identical 'veteran' dimension is found in Sweden – most likely because the question in the Swedish survey includes both past and present office – but indirectly we find a similar group identified by the two questions on whether party members have previously tried to be or have been nominated for public elections.

We find the ambassador, or 'outreach', dimension in all countries, although the activities included vary slightly. The online ambassador dimension is distinct in both the 2017 Norwegian and the 2015 Swedish surveys. In both Denmark and Sweden, this dimension also loads moderately on the issue of being a potential candidate. In the Danish case, we see a separate offline ambassador dimension, while the online/ offline activities are combined as in the Swedish case, and in Norway in 2017, the online ambassador comes out pure and simple. When discussing whether new online forms supplement or replace old-type electioneering, it is interesting to note that in Norway, online forms dominate the work of party ambassadors, in Sweden, they seem to blend, while in Denmark, different members engage in the two forms of activism (on Denmark, see Kosiara-Pedersen 2017, 128; on offline and online participation in Norway and Denmark, see, e.g., Pedersen and Saglie 2005).

Both the Norwegian and Swedish analyses identify a dimension related to the activities of party workers, and this activist dimension is also loading on influence seeking. In Norway, we have labelled this the 'party elite' dimension since it includes holding regional/national office within the party, participating in the selection of the regional/national leaders, contributing to decisions on the regional/national party manifesto, writing letters to the editor and making media appearances (TV, radio and newspapers) during election campaigns. It is interesting how it is possible to distinguish between more local activism and this higher-level activism due to the detailed questions in the 2017 Norwegian survey. In Sweden, a somewhat similar dimension (the 'election activist') includes decisions on the election manifesto in 2014 and membership ballots.

CONCLUSION

The purpose of this chapter is to explore dimensions in party member activism in order to (1) identify dimensions in party member activism in Scandinavian parties, and (2) analyse whether these change over time, in particular, whether it is possible to detect a lesser emphasis on labour and a larger emphasis on outreach.

Turning first to the question of identifying dimensions in party member activism in Scandinavian parties, the factor analyses identified a 'party worker' dimension as the most important in all Scandinavian member surveys. This captures a broad activity range: attending meetings, participating in campaign activities, influencing nominations and party policies, serving in party office and so forth. The party worker dimension accounts for between one-quarter and one-third of all variance. This group offers a chain of contact options, from meeting the voters, to contributing to internal party decision-making, to elected public office. The 'party worker' dimension shows the extent to which party member organizations provide traditional participatory linkage to the electorate.

The second dimension captures the old guard or 'veteran' member participation. This is the generation of members who have previously served their party in office. They know the trade but have a less comprehensive activity profile than today's party workers. Most likely, they are the party members who previously provided the kind of participatory linkage that the current 'party worker' dimension does. The 'veteran' dimension is present in all member surveys and captures from 8 to 15 per cent of the variance in the most recent country surveys.

The remaining dimensions differ between countries and over time. The online/offline ambassador dimensions are found in the Danish analyses and in the latest Norwegian and Swedish ones. Whereas credit card membership is a dimension of its own in Norway in 2000 and 2009, this activity is included in other dimensions in 1991 and 2017. The candidate dimension identified in Denmark in 2000 and 2012 is not found in the other countries. This may be due to real differences between the members or to differences between the questionnaires. We do not know.

Using the big brush, we find in all countries an activist dimension with broad, comprehensive participation. The party workers engaged in these activities are well positioned to seek out opinions in the electorate, bring them into party discussions, translate preferences into policies, present them to the public in election campaigns and finally, fight for party policies within public, democratic institutions. They provide membership-based participatory linkage. We also find that there are specialized participatory segments within party membership that can and do work actively within civil society to develop (or sell) party policies. There is no indication that members today are less involved in internal party work and more in outreach activities. Both types of activities are important to the members. The main message from the data is one of relative stability, although there are also clear indications that online activism is on the increase. This is certainly no surprise. Hence, the response to our second research question is 'no', it is not possible to detect a lesser emphasis on labour and a larger emphasis on outreach in the patterns of party member activism.

Party member activism is not 'one size fits all' – there are several dimensions. This has implications for how parties recruit, mobilize and organize party members and therefore also for how they contribute to representative democracy. First, by identifying the dimensions in their party member activism, parties may target mobilization and organization to the kind of activism that is of value to them. As argued in the first part of this chapter, party members may contribute to parties in several ways, but parties do not value all ways to the same extent. Hence, by recognizing the dimensions, parties may target specific segments among their (potential) members. This also implies that party membership linkage may take various forms across the parties as they develop their organizations.

Second, the dimensions in party member activism show how activism varies within the full-member group and not only across different types of party affiliation (cf. Scarrow 2015). The obvious example is the ambassador dimension, a kind of participation that is no different whether taken up by supporters with or without a membership 'card'. These groups differ in whether they provide a (in some parties) limited sum of dues, and in the legitimacy that may still stick to traditional dues-paying party members, but they do not differ in how they are active in promoting the party. Both groups may encourage voters to vote for the party and discuss party policies with the voters.

In addition, the variation in party member activism, and in particular the participatory dimensions identified, has implications for party member research. In particular, this has consequences for how we operationalize party member activism when explaining why party members participate. Whereas previous studies have tended to explain participation in the terms of the number of hours spent on party activities and by developing participation indices, the dimensions identified by the factor analyses open our eyes to the patterns in *how* party members participate. We discuss the implications of this in the following chapter (chapter 9), where we seek explanations for activism. Here we show how these explanations vary across different types of party member activism.

NOTES

1. Thanks to Marit Kvernenes, Tor Gaute Syrstad and Asmus Harre for efficient research assistance.

2. The first three Norwegian surveys were postal surveys, while the fourth in 2016-2017 was an online survey. In 1991 and 2000, 400 party members from each of the seven main parliamentary parties were randomly selected. The overall response rate was 68 per cent in 1991 and 61 per cent in 2000. In 2009 and 2016-2017, the team selected 1,000 party members from each party, and the overall response rate was 49 per cent in 2009 and 33 per cent in 2016-2017. The respondents have been compared with available variables for the total

membership (gender, region and age cohorts), and it was found that they are representative of the population of party members. See Heidar (2015).

The first Danish party member survey was a mail-back survey conducted in 2000 among members of all nine parties represented in parliament at that time (Bille and Elklit 2003; Hansen 2002; Pedersen 2003; Pedersen et al. 2004). A random sample of 1,000 in the three largest parties, Liberals, Social Democrats and Conservatives, and 800 in the remaining parties were drawn from parties' membership bases. The questionnaire was mailed to respondents, along with two reminders, one of which included a new questionnaire. The research team did not have access to the membership files, and the parties did not have access to the responses. See Kosiara-Pedersen (2015).

BIBLIOGRAPHY

Bille, Lars and Jørgen Elklit, eds. 2003. *Partiernes medlemmer*. Aarhus: Aarhus Universitetsforlag.
Elklit, Jørgen. 1991. 'Faldet i medlemstal i danske politiske partier. Nogle mulige årsager'. *Politica* 23 (1): 60–83.
Hansen, Bernhard. 2002. *Party Activism in Denmark*. Aarhus: Politica.
Heidar, Knut. 1994a. 'The Polymorphic Nature of Party Membership'. *European Journal of Political Research* 25 (1): 61–86.
———. 1994b. 'The Polymorphic Nature of Party Membership'. *European Journal of Political Research* 25: 61–86.
———. 2014. '"Little Boxes on the Hillside": Do All Party Members Look the Same?' Paper presented at the ECPR Joint Sessions of Workshops, Salamanca, April 2014.
———. 2015. 'Party Membership in Norway: Declining but Still Viable?' In *Party Members and Activists*, edited by Emilie van Haute and Anika Gauja, 151–68. London: Routledge.
Katz, Richard S. 1990. 'Party as Linkage: A Vestigial Function?' *European Journal of Political Research* 18 (1): 143–61.
Kosiara-Pedersen, Karina. 2015. 'Party Membership in Denmark: Fluctuating Membership Figures and Organizational Stability'. In *Party Members and Activists*, edited by Emilie van Haute and Anika Gauja, 66–83. London: Routledge.
———. 2017. *Demokratiets ildsjæle. Partimedlemmer i Danmark*. København: DJØF Forlag.
Mair, Peter. 1997. *Party System Change: Approaches and Interpretations*. Oxford: Oxford University Press.
Panebianco, Angelo. 1988. *Political Parties: Organization and Power*. Cambridge: Cambridge University Press.
Pedersen, Karina. 2003. *Party Membership Linkage: The Danish Case*. Denmark: Department of Political Science, University of Copenhagen.
Pedersen, Karina and Jo Saglie. 2005. 'New Technology in Ageing Parties: Internet Use in Danish and Norwegian Parties'. *Party Politics* 11 (3): 359–77.
Pedersen, Karina, Lars Bille, Roger Buch Jensen, Jørgen Elklit, Bernard Hansen and Hans Jørgen Nielsen. 2004. 'Sleeping or Active Partners? Danish Party Members at the Turn of the Millennium? Danish Party Members at the Turn of the Millennium'. *Party Politics* 10 (4): 367–84.
Scarrow, Susan E. 1994. 'The "Paradox of Enrollment": Assessing the Costs and Benefits of Party Memberships'. *European Journal of Political Research* 25: 41–60.

———. 1996. *Parties and Their Members: Organizing for Victory in Britain and Germany.* Oxford: Oxford University Press.

———. 2015. *Beyond Party Members: Changing Approaches to Partisan Mobilization.* Oxford: Oxford University Press.

Scarrow, Susan E., Paul D. Webb and Thomas Poguntke, eds. 2017. *Organizing Representation: Political Parties, Participation, and Power.* Oxford: Oxford University Press.

Seyd, Patrick and Paul Whiteley. 1992. *Labour's Grass Roots: The Politics of Party Membership.* Oxford: Clarendon Press.

———. 2002. *New Labour's Grassroots: The Transformation of the Labour Party Membership.* Basingstoke: Palgrave Macmillan.

Ware, Alan. 1996. *Political Parties and Party Systems.* Oxford: Oxford University Press.

Whiteley, Paul, Patrick Seyd and Jeremy Richardson. 1994. *True Blues: The Politics of Conservative Party Membership.* Oxford: Clarendon Press.

Appendix

Table A8.1. Activities included in the factor analyses.

Denmark 2012	Norway 2017	Sweden 2015
Legitimacy		
– recruit members*	– recruit members***	–
Financial		
– financial contributions*	–	–
Outreach		
– discuss party policies with non-members*	– discuss with non-members***	– discuss with non-members***
– online discussion*	– online discussion***	
– discuss party policies with non-members**	–	– convinced voters to vote for party**
– discuss party policies online**	– campaign online**	– online campaigning**
– encourage voters to vote for the party**	– campaign letters to the editor**	– friends or likes for politicians in social media**
–	– campaign media**	– campaigned among friends and colleagues**
–	– demonstrations***	–
Labour		
– canvassing**	– campaign canvassing**	–
– delivering campaign leaflets**	– leaflets**	– leaflets**
	– campaign leaflets**	– organized campaign meeting**
– put up election posters**	–	– put up election posters**

Denmark 2012	Norway 2017	Sweden 2015
– write letters to the editor*	– letters to the editor***	– voting on branch manifesto decisions**
Linkage		
– meeting attendance at any time	– any party event***	– party branch meeting***
– annual congress*	–	– branch meeting preparing manifesto***
– social and leisure activities*	–	– branch meeting for information***
–	–	– meetings for specific party groups**
Innovation/Political decisions		
– write political proposals*	– formulated policies***	– discussing with party leaders***
–	– party leader local	– contacted party leaders***
–	– party leader national	– developing election manifest**
–	– party manifesto local	–
–	– party manifesto national	–
Recruitment		
– participate in the nomination of candidate**	– candidate nomination local	– candidate nominations**
–	– candidate nomination national	– nominated or asked to be nominated for local/regional office
–	–	– nominated or asked to be nominated for national office
– recruitment potential	– recruitment potential among those asked***	– willing to take on party office
– elected representative for the party	– elected	–
– previously elected representative for the party	– previous elected	–
– party office	– intra-party office local	– have or have had party or public party office
–	– intra-party office national	–
– previously held party office	– previous intra-party office	–

Note: *At least once within the past five years. **At the latest election. *** Within the past year.

9

Explaining Party Member Activism

Anders Ravik Jupskås and Karina Kosiara-Pedersen

They are in the streets with folders, balloons and sweets at election time, their letters to the editor are found in the debate sections of newspapers, and they are clapping at the celebration of the party chair's speech in the televised transmission from the party's annual meeting. However, while many party members engage in a plethora of party activities, some clearly participate more than others (see chapter 7). What explains their participation? And are different types of party activism explained differently? The purpose of this chapter is to analyse why party members participate and hence contribute to party linkage.

We conceptualize party member activism rather narrowly as the activities members carry out in and for their parties. Hence, our approach includes neither forms of political participation outside of the party nor forms of activism carried out by party affiliates not enrolled as members (Gauja 2015; Faucher 2015; Kosiara-Pedersen and Kristiansen 2016; Scarrow 2015; Webb, Poletti and Bale 2017). This choice follows from this book's overall focus on the extent to which party member organizations provide democratic linkage in Nordic party democracies.

Chapters 7 and 8 show the extent to which parties provide participatory linkage with society by focusing on the amount and type of participation, respectively. We take these analyses one step further by looking into the character of the members who are participating, as this may have important implications for party linkage. In short, we argue that party linkage is weakened if participation is dominated by people with substantial resources since this implies that parties become less socially, and possibly less ideologically, representative. Parties may also become less ideologically representative of their electorates if ideologically deviant party members participate less than those who are completely in line with the party. Furthermore, we suggest that linkage is weaker if members with few expectations of intra-party democracy participate more than those who expect much, as this allows parties to

175

centralize power and decrease intra-party democracy. Finally, party linkage is weaker if members without ties to civil society dominate various forms of activism within the party, since parties thereby connect less to the organized society.

The novel contribution of this chapter is twofold. First, we analyse party member participation in general, but we also seek to explain members' participation in different types of activities. The main argument is that, since party member activism is multidimensional (see chapter 8), different types of activities require different explanations. We explore how party members' socioeconomic status and relationship with their party vary across the different types of activities. Second, besides socioeconomic characteristics and party members' relationship with their parties, we explore the extent to which party members' involvement in civil society organizations enhances or limits party activism. Are members of civil society providing a participatory linkage not only in their own organization but also in parties?

In this chapter, we first discuss the concept and operationalization of our dependent variable, 'party activism', before turning to theories explaining party member activism in the second part. We briefly present the data applied in the third part of the chapter, and in the fourth part, we present the empirical results for Denmark, Norway and Sweden. In the fifth and final part, we discuss the results and conclude that the empirical patterns of party activism among Scandinavian members do not indicate a weakening of parties' participatory linkage.

FORMS OF PARTY MEMBER ACTIVISM IN SCANDINAVIA

Party member activism is usually conceptually seen and empirically found to be multidimensional (Heidar 1994; see also chapter 8). For example, specific activities that members may carry out vary in terms of how formal they are, whether they concern intra-party decision-making or electoral activities and whether they are online or offline. Due to its multidimensional nature, some scholars measure party members' activism by asking about time (e.g. number of hours) devoted to party activities overall, rather than asking about involvement in specific activities (e.g. candidate selection or decision-making processes) (Cross and Young 2004; Gallagher and Marsh 2004; Hansen 2002; Pedersen et al. 2004; Seyd and Whiteley 1992; Whiteley, Seyd and Richardson 1994). The advantage of this measure is that it may include all sorts of activities as well as some indication of their intensity. However, the disadvantage is that members vary in terms of what they include, which makes any direct comparisons more problematic. Danish party members who indicate zero hours are still participating, for example, by attending the annual meeting, reading the party magazine or newsletter and encouraging voters to vote for the party (Kosiara-Pedersen 2017, 124). This is also the case with Swedish members.[1]

Another approach is to create activism indices (e.g. see Bale and Webb 2015; Seyd and Whiteley 1992; Webb, Poletti and Bale 2017). While these operationalizations are fruitful in deductive, theoretically based analyses of how party members, for example, contribute to specific tasks in the parties, they do to some extent collide with the nature of party members' participation. Party members do not necessarily follow the patterns set by researchers.

In this chapter, we take as our departure point the multidimensionality of party member activism as identified in chapter 8. However, we do not include 'the veterans' and 'the candidates' for the simple reason that we focus on current rather than previous ('the veterans') or potential ('the candidates') forms of activism (for an analysis of recruitment potential among Danish party members, see Kjær and Kosiara-Pedersen 2018; Kosiara-Pedersen and Harre 2017). Moreover, given that neither the dimensions nor the kinds of activities that are associated with them are identical across the three countries, we had to make a few adjustments as well as simplify the operationalization. In short, we distinguish between the meeting attendees, decision makers, campaigners, offline ambassadors and online ambassadors.

The two first types – meeting attendees and decision makers – reflect core activities within political parties. This is perhaps particularly the case in traditional mass parties, which entail meetings at the various levels not only with the purpose of deciding and delegating but also as the main channel of communication (cf. Duverger 1964). Arguably, members have less of a say in more recent electoral-professional and cartel parties. However, they still take part in important decision-making processes (Sartori 1976; Bille 1997, 2001). Both meeting attendance and decision-making are empirically associated with the dominant dimension of activism among Scandinavian parties, namely, the 'party worker' (see chapter 7). Attending meetings is, in fact, the internal activity with the highest frequency of participation in all three countries. We regard members as meeting attendees if they have participated an internal meeting during the past year, but we also distinguish between those who only have participated once and those who attend meetings more frequently. Decision makers refer to those who have participated in writing political proposals or in the nomination of candidates for the national election.

The third type of activism relates to campaigning, which is also empirically associated with the 'party worker' dimension. To be sure, campaigning has turned more capital intensive in the Scandinavian countries (Kosiara-Pedersen 2014), yet members are still important for (at least some) parties because they are a source of cheap labour or improve the public image of the party (e.g. see Lippert and Midtiby [2009] on the Danish Social Democrats). In our analyses, we see party members as campaigners if they delivered campaign leaflets, put up election posters and canvassed in the (most recent national or local) election prior to the survey.

The two final types of membership activism are offline and online ambassadors. While the offline ambassadors have been important at least since the 1980s (Scarrow 1996), online ambassadors have emerged more recently, enabled by the rise of new information and communication technologies (Römmele 2003). We distinguish between online and offline ambassadors for two reasons. First, the analysis of activism dimensions (see chapter 8) suggests that online ambassadorial activities constitute a distinct dimension in Norway and Sweden.[2] Second, a distinction between offline and online activities allows us to gauge the impact of new information and communication technologies. For example, is online activism further skewing political participation (in favour of those with more resources) or does it level the playing field (between those with and without resources) (cf. Pedersen and Saglie 2005)? In our study, members are offline ambassadors if they have discussed party policies with friends, family or colleagues or if they have encouraged voters to vote for their party. Members are online ambassadors if they have discussed online, made political statements defending the party in social media and forwarded campaign material via e-mail. In the appendix, we list the exact survey items used to operationalize our five types of party member activism.

EXPLANATIONS FOR PARTY MEMBER ACTIVISM

The traditional field of political participation forms the basis for studies of party member participation. More specifically, the comprehensive General Incentives Model, which includes resources, attitudes, values, norms, political interest and efficacy and cost-benefit analysis, among other things, aims to explain both why members enrol and why they participate (Seyd and Whiteley 1992, 2002; Whiteley and Seyd 1998; Whiteley, Seyd and Richardson 1994). We are not able to apply this (incredibly) comprehensive approach in this study, primarily due to lack of questions and uniformity across countries. Instead, we focus on four types of explanations: (1) resource explanations, (2) views on intra-party democracy, (3) political disagreement and (4) civil society integration.

Resource Explanations

Resource explanations focusing on aspects such as age, gender, education and class are often included in analyses of political participation, though the empirical support varies (Verba, Scholzman and Brady 1995). The main argument is that those with resources – more time, high income, high education, more experience, and more technological skills – are not only more likely to enrol (see chapter 4) but also to participate in parties because they are more likely to have the skills and interest inherent in party membership. Traditionally, scholars also considered being a man as a 'resource', though one may question the validity of such an assumption in more gender-equal societies such as the Scandinavian countries. However, we include gender in our analyses in order to see the extent to which men still participate more than women do.

To be sure, since party members already constitute a relatively well-off group of citizens (see chapter 4), we should not expect major effects of having resources. However, we do expect that members with higher education are likely to participate more in complex activities such as decision-making, and that those with more time (e.g. those without children in the household) are likely to participate more in time-consuming activities such as attending meetings and campaigning. Moreover, we also expect that young members are more likely to be online ambassadors due to them being 'digital natives' (Prensky 2001) or part of the 'Net generation' (Tapscott 1998).

> Hypothesis 1 (H_1): We expect that members with substantial resources are more likely to participate, particularly in complex activities like decision-making (for those with high education) and time-consuming activities like attending meetings and campaigning (for those without children in the household).

We include gender, age, education (college degree or not), income and whether children aged zero to sixteen years are living in the household.

Views on Intra-Party Democracy

We argue that at least two aspects of (views on) intra-party democracy are important when explaining party member activism. First, it matters how members view the role of members within a political party. Existing (organizational) models of parties point in rather different directions as regards the role of members – they have 'distinctive participatory cultures' (Heidar 2006, 308). The normative foundations and to some extent the empirical functioning of not only the traditional mass party but also the more recent form of amateur-activist parties encourage and enable extensive bottom-up participation by ordinary members (see Duverger 1964; Frankland, Lucardie and Rihoux 2008, 8; Katz and Mair 1995). Within other party types, however, such as catch-all, electoral-professional and cartel parties, participation of members is less of a concern, and more emphasis is put on how members provide legitimacy or constitute a recruitment pool of political personnel (Duverger 1964; Epstein 1967; Katz and Mair 1995; Panebianco 1988; see also, e.g. Krouwel 2006). In line with this reasoning, members who feel committed to a party culture of comprehensive participation are more likely to participate compared to those who favour a party culture with more restrictive and limited participation. Arguably, this is most likely the case with traditional mass party and rather time-consuming activities, such as attending meetings, decision-making and campaigning.

> Hypothesis 2a (H_{2a}): We expect that members with 'mass party perceptions' about their role are more likely to participate, particularly in mass party activities such as meeting attendance, decision-making and campaigning.

The second aspect of (views on) intra-party democracy concerns satisfaction. One thing is the role members expect to fill; another is the role they actually have and whether they are happy about it. Although some dissatisfied members might participate in order to change the party (Hirschman 1970), we believe that, generally speaking, satisfaction with intra-party democracy provides a more effective incentive for participation. Most importantly, this kind of satisfaction facilitates the feeling of being able and welcome to make a difference (Seyd and Whiteley 1992).

> Hypothesis 2b (H_{2b}): We expect that members who are satisfied with intra-party democracy are more likely to participate, particularly in time-consuming activities such as decision-making and meeting attendance.

We measure 'mass party perception' using a question about whether members should primarily support decisions made by the party leadership (i.e. catch-all, cartel or electoral-professional type) or not (i.e. mass party or amateur-activist type). With regard to satisfaction with democracy, no items are similar across all surveys (see also chapter 10). Instead, we use one question about whether the leadership is too strong (to compare Denmark and Norway) and one question about satisfaction with the organization (to compare Norway and Sweden).

Political Disagreement

Although the preferential agreement among members is quite high in Scandinavia (see chapter 6), some members clearly disagree more than others with the party's position on one or several issues. This may have an impact upon levels of participation. Somewhat similar to the case of intra-party democracy, members who dislike their party's direction, for example, because they are more ideologically extreme, might be motivated to remain and fight for change (Cross and Young 2008; Hirschman 1970; May 1973; Strøm 1990). However, members to a large extent enrol for political reasons (see chapter 3); hence, political agreement is expected to be even more motivating as a collective incentive for participation (Seyd and Whiteley 1992, 104). Moreover, party elites may also try to mobilize members who align with the party message in campaigns (Lilleker 2005).

> Hypothesis 3 (H_3): The more party members experience a political disagreement with their party, the less likely they are to participate, particularly in time-consuming activities such as decision-making and meeting attendance.

We measure political disagreement as the distance between party members' party and self-placement on the general left-right scale.

Civil Society Organizational Engagement

The core of the Nordic party systems was created by cleavages enhancing the link between parties and interest organizations (Hansen and Kosiara-Pedersen 2017). While the links between parties and interest organizations have loosened and changed at the organizational level (Allern, Aylott and Christiansen 2007; Allern and Verge 2017), they are still viable and considered to be important. In fact, new party families also seem to cultivate a close relationship with various interest organizations (Allern 2012), and some of them, such as the greens, even emerge from organized extra-parliamentary groups (Jupskås 2013).

Existing research has mainly focused on these links at the level of party and organizational elites. However, in line with the 'expectations-values-norms theory' (see Whiteley and Seyd 1996, 217), these links are likely to be present also at the level of ordinary (party) members for reasons of both expected benefits and social norms. First, given the strength of political parties in Scandinavia, it is quite rational for citizens who are politically committed to certain issues (e.g. members of interest groups or social movements) to participate in party activism. Second, members of extra-parliamentary organizations might be more likely to participate because they are already 'embedded in a network of social norms and beliefs, which provide internal and external motivations to behave in certain ways' (Whiteley and Seyd 2002, 45), including, in this case, taking part in organizational activities. At the same time, party members with organizational commitments outside of the party need to deal with the question of where to invest time and energy. Even if they wanted to, they might not have much time left to participate in party activism. As the party secretary of the Norwegian Socialist Left once said: 'members in the Socialist party are very active – just not in the party'[3]. We therefore expect members of other organizations to prioritize activities considered important for their overall political goals, such as decision-making and campaigning, and be less concerned with time-consuming or party-oriented activities, such as meeting attendance and ambassadorial outreach.

Hypothesis 4 (H_4): Party members with membership in civil society organizations are more likely to participate in various forms of activism, particularly when it comes to decision-making and campaigning.

We measure party members' engagement with civil society organizations in two ways. First, we assess party members' membership of these other organizations. Second, we look at activism (Denmark) or positions of trust (Norway) in these organizations.

DATA

We use data from the party member surveys of Denmark (2012), Norway (2017) and Sweden (2015) in our analysis of why party members participate (see chapter 1; Allern, Heidar and Karlsen 2015; Kölln and Polk 2016; Kosiara-Pedersen 2017). Tables A9.1 and A9.2 sum up the operationalization of the five dependent variables and the independent variables. Unfortunately, as noted in several other chapters, the surveys are not coordinated to the extent that they include identical questions. This means that we limit ourselves to analyses at the level of each of the three countries, and that we should be a bit cautious when comparing the results across countries (see chapter 1). We control for party but do not report on this.

EXPLAINING PARTY MEMBER ACTIVISM

In the three parts of this section, we present the results of each of the three country studies in turn. While we emphasize similarities and differences across countries as we go along, these will be discussed further in the conclusion of this chapter.

Explaining Danish Party Member Activism

Table 9.1 shows the results of one OLS and four logistic regressions that are to explain party member participation in (number of) party meetings, political decisions within the party, campaigning and offline and online ambassador participation. Women are less likely to participate in party decisions and online ambassador activities but more likely to be offline ambassadors, while there are no significant differences between women and men when it comes to meetings and campaigning. Similarly for age, this is positively correlated with participation in decision-making, negatively correlated with meeting attendance and online ambassador activities, and without significant impact on campaigning and offline ambassador activities. For both gender and age, the distinction between various activities shows variation in the explanations of their effect. However, there is no clear pattern in the variation.

It is easier to see a pattern in the effect of the more clear-cut 'resources': education, income and small children in the household. Education and income have a similar effect. Both a college degree and higher income correlate with less activism except when it comes to seeking political influence within the party (and being an offline ambassador in regard to income). Children (aged 0–16 years) in the household, as expected, limit participation in the more demanding and time-specific activities of meeting attendance, decision-making (ballots are not applied) and campaigning. However, children do not limit ambassador activities. Hence, except in the case of having children, we don't find support for the positive relationship between resources and participation (H_1).

The more party members agree with the statement that 'party members' most important task is to support decisions made by the party leadership', the less likely they are to participate. Hence, party members supporting an electoral-professional or elite party organization model are, as expected (H_{2a}), less likely to participate both as ambassadors and in activities central in mass party models such as attending meetings, decision-making and campaigning. Members who find that the leadership is too strong are more likely to be offline ambassadors, but otherwise it seems to have no effect. Hence, H_{2b} is not supported.

The larger the political disagreement party members find there to be between themselves and their party (based on self- and party placement on a left-right scale), the less likely they are to participate in all these kinds of activities except being an online ambassador. Hence, we find support for our hypothesis (H_3) in the Danish case.

We expect a positive relationship between membership in civil society organizations and party activism, particularly when it comes to activities during (or prior

Table 9.1. Denmark. Explaining party activism among Danish party members.

	Meetings	Decision	Campaign	Offline ambassador	Online ambassador
Gender, male (0, 1)	-0.131	-0.041 ***	-0.008	0.010 *	-0.062 ***
	(0.198)	(0.009)	(0.010)	(0.004)	(0.009)
Age	-0.027 ***	0.005 ***	0.0004	-0.0003	-0.007 ***
	(0.007)	(0.000)	(0.000)	(0.000)	(0.000)
Education (0, 1)	-0.505 **	-0.008	-0.082 ***	-0.008 *	-0.029 ***
	(0.197)	(0.009)	(0.009)	(0.004)	(0.009)
Income (log)	-0.554 **	-0.013	-0.027 **	0.005	-0.033 ***
	(0.182)	(0.009)	(0.009)	(0.004)	(0.008)
Children (0, 1)	-1.515 ***	-0.053 ***	-0.027 *	-0.0006	0.009
	(0.243)	(0.012)	(0.012)	(0.005)	(0.011)
Support decisions made by leadership (0–1)	-2.285 ***	-0.157 ***	-0.052 ***	-0.032 ***	-0.044 **
	(0.333)	(0.016)	(0.016)	(0.007)	(0.015)
Too-strong leadership (0–1)	0.454	-0.019	-0.004	0.032 ***	-0.030
	(0.368)	(0.017)	(0.018)	(0.008)	(0.017)
Political disagreement (0–1)	-2.601 **	-0.119 **	-0.152 ***	-0.035 *	0.006
	(0.861)	(0.041)	(0.042)	(0.016)	(0.039)
Membership of other organizations (0–1)	0.977 ***	0.073 ***	0.089 ***	0.019 ***	0.039 ***
	(0.242)	(0.012)	(0.012)	(0.005)	(0.011)
Activism in other organizations (0, 1)	0.008	0.078 ***	0.032 *	0.028 ***	0.008
	(0.340)	(0.016)	(0.016)	(0.007)	(0.016)
Control for party	+	+	+	+	+
Constant	7.130 ***	-1.231 ***	0.101	2.543 ***	1.790 ***
	(0.571)	(0.118)	(0.114)	(0.260)	(0.120)
n	11,695	12,994	13,102	13,102	13,102
adj. R^2	0.016	0.054	0.023	0.036	0.055
AIC	-0.131				

Note: Logistic regression. Average marginal effects (AMEs) and standard errors in parentheses. Significance: * $p < 0.05$, ** $p < 0.01$, *** $p < 0.001$.

to) elections such as decision-making and campaigning (H_4). This is supported in the Danish case except in regard to meeting attendance for those members active in other organizations (and online ambassador activities). The exception may exactly point to how civil society organizations and parties may compete for party members' time and attention. Whereas members active in other organizations are more likely to participate in decisions and campaigning, they are not more likely to attend meetings.

Explaining Norwegian Party Member Activism

Table 9.2 shows the results from analysis of the Norwegian data. As in the Danish analysis, this includes one OLS and four logistic regressions explaining general member activism (i.e. going to meetings) as well as taking part in decision-making, campaign activities and offline and online ambassador participation.

Female party members are more likely than male members to participate in campaigning and to be online ambassadors, while there are no clear gender differences as regards meetings, decision-making and offline ambassadors. Age, on the other hand, is negatively correlated with all kinds of membership activism, though the results are not significant when it comes to decision-making. Not surprisingly, age is particularly important when explaining online ambassadorial activism: younger members are much more likely to engage in such activities.

Education has no effect on any form of activism, while income seems to increase the likelihood of taking part in the campaign and online activity. Members with children at home are significantly less likely to attend meetings and participate in internal decision-making. However, having children at home has no significant impact on other forms of activism, though the coefficients are – as in Denmark – negative for campaigning and offline ambassador activities and positive for online ambassador activities. In sum, as in the Danish case, except in the case of having children, we don't find support for the hypothesis (H_1) about a positive relationship between resources and participation.

Party members' relationship with their party matters to participation. First, members who believe in a more amateur-activist model with active and critical members are – in line with expectations (H_{2a}) – much more likely to take part in decision-making. They also seem to be more active as offline ambassadors, whereas the relationship is insignificant for other types of activism (meetings, campaigns and online ambassador activities). Second, being satisfied with the functioning of the organization – that is, with the role granted to ordinary members, including rights and obligations – increases the likelihood of going to meetings, doing campaign activities and acting as an offline ambassador. Hence, H_{2b} is also at least partly supported when it comes to party members' satisfaction with how intra-party democracy works. However, whether the current leadership is too strong does not seem to influence levels of activism systematically. In fact, only when explaining the extent to which members act as offline ambassadors does this play a role – and in the opposite

Table 9.2. Norway. Explaining various forms of membership activism in Norway.

	Meeting	Decision	Campaign	Offline ambassador	Online ambassador
Gender, ref. male (0,1)	0.034	0.050	0.080 **	0.033	0.085 **
	(0.019)	(0.029)	(0.028)	(0.023)	(0.027)
Age	-0.003 ***	-0.001	-0.003 **	-0.003 ***	-0.009 ***
	(0.001)	(0.001)	(0.001)	(0.001)	(0.001)
Education (0,1)	-0.015	0.032	-0.053	-0.045	-0.047
	(0.020)	(0.030)	(0.029)	(0.024)	(0.028)
Income (log)	-0.016	0.147	0.232 **	0.066	0.323 ***
	(0.057)	(0.085)	(0.082)	(0.067)	(0.079)
Children (0,1)	-0.079 **	-0.072 *	-0.036	-0.011	0.008
	(0.023)	(0.034)	(0.033)	(0.027)	(0.032)
Support decisions made by leadership (0–1)	-0.041	-0.171 **	-0.025	-0.089 *	-0.016
	(0.034)	(0.051)	(0.049)	(0.040)	(0.047)
Too-strong leadership (0,1)	0.010	0.069	-0.020	0.111 *	0.016
	(0.039)	(0.059)	(0.056)	(0.046)	(0.054)
Satisfaction with organization (0–1)	0.162 *	0.142	0.172 *	0.256 ***	0.053
	(0.051)	(0.076)	(0.073)	(0.059)	(0.071)
Political disagreement (0–1)	-0.001	-0.004	-0.009	0.011	0.012
	(0.008)	(0.012)	(0.012)	(0.010)	(0.011)
Position of trust in other organizations (0,1)	0.049 ***	0.060 ***	0.051	0.094 ***	0.056
	(0.022)	(0.033)	(0.032)	(0.026)	(0.031)
Membership of other organizations (0–1)	0.125 *	0.181 *	0.192 ***	0.192 ***	0.187 ***
	(0.029)	(0.043)	(0.042)	(0.034)	(0.040)
Control for party	+	+	+	+	+
Constant	0.301	0.257	0.237	0.655	0.567
n	1,542	1,427	1,578	1,535	1,578
R^2	0.063	0.062	0.046	0.063	0.112
adj. R^2	0.052	0.050	0.035	0.052	0.102

Note: One linear (a) and four (b–e) ogistic regressions with five different dependent variables. Average marginal effects (AMEs) and standard errors in parentheses. Significance: * $p < 0.05$, ** $p < 0.01$, *** $p < 0.001$.

direction of what we expected. Members who see the current leadership as too strong are actually more likely to be offline ambassadors, possibly because they want to weaken the power of the current leadership.

We find no significant relationship between political disagreement and the five forms of participation and hence a complete dismissal of hypothesis 3 (H_3) in the Norwegian case. However, we do find marked support for our hypothesis 4 (H_4) that party members with membership in civil society organizations are more likely to participate in various forms of activism. Members who are well integrated into civil society are more likely to be active within the party. This is particularly the case for those with membership in other organizations: they go to meetings, take part in decision-making and campaign activities and act as offline and online ambassadors. These members are clearly of high value for the party. Those with positions of trust in other organization are also more likely to be active, but only when it comes to meetings and being offline ambassadors. Interestingly, this is contrary to the Danish case, where party members active in other organizations do not attend meetings more but participate in decision-making and campaigning.

Explaining Swedish Party Member Activism

Table 9.3 shows the results for Sweden. Here female members are more likely to take part in campaign activities and act as online ambassadors. There are no statistically significant relationships between gender and other forms of activism. Older members are less likely to attend meetings and to discuss policies with other people, either offline or online. However, they are more likely to be decision makers and, to a lesser extent, campaigners. The former makes sense – and is similar to the Danish results – given that older members often have a longer track record within the party organization. The latter, however, is a bit more surprising considering that older members often have more social and professional commitments that make it more difficult for them to participate in time-consuming activities, even if they are limited to a short period of campaigning.

When it comes to resources, education and income have opposite effects. While high education correlates with less activism, high income correlates with more activism. Members with high education are significantly less likely to be offline and online ambassadors. Other forms of activism, however, are not significantly influenced. Income, on the other hand, seems to positively influence levels of meeting attendance, decision-making and offline ambassador activities, while the relationship with campaign activities and online ambassador activities is positive but not statistically significant. Having children at home does not seem to make a (substantial) difference for Swedish members, though the coefficients are negative for time-consuming activities such as meeting attendance and decision-making. In fact, it significantly increases the likelihood of being an online ambassador. In sum, we find limited support for our hypothesis 1 about a positive relationship between resources and participation, particularly when it comes to demanding and decisive activities such as decision-making (H_1).

Table 9.3. Sweden. Explaining various forms of membership activism in Sweden.

	Hours	Decision	Campaign	Offline ambassador	Online ambassador
Gender, ref. male (0,1)	0.013 (0.008)	-0.011 (0.012)	0.036** (0.012)	0.001 (0.010)	0.055*** (0.011)
Age	-0.001*** (0.000)	0.004*** (0.000)	0.001* (0.000)	-0.002*** (0.000)	-0.006*** (0.000)
Education (0,1)	-0.012 (0.009)	0.008*** (0.012)	-0.012 (0.012)	-0.044*** (0.010)	-0.026* (0.011)
Income (log)	0.069*** (0.019)	0.125*** (0.026)	0.016 (0.027)	0.075*** (0.021)	0.035 (0.025)
Children (0,1)	-0.016 (0.011)	-0.026 (0.015)	0.011 (0.016)	-0.011 (0.013)	0.047** (0.014)
Support decisions made by leadership (0–1)	0.132*** (0.017)	0.051* (0.023)	0.130*** (0.024)	0.138*** (0.019)	0.126*** (0.022)
Satisfaction with organization (0–1)	0.001 (0.018)	0.038 (0.025)	0.019 (0.025)	0.074*** (0.020)	-0.011 (0.023)
Political disagreement (0–1)	-0.003 (0.003)	-0.001 (0.004)	0.002 (0.004)	0.002 (0.004)	0.004 (0.004)
Membership of other organizations (0,1)	0.102*** (0.015)	0.221*** (0.021)	0.149*** (0.021)	0.110*** (0.017)	0.163*** (0.019)
Control for party	+	+	+	+	+
Constant	0.313	-0.071	0.368	0.734	0.876
n	6,555	7,110	7,077	7,089	7,101
R^2	0.025	0.042	0.015	0.037	0.086
adj. R^2	0.023	0.041	0.014	0.035	0.085

Note: One linear (a) and four logistic (b–e) regressions with five different dependent variables. Linear coefficients (a)/Average marginal effects (AMEs) (b–e) and standard errors in parentheses. Significance: *$p < 0.05$; **$p < 0.01$; ***$p < 0.001$.

In sharp contrast to the Danish and Norwegian results, and our expectations (H_{2a}), Swedish members who believe that members should support decisions made by the party leadership, which is seen as an indicator of an electoral-professional party model, are more likely to carry out all five types of activism. The results might be driven by the fact that the item in the Swedish survey is slightly different than in the two other surveys. While the Danish and Norwegian surveys ask members whether they believe that supporting the leadership is *the most* important task for ordinary members, the Swedish survey only asks whether members in general should 'support decisions made by the party leadership'. In other words, the Danish and Norwegian surveys seem to measure obedience (towards the leadership), whereas the item in the Swedish survey is closer to loyalty (towards the leadership). This inter-pretation is supported by the fact that there are many more members in Sweden who agree with the statement than in the two other countries.

Turning to the satisfaction with the party organization, this does not play an important role when explaining types of activism among Swedish members. Being satisfied with the organization is positively correlated with decision-making, cam-paigning and offline ambassadorial activity, but only the latter relationship is sig-nificant. Hence, there is no marked support for our hypothesis that satisfaction is positively correlated with activism (H_{2b}).

We expected that the more party members experience political disagreement with their party, the less likely they are to participate, in particular, in the more demand-ing activities such as intra-party decision-making and meetings (H_3). This was the case in Denmark, but in Norway there are no correlations. The latter is also the case for Sweden. Party members' levels of political disagreement with their party show very low and non-significant coefficients.

However, as in Denmark and Norway, we find support for the hypothesis that party members who are also members of civil society organizations are more likely to participate in various forms of activism, particularly when it comes to activities during (or prior to) elections such as decision-making and campaigning; they are less likely to participate in activities between elections (H_4).

DISCUSSION AND CONCLUSION

In this chapter, we analyse the extent to which resources, views on intra-party democracy, political disagreement and civil society integration have an impact upon five distinct forms of party member activism: meeting attendance, decision-making, campaigning and offline and online ambassadorial behaviour. The analyses show that parties may mobilize different segments of their party memberships for differ-ent types of activities. Hence, we find support for a multidimensional understanding not only of the way in which party members are affiliated but also of traditional, dues-paying party membership. Party members are a mixed bunch whom parties can mobilize to different types of participation in various ways. However, our empirical results are not always in line with the more specific expectations.

First, we find some, but limited, support for the hypothesis about a positive relationship between resources and participation (H_1). Younger members are more likely to participate in all kinds of activities across all three countries, with the exception of decision-making. Those with children at home are consistently less likely to participate in demanding activities, but participation in offline and online ambassadorial activities is not affected. Men are more likely to participate as decision makers and online ambassadors in Denmark, but not in Norway and Sweden. In fact, and somewhat surprisingly, male party members in Norway and Sweden are actually significantly less likely to be online ambassadors. Moreover, male members are also less likely to be offline ambassadors (in Denmark) and campaigners (in Norway and Sweden). This could be explained by the higher levels of gender equality institutionalization in Norway and Sweden compared to Denmark (Christensen 1999). Higher education seems to limit participation, with the exception of decision-making, across all countries, possibly targeting participation to where it may have an impact. Higher income leads to more participation in certain activities in Norway and Sweden, while the opposite seems to be the case in Denmark, where high income decreases the likelihood of going to meetings, campaigning and being an online ambassador.

Second, we find some support for our expectation that members with views reflecting a 'mass party' participatory culture are more likely to participate (H_{2a}). This is particularly the case in Denmark, where such views correlate with higher levels of participation across all forms of activism, but also in Norway where it at least increases the likelihood of being a decision maker and offline ambassador. However, in Sweden, we find the opposite effect: those who hold 'mass party perceptions' are less likely to participate. While it might be the case that the Swedish members differ from Norwegian and Danish members in this regard, it is more likely that this result is due to the wording of the item we used. While the Danish and Norwegian survey asked whether supporting the leadership is the *most* important role as a member, the Swedish survey only asked whether it is important as a member to support decisions made by the leadership.

We find mixed results for our hypothesis about the positive relationship between satisfaction with intra-party democracy and participation (H_{2b}). On the one hand, it seems that (Norwegian and Swedish) party members who are satisfied with the organization are more likely to be offline ambassadors (in Sweden and Norway) as well as campaigners and meeting attendees (only in Norway). On the other hand (Danish and Norwegian) party members who believe that the current leadership is too strong are also more likely to participate as ambassadors. In short, this means that Scandinavian members seem motivated by both satisfaction (with the organization) and dissatisfaction (with a too-strong leadership). Moreover, it also means that satisfaction primarily affects the willingness to be an offline ambassador, that is, to stand up for the party among friends, family and colleagues.

Third, our analyses yield no support for the argument that members who agree with the party are more likely to participate than those who disagree (H$_3$). Among Swedish and Norwegian members, there is simply no significant relationship between ideological agreement (with the party) and levels of participation. Moreover, among Danish members, the relationship is actually the opposite of our expectation: with the exception of being an online ambassador, members who agree are less – not more – likely to participate in various forms of activism. In sum, we still do not know whether political disagreement has no effect, a negative effect, or perhaps a positive effect (in other countries) on party member activism. The jury is still out.

Fourth, and in contrast to most of our other expectations, we find strong support for the positive impact of civil society integration on participation (H$_4$). Across all countries, members who are part of the organized civil society – either ordinary members or those holding positions of trust – are much more likely to participate in all forms of activism. In other words, while these other civil society organizations may be the alternative that non-party members opt for, they do not inhibit activism among the members.

Turning to the implications of our results for how contemporary Scandinavian parties provide linkage, they show, first and most importantly, that participation in general does not seem to be more skewed than party membership as such. In other words, those with resources and those who are already over-represented in parties, in particular highly educated men, do not seem to dominate party activism. Hence, as a channel of participation, parties are mainly skewed at the entry point of recruitment into the party, not in regard to mobilization to various activities. This implies that when party members engage in explicit campaigning or in ambassadorial activities, they confer an image that is, at least as far as possible, heterogeneous.

Second, party members who support intra-party democracy are more active, which decreases the possibility of the party elite centralizing power. Members adhering to the mass party ideal are also more prone to be party activists. These are the members who, in the longer run, will keep the traditional party membership linkage alive. Furthermore, members who are dissatisfied with how intra-party democracy works are not more inclined to participate, whereby parties' participatory linkage is not built upon a foundation of opposition to party leadership. Members do not participate mainly to oppose the party leadership.

Third, the fact that political disagreement seems to matter very little for participation means that party activists are not (at least in their own eyes) less ideologically representative of inactive party members. Hence, those members engaging in decision-making within the party do not seem to skew the opinions of party members at large. In addition, when party members participate as offline and online ambassadors, they do not necessarily refer only to a narrow party line but may contribute to a more nuanced image of party policy.

Fourth, and finally, parties are not at all becoming isolated from the organized society more broadly. On the contrary, the levels of activism among party members with ties to civil society organizations strengthen party linkage. Although there are fewer members to create these ties (see chapter 2), current party members do not find these ties obsolete.

In conclusion, we find very little evidence for a weakened participatory linkage in terms of which members participate and why they do so.

NOTES

1. It is probably also the case with Norwegian members, but we do not really know since the Norwegian survey does not include a variable on time spent.

2. In Denmark, the online ambassadorial activities seem to be associated with 'the candidate' dimension.

3. Personal communication with Knut Heidar, who attended SV's annual meeting in 1985 and heard the speech of Secretary Erik Solheim.

BIBLIOGRAPHY

Allern, Elin Haugsgjerd. 2012. 'The Contemporary Relationship of "New Left" and "New Right" Parties with Interest Groups: Exceptional or Mainstream? The Case of Norway's Socialist Left and Progress Party'. *Scandinavian Political Studies* 36 (1): 67–90.

Allern, Elin Haugsgjerd and Tània Verge. 2017. 'Still Connecting with Society? Political Parties' Formal Links with Social Groups in the Twenty-First Century'. In *Organizing Representation: Political Parties, Participation, and Power*, edited by Susan E. Scarrow, Paul D. Webb and Thomas Poguntke, 106–35. Oxford: Oxford University Press.

Allern, Elin Haugsgjerd, Knut Heidar and Rune Karlsen. 2015. *After the Mass Party: Continuity and Change in Political Parties and Representation in Norway*. Lanham, MD: Lexington Books.

Allern, Elin Haugsgjerd, Nicholas Aylott and Flemming Juul Christiansen. 2007. 'Social Democrats and Trade Unions in Scandinavia: The Decline and Persistence of Institutional Relationships'. *European Journal of Political Research* 46 (5): 607–35.

Bale, Tim and Paul Webb. 2015. *Grunts in the Ground Game: UK Party Members in the 2015 General Election*. Paper prepared for the Gothenburg workshop on Intra-Party Politics, 17–18 September 2015.

Bille, Lars. 1997. *Partier i forandring*. Odense: Odense Universitetsforlag.

———. 2001. 'Democratizing a Democratic Procedure: Myth or Reality? Candidate Selection in Western European Parties, 1960–1990'. *Party Politics* 7 (3): 363–80.

Christensen, Ann-Dorte. 1999. 'Kvinder i de politiske partier'. In *Likestilte Demokratier? Kjønn Og Politikk I Norden*, edited by Christina Bergqvist, Viveca Ramstedt-Silén, Nina C. Raaum and A. Styrkársdottir, 65–87. Oslo: Universitetsforlaget.

Cross, William and Lisa Young. 2004. 'The Contours of Political Party Membership in Canada'. *Party Politics* 10 (4): 427–44.

———. 2008. 'Activism among Young Party Members: The Case of the Canadian Liberal Party'. *Journal of Elections, Public Opinion and Parties* 18 (3): 257–81.

Duverger, Maurice. 1964. *Political Parties*. London: Methuen & Co. Ltd.

Epstein, Leon D. 1967. *Political Parties in Western Democracies*. New York: Frederick A. Praeger.

Faucher, Florence. 2015. 'New Forms of Political Participation: Changing Demands or Changing Opportunities to Participate in Political Parties?' *Comparative European Politics* 13: 409–59.

Frankland, E. Gene, Paul Lucardie and Benoît Rihoux, eds. 2008. *Green Parties in Transition: The End of Grass-Roots Democracy?* Farnham: Ashgate Publishing.

Gallagher, Michael and Michael Marsh. 2004. 'Party Membership in Ireland: The Members of Fine Gael'. *Party Politics* 10 (4): 407–25.

Gauja, Anika. 2015. 'The Construction of Party Membership'. *European Journal of Political Research* 54 (2): 232–48.

Hansen, Bernhard. 2002. *Party Activism in Denmark*. Aarhus: Politica.

Hansen, Kasper Møller and Karina Kosiara-Pedersen. 2017. 'Nordic Voters and Party Systems'. In *Routledge Handbook on Scandinavian Politics*, edited by Peter Nedergaard and Anders Wivel, 114–23. London: Routledge.

Heidar, Knut. 1994. 'The Polymorphic Nature of Party Membership'. *European Journal of Political Research* 25 (1): 61–86.

———. 2006. 'Party Membership and Participation'. In *Handbook of Party Politics*, edited by Richard S Katz and William J Crotty, 301–15. London: SAGE.

Hirschman, Albert O. 1970. *Exit, Voice, and Loyalty*. Cambridge, MA: Harvard University Press.

Jupskås, Anders Ravik. 2013. 'Miljøpartiet de grønne og det "politiske rommet"'. *Norsk statsvitenskapelig tidsskrift* 29 (02): 131–43.

Katz, Richard S. and Peter Mair. 1995. 'Changing Models of Party Organizations and Party Democracy: The Emergence of the Cartel Party'. *Party Politics* 1 (1): 5–28.

Kjær, Ulrik and Karina Kosiara-Pedersen. 2018. 'The Hourglass of Women's Representation'. *Journal of Elections, Public Opinion & Parties*. doi: 10.1080/17457289.2018.1530678.

Kölln, Ann-Kristin and Jonathan Polk. 2016. 'The 2015 Swedish Party Membership Survey'. http://partiforskning.gu.se/Forskning+om+partier/partimedlemsundersokning/party-membership-survey-2015.

Kosiara-Pedersen, Karina. 2014. 'Partiernes kampagneudgifter'. In *Folketingsvalgenkampen 2011 i perspektiv*, edited by Kasper Møller Hansen and Karina Kosiara-Pedersen, 57–66. Copenhagen: Djøf Publishing.

———. 2017. *Demokratiets ildsjæle: Partimedlemmer i Danmark*. Copenhagen: Djøf Publishing.

Kosiara-Pedersen, Karina and Amalie Munkner Kristiansen. 2016. 'Alternativt partimedlemskab'. In *Statskundskab i praksis. Klassiske teorier og moderne problemer*, edited by Karina Kosiara-Pedersen, Gustav Nedergaard and Emil Lobe Suenson, 15–31. Copenhagen: Karnov Group.

Kosiara-Pedersen, Karina and Asmus Harre. 2017. 'Kandidatrekruttering i politiske partier'. *Økonomi og Politik* 90 (3): 40–51.

Krouwel, André. 2006. 'Party Models'. In *Handbook of Party Politics*, edited by Richard S. Katz and William J. Crotty, 350–69. London: SAGE.

Lilleker, Darren G. 2005. 'The Impact of Political Marketing on Internal Party Democracy'. *Parliamentary Affairs* 58 (3). doi: https://doi.org/10.1093/pa/gsi052.

Lippert, Søren and Lars Midtiby. 2009. 'Græsrødderne ER kampagnen'. *Kommunikationsforum*, 20 November 2009. www.kommunikationsforum.dk/artikler/graesroedderne-er-kampagnen.

May, John D. 1973. 'Opinion Structure of Political Parties: The Special Law of Curvilinear Disparity'. *Political Studies* 21 (2): 135–51.

Panebianco, Angelo. 1988. *Political Parties: Organization and Power*. Cambridge: Cambridge University Press.

Pedersen, Karina and Jo Saglie. 2005. 'New Technology in Ageing Parties: Internet Use in Danish and Norwegian Parties'. *Party Politics* 11 (3): 359–77.

Pedersen, Karina, Lars Bille, Roger Buch Jensen, Jørgen Elklit, Bernard Hansen and H. J. Nielsen. 2004. 'Sleeping or Active Partners? Danish Party Members at the Turn of the Millennium'. *Party Politics* 10 (4): 367–84.

Prensky, Marc. 2001. 'Digital Natives, Digital Immigrants Part 1'. *On the Horizon* 9 (5): 1–6.

Römmele, Andrea. 2003. 'Political Parties, Party Communication and New Information and Communication Technologies'. *Party Politics* 9 (1): 7–20.

Sartori, Giovanni. 1976. *Parties and Party Systems: A Framework for Analysis.* Cambridge: Cambridge University Press.

Scarrow, Susan E. 1996. *Parties and Their Members: Organizing for Victory in Britain and Germany.* Oxford: Oxford University Press.

———. 2015. *Beyond Party Members: Changing Approaches to Partisan Mobilization.* Oxford: Oxford University Press.

Seyd, Patrick and Paul Whiteley. 1992. *Labour's Grass Roots: The Politics of Party Membership.* Oxford: Clarendon Press.

———. 2002. *New Labour's Grassroots: The Transformation of the Labour Party Membership.* Basingstoke: Palgrave Macmillan.

Strøm, Kaare. 1990. 'A Behavioral Theory of Competitive Political Parties'. *American Journal of Political Science* 34 (2): 565–98.

Tapscott, D. 1998. *The Rise of the Net Generation: Growing Up Digital.* New York: McGraw Hill.

Verba, Sidney, Kay Lehman Scholzman and Henry E. Brady. 1995. *Voice and Equality: Civic Voluntarism in American Politics.* Cambridge, MA: Harvard University Press.

Webb, Paul, Monica Poletti and Tim Bale. 2017. 'So Who Really Does the Donkey Work in "Multi-Speed Membership Parties"? Comparing the Election Activities of Party Members and Party Supporters', *Electoral Studies*, 46: 64–74.

Whiteley, Paul and Patrick Seyd. 1998. 'The Dynamics of Party Activism in Britain: A Spiral of Demobilization?' *British Journal of Political Science* 28 (1): 113–37.

———. 2002. *High-Intensity Participation: The Dynamics of Party Activism in Britain.* Ann Arbor, MI: University of Michigan Press.

Whiteley, Paul, Patrick Seyd and Jeremy Richardson. 1994. *True Blues: The Politics of Conservative Party Membership.* Oxford: Clarendon Press.

Appendix

Table A9.1. Operationalization of the dependent variables.

	DENMARK	NORWAY	SWEDEN
Meeting attendance	Log of number of meetings attended within the past year	Only possible with 6 values: 0 meetings 1 meeting 2–4 meetings 5–9 meetings 10–20 meetings > 20 meetings (98=don't know 99=missing)	Log of number of hours devoted to party activities in the average month
Decision makers (0, 1)	Wrote political proposals and/ or participated in the nomination of candidate (in 2011)	Formulated policies and/or candidate nomination (for national elections)	Developing the electoral manifesto at the national level (13%) and/or candidate selection for national elections
Campaigners (0, 1)	Delivered campaign leaflets, put up election posters, and/or canvassed	Delivered campaign leaflets and/or canvassed	Delivered campaign leaflets and/or put up election posters

	DENMARK	NORWAY	SWEDEN
Offline ambassadors (0, 1)	Discussed party policies with friends, family, or colleagues 'at the general election' and/or 'within the last five years', and/or whether they encouraged voters to vote for their party at the general election	(1) Discussed the party's policies with people who are not members of the party 'during the last year'	(1) Political debate with another party 'in the last 12 months' and /or (2) persuaded others to vote for the party 'during the last month before the election'
Online ambassadors (0, 1)	Discussed party policies online at and between elections	(1) Wrote in social media defending your own party's policies or criticizing other parties' policies 'during the last year', (2) wrote comments with political content on social media, and/or (3) forwarded campaign material via e-mail or social media 'in the campaign'.	(1) Posted comments of a political nature on a social networking profile, blog, or home page 'in the last month of the campaign' and/or (2) forwarded campaign content to friends, family, or colleagues via e-mail, Twitter, or Facebook 'in the last month of the campaign'.

Table A9.2. Operationalization of the independent variables when explaining party member activism.

	DENMARK	NORWAY	SWEDEN
Gender	0=man 1=women	0=man 1=women	0=man 1=women
Age	Continuous	Continuous	Continuous
Education **(0, 1)**	College/university (academic) degree (1) or not (0).	College/university (academic) degree (1) or not (0) (Q77)	College/university (academic) degree (1) or not (0)
Income **(logarithm)**	16 categories. Logarithm because increase from 0 to 100,000 matters more than increase from 900,000 to 1,000,000.	9 values	12 values
Children **(0,1)**	Two values: 0=0 children or children over 16 years old, 1=Children aged 0–16 years old in the household	Two values: Whether respondent has children below 16 years or not	Two values: 0=0 children or children over 16 years old, 1=Children aged 0–16 years old in the household
Perceptions of internal democracy/party			
Perceptions about the role of party members (0–1): 0 completely disagree 0.25 disagree 0.5 neither 0.75 agree 1 completely agree	The most important task of party members is to support decisions made by the party leadership	The most important task of party members is to support decisions made by the party leadership	My role as a member is to support decisions made by the party leadership
Too-strong leadership (0–1): 0 completely agree 0.25 agree 0.5 neither 0.75 disagree 1 completely disagree	A problem with the party today is that the leadership is too strong	A problem with the party today is that the leadership is too strong	Not available

	DENMARK	NORWAY	SWEDEN
Satisfaction with the organization (0–1): 0 dissatisfaction 0.25 0.5 neither 0.75 1 satisfaction	Not available	Satisfaction with the functioning of the organization (role granted to members, rights & obligations)	Satisfaction with the functioning of the organization (role granted to members, rights & obligations)
Political disagreement Item (0–10)	Difference between self-placement on left-right and placement of party on left-right	Difference between self-placement on left-right and placement of party on left-right	Difference between self-placement on left-right and placement of party on left-right
Civil society integration			
Activism (0, 1): 0=No active memberships/ posts1=One or more activememberships/ posts	Activism in other organizations	Position of trust in other organizations	Not available
Membership: 0=No membership 0.25=One membership 0.5=Two memberships 0.75=Three memberships 1=Four or more memberships	Membership in other organizations	Membership in other organizations	Membership in other organizations: only six different types: – trade union – employer union – religious organization – environmental organization – humanitarian/ human rights/ peace – sports club

IV

INFLUENCE

PERCEPTIONS OF POWER AND DEMANDS FOR VOICE

10

Party Members' Perception of Intra-Party Democracy

Niklas Bolin and Karina Kosiara-Pedersen

Internally democratic parties are not a prerequisite for representative democracy since democracy lies in the electoral competition among parties (Allern and Pedersen 2007). However, as shown in chapter 1, in the European model of party democracy, parties not only provide the electorate with alternatives on election day, but they are also supposed to guarantee their members influence over intra-party decision-making and thereby a supplementary channel of linkage between voters and the state. Surely most political parties like to envisage themselves providing some form of participatory linkage, and there is a strong tradition of officially being very favourable to intra-party democracy. Most parties have, at least formally, democratic structures (Aylott and Bolin 2017, 57) with representative bodies in charge of taking important decisions, formulating policies, selecting leadership and nominating election candidates. In these ways, the mass party structure is alive and kicking. However, the Michelian (Michels [1915] 1962) view holds that political parties are bound to end up like oligarchies; while ostensibly democratic, party elites in reality run party organizations.

The perception of parties as leader-centred organizations with little influence for ordinary members has not passed unnoticed by party leaders themselves. Parties have gone from enrolling large shares of the electorates to become restricted clubs with only a limited share of citizens interested in membership (see chapter 2, and, e.g., Scarrow 2015; van Biezen, Mair, and Poguntke 2012). As a response, new counter-strategies have been adopted in order to enhance the linkage capacity of their membership organizations. One way in which the challenge of declining membership levels has been met has been to formally democratize parties internally. By giving members greater incentives to enrol and participate, it is argued, parties' membership losses could be halted or even reversed (but see Katz 2013). Several studies have shed light on the extent to which party members increasingly are being included in core intra-party decision-making processes (e.g. Bille 2001; Cross and Blais 2012b; Hazan and Rahat 2010) in general (Cross and Katz 2013), as well as specifically in regard to party leader selection (Cross and Blais 2012a; Cross and Pilet 2015; Pilet and Cross 2014; Scarrow 2015), candidate selection (Pilet, van Haute and Kelbel 2015) and decisions on the political programme (Gauja 2013, 2015; Scarrow 2015).

However, the literature also questions the extent to which these inclusionary measures have actually increased members' influence over party decisions or, perhaps somewhat paradoxically, have further empowered the leadership, as was argued in the cartel party thesis (Katz and Mair 1995) from the perspective of what might be called a 'fake-democratization thesis' (Aylott and Bolin 2018). Ignazi (2018), for example, argues that more direct forms of intra-party democracy undermine pluralism as well as deliberation within parties as they tend to estrange members from each other and to marginalize mid-level activists. This implies that intra-party reforms increase the power of party leaders rather than diffusing intra-party power. Hence, there may be a contradiction between the formal story of the statutes and the real, de facto story of 'praxis'.

In sum, we are left with two contradictory perspectives on the current state of intra-party democracy in parties' participatory linkages: the formal strengthening of individual rank-and-file members and the possible de facto strengthening of the party leadership. While our goal is not to settle this dispute, we shed light on the extent to which any of these views are more prevalent among Scandinavian party members. In other words, to relate to the overall aim of this volume we confine ourselves in this chapter to investigating (1) the extent to which the participatory linkage parties are providing comes with member influence as perceived by the party members themselves, and (2) what may explain these perceptions (cf. Bernardi, Sandri and Seddone 2016; Sanches et al. 2018).

In at least two respects, the Scandinavian countries are of great interest in this context. First, Denmark, Norway and Sweden are regularly identified as among the most democratic countries in the world (V-Dem Institute 2018, 72). Since parties tend to adapt to their environment (Harmel and Janda 1994), it is reasonable to expect that a high level of state-level democracy is associated with highly democratic party organizations (Bolin et al. 2017). Norwegian parties have adopted a higher level of formal intra-party democracy than Swedish and Danish parties (Bolin et al. 2017). Hence, we have some variation within this rather similar context (in addition, see chapter 1). Second, political parties have traditionally been very strong in the Scandinavian countries. Not only do they have a history of relatively high levels of enrolment, the level of trust in Scandinavia is also very high in a comparative perspective (Norris 2011, 76; Whiteley 2014, 380). Taken together, we therefore contribute to the literature by further investigating how party members perceive intra-party democracy in countries with a deep-rooted tradition of democratic practices at both the state and party levels.

In the next section, we present the chapter's theoretical base and hypotheses. In the following methods section, we briefly present the cases, dependent and independent variables and the analytical strategy. Our main empirical findings are presented in the next section, whereafter we conclude.

INTRA-PARTY DEMOCRACY

Intra-party democracy is indeed an elusive concept that is hard to define and empirically assess. However, if we begin with an understanding of democracy as a political system ruled by its citizens, it is reasonable to equate intra-party democracy with a concept denoting that parties are ruled by their members (Bolin et al. 2017; Rahat and Shapira 2017). Although this understanding seems to be commonly agreed upon, conceptualizations differ. While some aspects such as decentralization (von dem Berge and Obert 2017) and transparency (Rahat and Shapira 2017) are included in single studies, the inclusion of members is a necessary condition for a minimum level of intra-party democracy implicit in all accounts.

In this chapter, we understand intra-party democracy to be a concept covering the extent to which party members are included in decision-making processes within the party. Importantly, however, this does not necessarily mean by direct vote alone. Democracy at the state level can come in different forms such as representative democracy and direct democracy. Similarly, intra-party democracy might entail both selection of representatives and membership votes. Hence, the participatory linkage may entail different ways of involving party members and supporters.

Much research on intra-party democracy has been based on content analysis of party statutes. The 'official story' is not necessarily the 'real story', but the official story sets the limits within which the real story unfolds (Katz and Mair 1992). This research has shown that there is a general trend towards more inclusive decision-making processes both in regard to leader selection (Cross and Blais 2012b; Pilet and Cross 2014; Sandri and Seddone 2015) and candidate selection (Hazan and Rahat 2010). Hence, rank-and-file party members are increasingly given a direct vote on important party decisions. A number of recent attempts have estimated more generally how internally democratic parties are by developing intra-party democracy indices that take into account several aspects of internal processes (Bolin et al. 2017; Rahat and Shapira 2017; von dem Berge and Poguntke 2017; von dem Berge et al. 2013).

Due to the focus on party statutes, many studies so far have taken a party-level perspective (Cross and Katz 2013). With the development of indices to capture levels of intra-party democracy, recent research has also taken us down the comparative road. Bolin et al. (2017), for example, compare the level of intra-party democracy in 121 parties in democratic societies. One important conclusion from their study is that there is indeed significant variation between parties. Primarily they find that variation is greater between countries than within countries, suggesting that parties tend to adjust their structures to other parties within the same party system. There is a contagion within political systems.

Looking more closely at the Scandinavian countries, Bolin et al. (2017) find that Norwegian parties, on average, are among the most internally democratic, whereas Danish and Swedish parties generally have average levels of intra-party democracy. However, there are different degrees of variation within countries. Norway is in fact the country with the least variation across parties within the whole Political Party Database project (see www.politicalpartydb.org). Denmark, on the other hand, is among the countries with the largest variation among parties. Sweden scores roughly in the middle.

More recently light has also been shed on intra-party democracy in the perspective of party members and voters with a focus on their view on how the internal party democracy of their party works, their satisfaction with this, and their perception of how it should be (Bernardi, Sandri and Seddone 2016; Sanches et al. 2018; Sandri 2012). Similar to these studies, we map and explain individual party members' perceptions of intra-party democracy in their respective parties and hence provide a more comprehensive account of the character of parties' participatory linkage.

Hypotheses

The purpose of this chapter is to map and explain variation in party members' perceptions of intra-party democracy. We seek explanations at the aggregate, country level, at the level of party families and at the individual level.

We map party members' perception of intraparty democracy at the country and party levels. Bolin et al. (2017) show the extent to which parties vary in their level of intra-party democracy according to the party statutes. At the aggregate level, they find that Norwegian parties are among the most internally democratic whereas their Danish and Swedish counterparts score about average in a sample of nineteen 'Western' countries (Bolin et al. 2017, 171). On the basis that there is a correlation between the formal level of intra-party democracy and party members' satisfaction with intra-party democracy , we expect that Norwegian party members are also more satisfied with how intra-party democracy works.

> H_1. Norwegian party members have, on average, a more favourable perception of intra-party democracy than Swedish and Danish party members.

Research on party leader selection and candidate selection uniformly finds that, over time, party members have been given expanded rights concerning selecting their leaders and candidates as well as how they organize policy formulation. On the one hand, this change could be expected to take place to a varying extent in different types of parties. For instance, it is often argued that ideology is reflected in how the party organizes; in green parties, for example, inclusive intra-party processes are considered important in their own right (Bolin 2012, 106; Poguntke 1987; Rüdig and Sajuria 2018). In contrast, the populist radical right is often claimed to have very centralized organizations (Heinisch and Mazzoleni 2016; Mudde 2007; Pedersen and Ringsmose 2004). On the other hand, one of the main findings from the first round of the Political Parties Data Base project based primarily on party statutes was that parties adapt organizationally to their national competitors rather than to party family members of other countries (Bolin et al. 2017). Based on the expected relation between formal statutes and party members' satisfaction, our expectation is:

H$_2$. There are no systematic differences across party families in their party members' perception of intra-party democracy.

After mapping party members' perception of intra-party democracy at the country and party family levels, we turn to our second research question to explain this at the individual level. We focus on four explanations for party members' perception of intra-party democracy, namely, whether they are elected or hold intra-party office, whether they participate in party meetings, their political distance from their party and their expectations of intra-party democracy.

The level of intra-party democracy does not matter equally to all party members. Passive members who do nothing but pay their dues and possibly discuss party policies with non-members and encourage them to vote for their party may not care much about centralized and selective decision-making. However, to the activist, it matters more (Bille 2001; Katz and Mair 1995; Strøm 1990). Activists seek influence through their participation; they make use of the intra-party democracy. This leads to two expectations.

First, in short, it is about what position a party member has in regard to a party's internal structure, that is, both the formal rules and regulations on intra-party democracy and how these are applied in practice. Even though elected officials to different extents are constrained by intra-party democracy (Pedersen 2010), they have their parliamentary platform and make up the party elite together with selected people from party headquarters. This could be argued about those holding intra-party office as well. Due to their position, they have a role to play in intra-party democracy – or at least a platform from which to make an impact.

H$_3$. Party members who are elected officials or hold intra-party office perceive their party's intra-party democracy to be higher than rank-and-file members.

Second, we expect a positive relationship between participation and perception, so that those who actually take part in the intra-party democracy perceive this more favourably. This is supported by Sanches et al. (2018) who find that activism is positively related to satisfaction with intra-party democracy.

H$_4$. Party members having attended party meetings perceive a higher level of intra-party democracy.

Intra-party democracy is expected to matter more if there is something at stake not only in position but also in content. Hence, the stakes are higher for party members who disagree with the political position of their party – in general or on specific issues. A (perceived) low level of intra-party democracy does not make a difference to members if they agree with the political decisions of their party, whether it be on personnel or policies. However, it matters if there is disagreement and the members choose to stay and fight their case and not simply stay silent or leave (cf. Hirschman 1970). Political disagreement is expected to enhance dissatisfaction with the party leadership and hence intra-party democracy.

> H_5. The larger the political distance party members perceive between themselves and their party, the lower the level of intra-party democracy they perceive.

Our fourth, and final, hypothesis at the individual level (and sixth in total) concerns the impact of party members' demand for intra-party democracy. There are differences in the extent to which party members think they should have a say within their parties, and these expectations are expected to affect their perception of intra-party democracy. In other words, satisfaction might be an effect of low demands of inclusiveness rather than great supply of democratic practices (cf. Norris 2011). If party members believe that the leadership should be powerful within the party, they will not be dissatisfied with a low level of party member involvement in important party decisions.

> H_6. The higher the demand of intra-party democracy, the lower the level of intra-party democracy perceived by the party members.

DATA AND ANALYTICAL STRATEGY

In order to measure party members' perception of intra-party democracy, we use data from the party member surveys of Denmark (2012), Norway (2017) and Sweden (2015).[2] Unfortunately, the surveys are not coordinated to the extent that they include identical questions. While there are questions that overlap in two countries, there are no questions on intra-party democracy included in all three surveys. As in the other chapters of this book, we will make the best of what is available. The strategy employed is, first, to conduct a number of separate country-based analyses with different operationalizations of perceptions of intra-party democracy and, second, to make pairwise comparisons between countries where we include identical dependent variables.

Dependent Variables

The operationalization of party members' perception of intra-party democracy is based on items from each country survey where members were asked to state their opinions about different propositions on the workings of intra-party democracy in their parties. Members were asked to respond on a five-point Likert scale.[3] Some of the items are coded in different directions for different countries, and these have been converted so that higher values indicate a perception of higher-level intra-party democracy.

Parties involve their members in decision-making to different degrees and also partly according to different principles. Whereas some parties, sometimes, allow members to have a direct say using membership ballots, the representative principle, where lower levels send delegates to higher levels, is the dominant principle. While the principles differ in how members may influence their parties, none of them is more democratic per se. Hence, in order to respect the variation in party organization principles, party members' perception of intra-party democracy is here based on how they view their parties, in particular, party leadership. Three different items are used to measure party members' perception of intra-party democracy. The first question asks about whether 'it is a problem for the party that the leadership is too strong'. This question is found in the Danish and Norwegian surveys. The second and third questions are available in the Norwegian and Swedish surveys and ask about party members' 'satisfaction with the leadership' and 'satisfaction with the functioning of the organization (role granted to members, rights & obligations)', respectively.

Independent Variables in the Individual-Level Analyses

Our first individual-level hypothesis suggests that high-ranking members are more satisfied with intra-party democracy than rank-and-file members (H_3). In order to test this hypothesis, we construct a dichotomous variable, *position*, indicating whether the member is holding or has held any public office representing the party or any position within the party organization.

Second, we also expect that the level of participation in party activity should be associated with the perception of intra-party democracy (H_4). To test this, we create a dichotomous variable, *participation*, which indicates whether the member has participated in any party meeting during the past year.

Third, we hypothesize that party members perceive there to be a lower level of intra-party democracy if their perceived political distance from their party is larger (H_5). To assess this expectation, we simply construct a variable, *distance*, that takes the absolute value of the difference between the self- and party placement of the member on a 10/11-point left-right scale.

Fourth, since we expect that perceptions of intra-party democracy are dependent on how much influence party members demand, we construct a variable, *expectation*, from an item that asks about the extent to which respondents agree with the statement 'the most important role as a member is to support decisions made by the party leadership'.[4] Again, similar to the construction of the dependent variables, we need to take into account that the response scales are in different directions for the different surveys. Danish and Norwegian respondents were asked to respond on a scale from 'fully agree' (1) to 'fully disagree' (5), whereas responses in the Swedish survey go in the other direction. We therefore recoded Swedish responses so higher values indicate higher levels of expectation.

Finally, we also control for socioeconomic characteristics by including variables for age and gender, and we include party dummies to control for omitted party-level characteristics. The dependent variables are ordinal scale variables with five possible outcomes. However, as the dependent variables are approximately normally distributed and for reasons of interpretability, we run OLS regression models. To check the robustness of our models, we also run ordinal logistic regression (see appendix). These estimations produce similar results as the OLS regression models.

PARTY MEMBERS' PERCEPTION OF INTRA-PARTY DEMOCRACY

To what extent is intra-party democracy perceived by party members to characterize participatory linkage, and how may differences be explained? In order to show the extent to which we find variation among parties, countries and party families, in this first section, we map the aggregate level of party members' perception of intra-party democracy. We also present the extent to which party members want, or expect, intra-party democracy. In the second section, we analyse our second research question concerning the extent to which position, traditional participation, political distance and expectations of intra-party democracy may explain party members' perception of intra-party democracy at the individual level.

Perception and Expectation of Intra-Party Democracy at the Country and Party Levels

In figure 10.1 (see also tables A10.3 through A10.5), we present Scandinavian party members' perception of intra-party democracy. Overall, the data suggest that party members are reasonably happy with the intra-party democracy of their parties. For all parties, the average level of perception of intra-party democracy is above 3, that is, the middle option indicating neither agreement nor disagreement with statements about the party's intra-party democracy.

A pairwise comparison of the country-level averages also reveals that perceptions of intra-party democracy are highest in Norway. Norway scores higher than Sweden on both satisfaction with the organization (3.90 vs. 3.54) and satisfaction with the leadership (4.03 vs. 3.67), and it scores higher than Denmark on the statement about whether the leadership is too strong (3.91 vs. 3.73); that is, Norwegian party members are less likely to find that their party leadership is too strong. As there are no overlapping items between Denmark and Sweden, we cannot make any well-grounded claims about their mutual ordering. The results suggesting that Norwegian

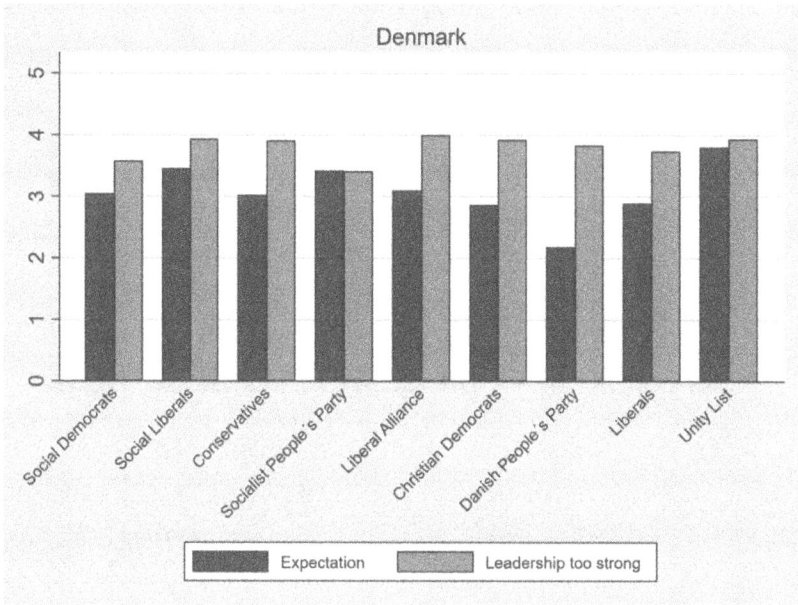

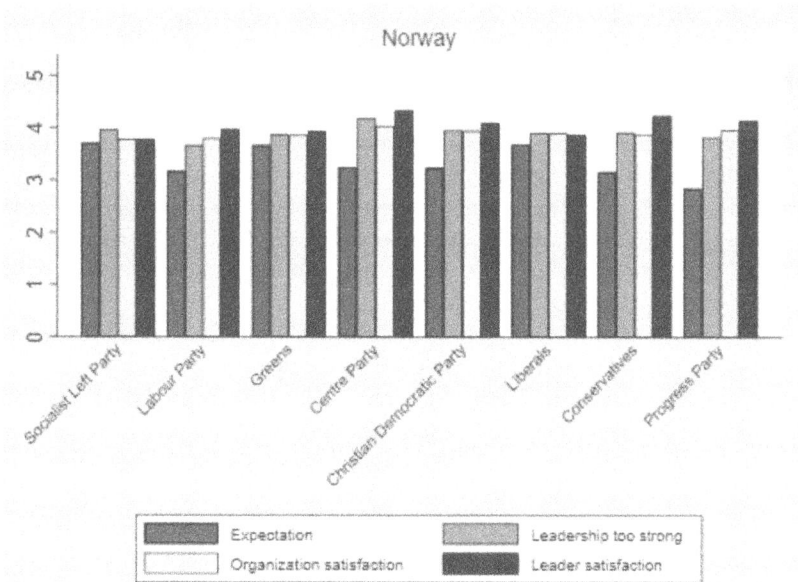

Figure 10.1.   Average levels of intra-party democracy perceptions and expectations.

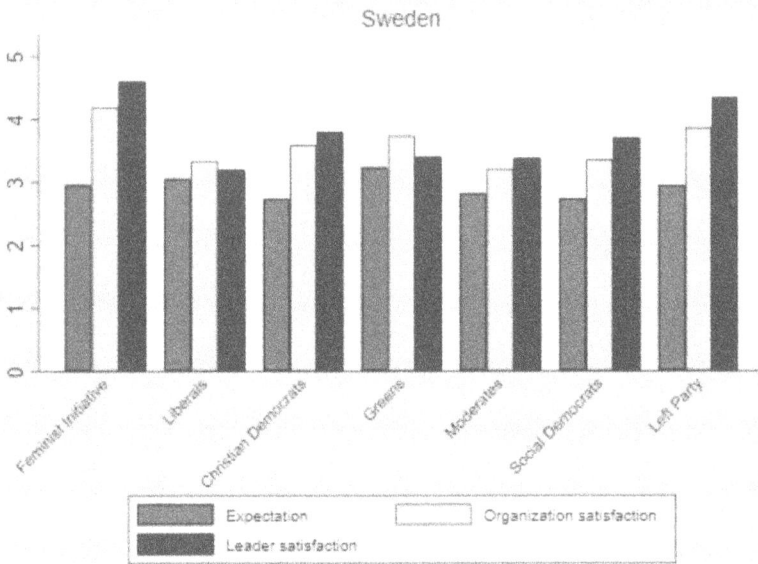

Figure 10.1. (continued)

party members are somewhat more satisfied than their Scandinavian neighbours support our hypothesis that there is a correlation between party members' perception and the level of intra-party democracy granted in party statutes. Furthermore, and again in line with the findings of Bolin et al. (2017), we also find that within-country variation is smaller in Norway than in Denmark and Sweden. These aggregated data, hence, suggest that there is an association between party-level intra-party democracy based on party statutes ('the official story') and party members' perception of their parties' democratic practice ('the real story').

When we turn to the level of party family, however, we find that the variation is rather small. First, as reported in tables A10.3 through A10.5, the between-group variance explained by party differences is low. The effect sizes are low (Eta squared values of 0.14 and below); hence, we expect that individual-level factors are generally more important than party level-factors in explaining levels of perception of intra-party democracy. This conclusion is further corroborated by our calculations of the mean levels of members' perception of intra-party democracy across party family presented in table 10.1. Here we have simply taken the average values of the aggregated data for all intra-party democracy variables presented in tables A10.3 through A10.5 (expectation excluded) and presented them according to party family.

Since the data across countries are not fully comparable, we must be cautious if comparing absolute values. However, if we instead compare the party families' mutual rank order, we may at least draw some tentative conclusions about variations

Table 10.1. Party members' perception of intra-party democracy across party family.

	Denmark	Norway	Sweden
	Mean (rank)	Mean (rank)	Mean (rank)
Christian Democrat	3.93 (1)	3.87 (1)	3.70 (2)
Conservative	3.92 (2)	3.77 (6)	3.30 (5)
Green	–	3.80 (5)	3.57 (3)
Left Socialist	3.68 (5)	3.81 (4)	4.11 (1)
Liberal	3.89 (3)	3.84 (2)	3.28 (6)
Radical right	3.84 (4)	3.82 (3)	–
Social Democrat	3.58 (6)	3.61 (7)	3.54 (4)

Note: In those cases (Left Socialist and Liberals in Denmark) where there is more than one party per party family, the mean intra-party democracy value is presented. The Social Liberals are included in the liberal party family of Denmark. Party families with only one party are excluded. This means the Norwegian Centre Party and the Swedish Feminist initiative are not included.

in perceptions of intra-party democracy. Overall, we find only small differences in table 10.1. With two exceptions, party families seem to be very similar. First, members of the christian democrats stand out as being the most positive. The level of their members' satisfaction is highest in both Denmark and Norway and is second-highest behind the Left Party in Sweden. Second, social democratic members are generally the most negative. In both Denmark and Norway, they show the lowest level of perceived intra-party democracy while their Swedish counterparts are somewhat less dissatisfied. Since all three social democratic parties were in government at the time of the survey, government participation, which implies more power to the party elite and often less of an ear for the rank-and-file, cannot explain this cross-country difference. Importantly, however, some of the differences in rank order are based on very small differences in average levels of perception of intra-party democracy.

Individual-Level Explanations for the Perception of Intra-Party Democracy

So far, our analyses suggest that factors at the country and party family levels poorly explain party members' perception of intra-party democracy, hence, we now turn to an analysis of the individual determinants of individual-level perceptions of intra-party democracy. We run OLS regression models based on three different dependent variables (see table 10.2). In the first set of models (1 and 2), we analyse Swedish and Norwegian party members and their satisfaction with the functioning of their party organizations. The second set of models (3 and 4) deals with the same countries but uses party members' satisfaction with their party leadership as the dependent variable. Finally, our third set of models (5 and 6) predicts the extent to which party members in Norway and Denmark perceive it as a problem that their leadership is too strong.

Table 10.2. Explaining levels of party members' perception of intra-party democracy (OLS regression).

Dependent variable	Satisfaction with functioning of organization		Satisfaction with leadership		It is a problem for party that leadership is too strong	
	Model 1: Sweden	Model 2: Norway	Model 3: Sweden	Model 4: Norway	Model 5: Norway	Model 6: Denmark
Position	−0.023	0.034	−0.054**	0.019	−0.042	0.040**
	(0.023)	(0.042)	(0.022)	(0.044)	(0.053)	(0.020)
Participation	−0.021	0.114***	0.004	0.105**	0.093*	−0.061**
	(0.024)	(0.039)	(0.023)	(0.041)	(0.049)	(0.025)
Distance	−0.149***	−0.147***	−0.184***	−0.198***	−0.145***	−0.099***
	(0.008)	(0.015)	(0.007)	(0.015)	(0.019)	(0.008)
Expectation	−0.221***	−0.112***	−0.276***	−0.107***	−0.072***	0.032***
	(0.010)	(0.015)	(0.009)	(0.016)	(0.020)	(0.009)
Age	0.003***	0.005***	−0.001*	0.001	0.000	−0.001
	(0.001)	(0.001)	(0.001)	(0.001)	(0.001)	(0.001)
Gender	0.089***	0.083**	0.074***	0.205***	0.058	0.143***
	(0.021)	(0.035)	(0.020)	(0.037)	(0.045)	(0.021)
Constant	−2.206*	−6.181***	7.883***	1.494	3.394	5.104***
	(1.296)	(2.016)	(1.259)	(2.157)	(2.607)	(1.313)
Adjusted R^2	0.180	0.100	0.294	0.146	0.060	0.063
N	8,462	1,989	9,200	2,138	1,976	10,579

Note: $*p<0.1$, $**p<0.05$, $***p<0.01$. OLS regression with unstandardized b-coefficients and standard errors within parentheses. All models include party dummies.

Table 10.2 shows that our individual-level hypotheses obtain mixed support. The hypothesis most strongly supported is the effect of political distance (H_5). As expected, the *distance* predictor is highly and negatively associated with perception of intra-party democracy. The larger the political distance party members indicate between themselves and their party on the left-right scale, the less intra-party democracy they perceive their party to exhibit. Members with larger self-perceived political disagreement with their party are more dissatisfied with the way in which parties provide a participatory linkage by giving members 'a say' in important party decisions.

Since significant effects are not the same as substantial effects, we need to look at the coefficients. The coefficients of the distance predictor range from about −0.10 (model 6) to −0.20 (model 5). In other words, one further step difference between the position of members and their party is associated with 0.10 to 0.20 lower level of intra-party democracy perception on a scale ranging from 1 to 5. The effect is strongest for Norwegian party members followed by the Swedish and, last, the Danish. These results imply that parties with a higher level of intra-party political disagreement, or the parties that are less harmonious, that are providing less of a 'policy' linkage through their party member organization, are also providing a weaker linkage in intra-party democracy terms, at least in the eyes of their members. Policy and intra-party democracy go hand in hand when providing linkage through party membership organizations.

We also get strong support for the expectation that the higher the demand of intra-party democracy, the lower the level of perceived intra-party democracy (H_6). In all but model 6, the Danish case, the expectation of intra-party democracy is strongly and negatively related to intra-party democracy perception, indicating that lower demand for internally democratic processes is associated with higher satisfaction. In other words, perceptions of intra-party democracy are not only driven by actual practices but also by what party members expect from their parties. The effect of the expectation predictor is somewhat more varied. While a one-step increase in expectation on a five-step scale is associated with a 0.22 to 0.28 step decrease in satisfaction with intra-party democracy for Swedish members, a similar change is only associated with about 0.10 step decrease for Norwegian parties. The fact that model 6 shows that Danish party members' satisfaction with intra-party democracy is partly driven by their demand, but in a positive direction, is surprising. However, the fact that the coefficient is considerably smaller than in the other models suggests that the substantial effect, even if significant, is close to negligible. Further, if the analysis is broken down by party, we see that the significant positive relationship does not hold for all parties. For some parties, the positive relation is not significant, and for two parties, the Danish People's Party and the Socialist People's Party, we actually find a negative relationship, although significant only for the latter.

The results from our two remaining main independent variables generally do not give any support for the corresponding hypotheses. Having participated in at least one party meeting during the last twelve months is significantly related to increasing levels of perceived intra-party democracy in three out of six models, but it is also significantly related to decreasing levels of perceived intra-party democracy in one model (model 6). More specifically, our participation hypothesis, that party members who have attended party meetings perceive a higher level of intra-party democracy (H_4), is supported only in Norway, whereas no such conclusion can be drawn based on the Swedish and Danish data. Hence, Norwegian party members who participate in party meetings find that the level of intra-party democracy is higher than to party members who do not participate. The opposite is the case for Danish party members.

Finally, our data suggest that the hypothesis that party members who are elected officials or hold intra-party office perceive their party's intra-party democracy to be higher than rank-and-file members do (H_3) should be rejected. While office holding is significant in two models, the direction of the relation varies. In other words, there are no significant differences in perception of intra-party democracy that are dependent on experience of holding elected or intra-party positions.

Finally, it is also interesting to note the results of our control variables. Being a woman is significantly associated with higher levels of perceived intra-party democracy in all but one of our (Norwegian) models, hence, women tend to be more satisfied with intra-party democracy, also when 'controlling' for office, political agreement and participation. However, the coefficients of the gender predictor in most models suggest that the substantial effect is generally rather weak. Two models (models 4 and 6), however, show somewhat greater coefficients and consequently substantial effects. These results indicate that a more gender-balanced party membership may in general be more satisfied but that the difference is not expected to be major (see chapter 4 on the gender balance of Nordic party members). The results from our age variable indicate that this is not an important predictor of intra-party democracy perceptions. Hence, this result points to the absence of a generation or life-cycle effect where younger party members are more disgruntled – or older party members more satisfied about how it worked in the good old days of the mass parties.

Finally, a few words on comparing models with overlapping operationalization of the dependent variable. The comparisons of models 1 and 2 and models 3 and 4 suggest that the effects at work are similar in Sweden and Norway, whereas Denmark is the odd one out. Although the substantial effect is small and the pattern does not hold up for all parties, this finding calls for further research. Last, a couple of methodological points. First, the performance of the models in table 10.2 varies in regard to predicting perceived levels of intra-party democracy, and adjusted R^2 levels between 0.06 and 0.29 show that some variables of interest have been omitted. Second, besides running OLS regression models, we have also run ordered logistic regressions to check the robustness of our results; the results of the importance of individual variables are very similar to those from the OLS regression models.

CONCLUSION

While the study of intra-party democracy has a long tradition, we have only recently developed the tools to make systematic large-N comparisons at the party level. While this is an important contribution to the party literature, it says little about how party members actually perceive intra-party democratic procedures of their parties and hence whether parties include political decision-making power in their participatory linkage. With this chapter, our objective has been to contribute to this area. Using party member surveys of the three Scandinavian countries, we have made a first attempt to map and explain variations in party members' perceptions of intra-party democracy. While our data only allow us to draw preliminary conclusions of comparative character, we reveal some interesting findings.

First, our data suggest that Scandinavian party members are generally happy with the inclusiveness of their intra-party processes. In fact, the mean value for all included items tapping into intra-party democracy is above 3 for all parties on a 1 to 5 scale. On a general level, Norwegian party members are somewhat more satisfied than their Swedish and Danish counterparts. The differences are small and the analysis is based on partly different operationalizations of intra-party democracy perceptions; hence, we need to be cautious. However, a cautious conclusion is that we find support for our hypothesis that Norwegian party members, on average, have a more favourable perception of intra-party democracy than Swedish and Danish party members (H_1). This implies that there seems to be an association between party-level intra-party democracy based on party statutes and party members' perception of their parties' democratic practice. Norwegian parties' stronger mass-party tradition plays out in the statutes where they have a higher level of intra-party democracy. Party members are granted a larger say in Norwegian parties – and they also perceive there to be a higher level of intra-party democracy.

At the party family level, we find no systematic differences across party families in their party members' perception of intra-party democracy (H_2). The main conclusion from our analysis at the party level is that individual-level characteristics seem more important for understanding variations in perceptions of intra-party democracy than formal rules and practices at the party level.

Turning to our individual-level explanations for party members' perception of intra-party democracy, we tested four hypotheses. The most strongly confirmed one is that the larger the political distance party members perceive between themselves and their party, the lower the level of intra-party democracy they perceive (H_5). We also found that party members' expectation of having a say in intra-party politics is of importance. The higher the demand of intra-party democracy, the lower the level of intra-party democracy perceived by the party members (H_6). Our participation and position hypotheses, that is, those party members who have attended party meetings (H_4) or who hold office (H_3) perceive a higher level of intra-party democracy, only gained weak support. Finally, our data also suggest that women are significantly more satisfied with intra-party democracy than men are.

While party members are in general more satisfied than dissatisfied with the intra-party democracy, not all members are happy about it. And it does have implications for how parties provide participatory linkage. Party members who find a lack of intra-party democracy are more likely to consider leaving their party (Kosiara-Pedersen 2017, ch. 13; Polk and Kölln 2018). On the other hand, at least in the Danish case, they are also more likely to participate within the party and be potential candidates (Kosiara-Pedersen 2017, ch. 7).

So what does all of this mean for linkage and explanations of intra-party democracy? Besides being one of the first attempts to study perceptions of intra-party democracy, it also leaves us with some lessons. Together with other recent re-evaluations of the party decline thesis (e.g. Scarrow 2015), our results suggest that Scandinavian political parties are in better shape than some scholars and pundits suggest. Current party members are rather satisfied. In terms of the overall aim of this volume, we might therefore conclude that Scandinavian parties, at least to some extent, do provide their members with a say over important intra-party processes. Influence on party decisions seems to be part of the participatory linkage that party member organizations provide. In other words, the European Party Democracy model, where parties present different alternatives at the ballot box but also provide an additional intra-party channel of influence, cannot be ruled out as a valid illustration of how parties organize.

NOTES

1. Thanks to participants in the workshop on parties at the XVIII Nordic Political Science Association (NOPSA) Conference, University of Southern Denmark, Odense, Denmark, 8–11 August 2017, and the Swedish Political Science Association (SWEPSA) annual conference, Karlstad University, 4–6 October 2017 for useful comments on our first draft.
2. See chapter 1, for details and references.
3. See appendix, for references to survey items.
4. The Swedish survey item does not include the introductory words 'most important'.

BIBLIOGRAPHY

Allern, Elin Haugsgjerd and Karina Pedersen. 2007. 'The Impact of Party Organisational Changes on Democracy'. *West European Politics* 30 (1): 68–92.

Aylott, Nicholas and Niklas Bolin. 2017. 'Managed Intra-Party Democracy: Precursory Delegation and Party Leader Selection'. *Party Politics* 23 (1): 55–65. doi: 10.1177/1354068816655569.

———. 2018. 'The Scope of Party Leadership: Re-Examining the Terms on which Political Parties Select Their Leaders'. PUPOL 3rd International Conference, Stockholm, 19–20 April.

Bernardi, Luca, Giulia Sandri and Antonella Seddone. 2016. 'Challenges of Political Participation and Intra-Party Democracy: Bittersweet Symphony from Party Membership and Primary Elections in Italy'. *Acta Politica* 52 (2): 218–40. doi: 10.1057/ap.2016.4.

Bille, Lars. 2001. 'Democratizing a Democratic Procedure: Myth or Reality? Candidate Selection in Western European Parties, 1960–1990'. *Party Politics* 7 (3): 363–80.

Bolin, Niklas. 2012. *Målsättning riksdagen: Ett aktörsperspektiv på nya partiers inträde i det nationella parlamentet.* Umeå: Umeå universitet.

Bolin, Niklas, Nicholas Aylott, Benjamin von dem Berge and Thomas Poguntke. 2017. 'Paterns of Intra-Party Democracy around the World'. In *Organizing Representation: Political Parties, Participation, and Power*, edited by Susan Scarrow, Paul Webb and Thomas Poguntke, 158–84. Oxford: Oxford University Press.

Cross, William P. and André Blais. 2012a. *Politics at the Centre: The Selection and Removal of Party Leaders in the Anglo Parliamentary Democracies.* Oxford: Oxford University Press.

———. 2012b. 'Who Selects the Party Leader?' *Party Politics* 18 (2): 127–50. doi: 10.1177/1354068810382935.

Cross, William P. and Jean-Benoit Pilet, eds. 2015. *The Politics of Party Leadership: A Cross-National Perspective.* Oxford: Oxford University Press.

Cross, William P. and Richard S. Katz, eds. 2013. *The Challenges of Intra-Party Democracy.* Oxford: Oxford University Press.

Gauja, Anika. 2013. 'Policy Development and Intra-Party Democracy'. In *The Challenges of Intra-Party Democracy*, edited by William P. Cross and Richard S. Katz, 116–35. Oxford: Oxford University Press.

———. 2015. 'The Individualisation of Party Politics: The Impact of Changing Internal Decision-Making Processes on Policy Development and Citizen Engagement'. *The British Journal of Politics and International Relations* 17 (1): 89–105. doi: 10.1111/1467–856x.12035.

Harmel, Robert and Kenneth Janda. 1994. 'An Integrated Theory of Party Goals and Party Change'. *Journal of Theoretical Politics* 6 (3): 259–87. doi: 10.1177/0951692894006003001.

Hazan, Reuven Y. and Gideon Rahat. 2010. *Democracy within Parties: Candidate Selection Methods and Their Consequences.* Oxford: Oxford University Press.

Heinisch, Reinhard and Oscar Mazzoleni, eds. 2016. *Understanding Populist Party Organisation: The Radical Right in Western Europe.* London: Palgrave Macmillan.

Hirschman, Albert O. 1970. *Exit, Voice, and Loyalty.* Cambridge, MA: Harvard University Press.

Ignazi, Piero. 2018. 'The Four Knights of Intra-Party Democracy: A Rescue for Party Delegitimation'. *Party Politics.* doi: 10.1177/1354068818754599.

Katz, Richard S. 2013. *The Challenges of Intra-Party Democracy,* edited by William P. Cross and Richard S. Katz, 49–64. Oxford: Oxford University Press.

Katz, Richard S. and Peter Mair. 1992. 'Introduction'. In *Party Organizations: A Data Handbook,* edited by Richard S. Katz and Peter Mair, 1–20. London: SAGE.

———. 1995. 'Changing Models of Party Organization and Party Democracy: The Emergence of the Cartel Party'. *Party Politics* 1 (1): 5–28.

Kosiara-Pedersen, Karina. 2017. *Demokratiets ildsjæle – Partimedlemmer i Danmark.* Copenhagen: Djøf Publishing.

Michels, Robert. (1915) 1962. *Poltical Parties: A Sociological Study of the Oligarchical Tendencies of Modern Democracy.* New York: Free Press.

Mudde, Cas. 2007. *Populist Radical Right Parties in Europe.* Cambridge: Cambridge University Press.

Norris, Pippa. 2011. *Democratic Deficit: Critical Citizens Revisited.* Cambridge: Cambridge University Press.

Pedersen, Helene Helboe. 2010. *Partiers interne organisering og parlamentariske adfærd.* Aarhus: Politica.

Pedersen, Karina and Jens Ringsmose. 2004. 'From the Progress Party to the Danish People's Party: From Protest Party to Government Supporting Party'. ECPR Joint Session of Workshops, Uppsala, 13–18 April.

Pilet, Jean-Benoit and William P. Cross. 2014. 'The Selection of Party Leaders in Comparative Perspective'. In *The Selection of Political Party Leaders in Contemporary Parliamentary Democracies: A Comparative Study,* edited by Jean-Benoit Pilet and William P. Cross, 222–39. New York: Routledge.

Pilet, Jean-Benoit, Emilie van Haute and Camille Kelbel. 2015. *Candidate Selection Procedures for the European Elections.* Brussels: Study for the European Parliament, Directorate General for Internal Policies – Directorate C: Citizens' Rights and Constitutional Affairs.

Poguntke, Thomas. 1987. 'New Politics and Party Systems: The Emergence of a New Type of Party?' *West European Politics* 10 (1): 76–88.

Polk, Jonathan and Ann-Kristin Kölln. 2018. 'Electoral Infidelity: Why Party Members Cast Defecting Votes'. *European Journal of Political Research* 57 (2): 539–60. doi: doi:10.1111/1475–6765.12238.

Rahat, Gideon and Assaf Shapira. 2017. 'An Intra-Party Democracy Index: Theory, Design and a Demonstration'. *Parliamentary Affairs* 70 (1): 84–110. doi: https://doi.org/10.1093/pa/gsv068.

Rüdig, Wolfgang and Javier Sajuria. 2018. 'Green Party Members and Grass-Roots Democracy: A Comparative Analysis'. *Party Politics.* doi: 10.1177/1354068818754600.

Sanches, Edalina Rodrigues, Marco Lisi, Isabella Razzuoli and Paula do Espírito Santo. 2018. 'Intra-Party Democracy from Members' Viewpoint: The Case of Left-Wing Parties in Portugal'. *Acta Politica* 53 (3): 391–408. doi: 10.1057/s41269–017–0057-x.

Sandri, Giulia. 2012. 'Perceptions of Intra-Party Democracy and Their Consequences on Activism: A Comparative Analysis of Attitudes and Behaviors of Grass-Roots Party Members'. 22nd IPSA World Congress, Madrid.

Sandri, Giulia and Antonella Seddone. 2015. 'Introduction: Primary Elections across the World'. In *Party Primaries in Comparative Perspective*, edited by Giulia Sandri, Antonella Seddone and Fulvio Venturino, 1–20. London: Routledge.

Scarrow, Susan E. 2015. *Beyond Party Members: Changing Approaches to Partisan Mobilization.* Oxford: Oxford University Press.

Strøm, Kaare. 1990. 'A Behavioral Theory of Competitive Political Parties'. *American Journal of Political Science* 34 (2): 565–98.

van Biezen, Ingrid, Peter Mair and Thomas Poguntke. 2012. 'Going, Going, . . . Gone? The Decline of Party Membership in Contemporary Europe'. *European Journal of Political Research* 51 (1): 24–56.

V-Dem Institute. 2018. 'Democracy for All? V-Dem Annual Democracy Report 2018'. Accessed 7 November 2018 at https://www.v-dem.net/en/news/democracy-all-v-dem-annual-democracy-report-2018/.

von dem Berge, Benjamin and Peter Obert. 2017. 'Intraparty Democracy in Central and Eastern Europe: Explaining Change and Stability from 1989 until 2011'. *Party Politics.* doi: 10.1177/1354068816688364.

von dem Berge, Benjamin and Thomas Poguntke. 2017. 'Varieties of Intra-Party Democracy: Conceptualisation and Index Construction'. In *Organizing Political Parties. Representation, Participation, and Power*, edited by Susan E. Scarrow, Paul D. Webb and Thomas Poguntke, 136–57. Oxford: Oxford University Press.

von dem Berge, Benjamin, Thomas Poguntke, Peter Obert and Diana Tipei. 2013. *Measuring Intra-Party Democracy: A Guide for the Content Analysis of Party Statutes with Examples from Hungary, Slovakia and Romania.* Berlin, Heidelberg: Springer.

Whiteley, Paul. 2014. 'Does Regulation Make Political Parties More Popular? A Multi-Level Analysis of Party Support in Europe'. *International Political Science Review* 35 (3): 376–99.

Appendix

Table A10.1. Items from surveys.

VARIABLE	Denmark	Norway	Sweden
		SURVEY ITEMS	
Satisfaction with organization		How satisfied are you with the functioning of the organization (role granted to members, rights and obligations)? (Q49_2)	How satisfied are you with the functioning of the organization (role granted to members, rights & obligations)? (Q91_3)
Satisfaction with leadership		How satisfied are you with the leadership? (Q49_3)	How satisfied are you with the leadership? (Q91_2)
Leadership is too strong	It is a problem for the party that its leadership is too strong. (s_54_4)	It is a problem for the party that its leadership is too strong. (Q40_2)	
Position	Have you been elected to intra-party or elected office at the local, regional or national level?	Do you currently hold or have you in the past held any position within the party organization?	Do you currently hold or have you in the past held any public office representing the

(continued)

SURVEY ITEMS

VARIABLE	Denmark	Norway	Sweden
	(six individual questions) (s_30_1–s_30_5, s_30_10)	(local, regional or national branch) or any public office representing the party (local, regional or national level)? (Q26, Q27)	party (e.g. local councillor, mayor and MP) or any position within the party organization (e.g. local branch treasurer/secretary)? If yes, please specify which and on which level. (Q67)
Participation	How many times within the past year have you been at a meeting in your local branch (all kinds of meetings, events)? (s_24)	Have you participated in a party event such as a meeting of the party branch, courses, seminars, rallies or parties in the last 12 months? (Q12)	Could you please indicate whether you have participated in a regular meeting of the party branch in the past 12 months? (Q83)
Distance	In politics, we often talk about left and right. Where would you place yourself and the parties? (s_48_1–s_48_10)	In politics, we sometimes talk about left and right. Where would you place yourself and the parties? (Q19, Q20)	Political opinions are often said to be left or right. When you think about your own/party's opinions, where would you place them on the scale below? (Q34, Q35)
Expectation	The most important role of party members is to support the party leadership's decisions. (s_54_1)	The most important role of party members is to support the party leadership's decisions. (Q40_4)	My role as a member is to support decisions made by the party leadership. (Q93_5)

Table A10.2. Descriptive statistics.

	Denmark			Norway			Sweden		
	N	Mean (std. dev.)	Min–Max	N	Mean (std. dev.)	Min–Max	N	Mean (std. dev.)	Min–Max
Satisfaction with organization				2,266	3.895 (0.754)	1–5	9,524	3.544 (1.033)	1–5
Satisfaction with leadership				2,459	4.032 (0.846)	1–5	10,179	3.670 (1.111)	1–5
Leadership is too strong	16,434	3.726 (1.018)	1–5	2,202	3.907 (0.945)	1–5			
Position	21,182	0.416 (0.493)	0–1	2,599	0.654 (0.476)	0–1	10,074	0.643 (0.479)	0–1
Participation	13,773	0.782 (0.413)	0–1	2,575	1.606 (0.489)	1–2	10,258	0.643 (0.479)	0–1
Distance	18,047	0.947 (1.497)	0–11	2,508	1.040 (1.139)	0–9	10,125	1.346 (1.404)	0–10
Expectation	16,654	3.170 (1.174)	1–5	2,422	3.362 (1.102)	1–5	10,138	2.950 (1.081)	1–5
Year of birth	17,108	1959.241 (15.572)	1910–1998	2,506	1963.862 (16.668)	1925–2001	10,296	1960.030 (16.577)	1921–2015
Gender	17,111	0.352 (0.478)	0–1	2,566	0.375 (0.484)	0–1	10,199	0.411 (0.492)	0–1

Table A10.3. Party members' perception of intra-party democracy in Denmark.

	(1) It is a problem for the party that the leadership is too strong
	Mean (std. dev.)
Social Democrats	3.58 (0.99)
Social Liberals	3.94 (0.92)
Conservatives	3.92 (0.97)
Socialist People's Party	3.42 (1.04)
Liberal Alliance	4.00 (0.95)
Christian Democrats	3.93 (0.86)
Danish People's Party	3.84 (1.09)
Liberals	3.74 (0.94)
Unity List	3.94 (1.03)
Mean (std. dev.)	3.73 (1.02)
N	16,434
Eta squared	0.04***

Note: Higher values indicate disagreement, that is, a more positive perception of intra-party democracy. Eta squared refers to the between-groups variance explained by party differences.

***$p<0.01$, **$p<0.05$.

Table A10.4. Party members' perception of intra-party democracy in Norway.

	(1) It is a problem for the party that the leadership is too strong	(2) Satisfaction with the functioning of the organization	(3) Satisfaction with the leadership
	Mean (std. dev.)	Mean (std. dev.)	Mean (std. dev.)
Labour Party	3.67 (1.01)	3.80 (0.79)	3.98 (0.82)
Progress Party	3.83 (1.00)	3.97 (0.77)	4.14 (0.80)
Conservative Party	3.92 (0.94)	3.88 (0.77)	4.23 (0.80)
Socialist Left Party	3.97 (0.91)	3.78 (0.75)	3.78 (0.88)
Centre Party	4.18 (0.86)	4.04 (0.67)	4.33 (0.71)
Christian Democratic Party	3.95 (0.87)	3.95 (0.65)	4.10 (0.82)
Liberal Party	3.90 (0.89)	3.90 (0.75)	3.88 (0.87)
Greens	3.89 (1.00)	3.87 (0.81)	3.94 (0.89)
Mean (std. dev.)	3.91 (0.95)	3.90 (0.75)	4.03 (0.85)
N	2,202	2,266	2,459
Eta squared	0.02***	0.01***	0.04***

Note: See table A10.3.

Table A10.5. Party members' perception of intra-party democracy in Sweden.

	(1) Satisfaction with the functioning of the organization	(2) Satisfaction with the leadership
	Mean (std. dev.)	Mean (std. dev.)
Social Democrats	3.36 (0.99)	3.71 (0.97)
Left Party	3.87 (0.92)	4.34 (0.82)
Green Party	3.74 (1.03)	3.40 (1.09)
Feminist Initiative	4.19 (0.90)	4.60 (0.64)
Liberals	3.35 (0.95)	3.20 (1.16)
Christian Democrats	3.60 (0.97)	3.80 (1.02)
Moderate Party	3.22 (1.08)	3.38 (1.13)
Mean (std. dev.)	3.54 (1.03)	3.67 (1.11)
N	9,524	10,179
Eta squared	0.07***	0.14***

Note: See table A10.3.

Table A10.6. Explaining levels of party members' perception of intra-party democracy (ordinal logit regression).

Dependent variable	Satisfaction with the functioning of the organization		Satisfaction with the leadership		It is a problem for the party that the leadership is too strong	
	Model 7: Sweden	Model 8: Norway	Model 9: Sweden	Model 10: Norway	Model 11: Norway	Model 12: Denmark
Position	−0.032	0.124	−0.123***	0.070	−0.093	0.084**
	(0.045)	(0.116)	(0.045)	(0.105)	(0.109)	(0.038)
Participation	−0.021	0.325***	0.013	0.294***	0.216**	−0.089**
	(0.047)	(0.106)	(0.046)	(0.098)	(0.100)	(0.045)
Distance	−0.285***	−0.392***	−0.356***	−0.450***	−0.278***	−0.169***
	(0.015)	(0.042)	(0.015)	(0.039)	(0.039)	(0.015)
Expectation	−0.439***	−0.277***	−0.552***	−0.244***	−0.136***	0.086***
	(0.020)	(0.043)	(0.020)	(0.040)	(0.041)	(0.017)
Age	0.008***	0.015***	−0.002	0.005*	0.001	−0.000
	(0.001)	(0.003)	(0.001)	(0.003)	(0.003)	(0.001)
Gender	0.203***	0.230**	0.156***	0.500***	0.109	0.259***
	(0.042)	(0.096)	(0.041)	(0.090)	(0.090)	(0.039)
Cutpoint 1	9.900	23.704	−8.734	4.605	−2.119	−4.587
	(2.591)	(5.617)	(2.538)	(5.258)	(5.250)	2.417)
Cutpoint 2	11.541	25.646	−7.083	6.220	−0.072	−3.119
	(2.591)	(5.612)	(2.537)	(5.255)	(5.247)	2.416)
Cutpoint 3	13.019	27.010	5.908	7.077	1.244	−1.455
	(2.591)	(5.613)	(2.537)	(5.254)	(5.247)	2.416)
Cutpoint 4	15.286	30.644	−3.582	10.367	3.242	0.153
	(2.593)	(5.623)	(2.536)	(5.257)	(5.248)	2.417)
Pseudo R^2	0.070	0.047	0.128	0.064	0.025	0.024
N	8,642	1,989	9,200	2,138	1,976	10,579

Note: *p <0.1, **p<0.05, ***p<0.01, standard errors within parentheses.

11

A Break in the Representative Chain

Party Members' Ideological Disagreement with Candidates and Demands for Intra-Party Democracy

Ann-Kristin Kölln and Jonathan Polk[1]

Party organizations in Europe have undergone substantial changes over the decades since the term 'mass organizations' was coined (Katz and Mair 1995). Today's political parties are often characterized by at least two common features. First, almost all European parties have suffered from substantial membership loss over the past decades and are today recording often record-low figures of formal membership (e.g. Kölln 2016; Scarrow and Gezgor 2010; van Biezen, Mair and Poguntke 2012). Second, and partly as a consequence of the membership decline, many European party organizations have increased the formal decision-making power of their members, even though, informally, the party leadership has often been empowered over this time period (e.g. Cross and Katz 2013; Katz and Mair 1995, 2009; Poguntke et al. 2016; Scarrow, Webb and Farrell 2000; Schumacher and Giger 2017). The logical consequence of both developments is that today's party members have more internal power (at least formally) and higher chances of eventually standing for and obtaining elected office than ever before.

Even though members and candidates share many important attitudes towards their party, several studies provide empirical evidence that breaks up the unitary actor assumption of a political party. We followed this tradition in chapter 5 and investigated May's Law of Curvilinear Disparity (1973) across four countries and three levels of the party. This chapter uses this disagreement within parties on general ideology as well as on particular issues to study the potential consequences this may have for members' preferences for intra-party democracy. We conceptualize internal party disagreement as differences in ideological leanings and issue preferences between party members and candidates running for national parliamentary elections across three Scandinavian countries: Denmark, Norway and Sweden. We draw on the theory of exit, voice and loyalty (Hirschman 1970) and institutionalist theories of delegation to study the consequences of tensions within parties.

Our chapter contributes to the book's dimensions of membership representation and influence. Preceding chapters examined the role of members in the representation process with a focus on the descriptive representation of party members (chapter 4) and the ideological agreement between a party's voters, members and candidates (chapter 5). Here, we extend the analysis to a separate link in the chain of representation of societal interests in the political process: the relationship between a party's members and its candidates for national legislative office. We further contribute to a deeper understanding of member-based representation by pushing beyond the general left-right dimension to look at member-candidate (dis)agreement on substantive issues other than (and often orthogonal to) left-right issues.

Another major theme of this book revolves around the amount and types of influence that party members have within their parties. Our work here clearly speaks to this topic in its focus on understanding variation in the demand within a party's membership for more influence in the party's decision-making. Here, the chapter connects to the findings of both the preceding chapters' interest in ideological agreement within parties and its examination of intra-party democracy discussed in chapter 10. As the introductory chapter of the book anticipates, in practice, questions related to representation and influence connect with one another in theoretically explicable patterns.

Within this chapter, we seek to answer an overarching research question related to member-based representation and influence and hence on how party members contribute to parties' participatory linkage. Acknowledging the existence of intra-party disagreement, we ask if party members who see themselves as more ideologically distant from the positions of their parties' candidates are more likely to favour heightened power for members on internal party decision-making. In order to answer this question, we combine data on candidates from the Comparative Candidate Survey (CCS) for the first time with independent surveys of party members in Denmark (Kosiara-Pedersen 2017), Norway (Jupskås and Heidar 2009) and Sweden (Kölln and Polk 2017).

The chapter's findings directly contribute to two of the book's themes: representation and influence. Our results show that ideological disagreement between party members and party candidates in the three Scandinavian countries is associated with more support for direct democratic internal party decision-making from party members. More specifically, our analysis suggests that greater member-candidate incongruence on general left-right (all three countries), immigration preferences (only in Norway and Sweden) and European integration (only in Sweden) are each associated with more support for important decisions facing the party being taken directly by the entire membership.

CANDIDATES, MEMBERS AND IDEOLOGICAL PREFERENCES

Research stressing the representative character of political parties argues that party members fulfil functions of social and opinion representation that are important for democratic politics (e.g. see Kölln 2017; May 1973; Müller and Katz 1997; Scarrow and Gezgor 2010; Widfeldt 1995, 1999). Since members can directly influence policy output without being democratically legitimized, for example, via candidate selection (Lundell 2004), it is important to know if the opinions of party members resemble those of a party's candidates for elected office. In other words, according to theories of representative democracy, party candidates should ideally match members' ideological position.

But ideological congruence between candidates and members is also important from an accountability point of view. The delegation model of representation stresses what happens within parties. Party members or congresses select candidates to run for office and thus delegate to candidates, which makes members or party congress the principal and candidates the agents (see Wolkenstein 2018; but also Müller 2000; Neto and Strøm 2006). If the political preferences of candidates do not match those of members, delegation has failed, at least in part. Both perspectives share the understanding that congruence in political preferences between party candidates and members is beneficial.

Existing theoretical and empirical literature has already investigated the opinion structure within political parties. John May (1973) famously asserted that mid-level elites, such as party members, are more likely to hold ideologically extreme views than the party elite (MPs, members of the executive or election candidates) or the non-elite – party voters (May 1973, 135–36; Narud and Skare 1999, 46–47). Although many studies have looked at the ideological agreement between a party's leadership, its mid-level elite and a party's voters, fewer have done so in a cross-national setting. Further, while a growing number of congruence studies examine the positions of parliamentary candidates (e.g. Andreadis and Stavrakakis 2017; Costello, Thomassen and Rosema 2012; Leimgruber, Hangartner and Leemann 2010), we are not aware of any study that compares party members and parliamentary candidates within such a framework.

In this chapter, we take this up by examining the extent to which a distinct group of the mid-level elite, party members, differs in its ideological positions from a distinct part of the party elite, candidates for office, and if so, with what consequences. Our focus on the relationship between members and candidates concerns a key intermediary in the chain of representation and a possible source of tension for party-based governance.

Albert Hirschman's (1970) theory of exit, voice and loyalty (EVL) has been widely used in various aspects of political science (see Clark, Golder and Golder [2017] for a recent overview). From the perspective of research on party members, we see a number of ways that this general theory of varied responses to organizational decline could be productively applied to parties in an era of diminishing membership. For example, prior research provides evidence that members are more likely to consider voting for another party (disloyalty) or even quitting their current party (exit) if they disagree with the ideological position of the party leadership (Kölln and Polk 2017; Kosiara-Pedersen 2016; Polk and Kölln 2018; van Haute and Carty 2012). Here we focus on a different aspect of the EVL framework, namely voice, by examining the effect of ideological disagreement (or incongruence) between members and candidates on members' attitudes towards intra-party decision-making.

This perspective complements research on principal-agent relationships in party-based parliamentary democracies (see Müller 2000; Neto and Strøm 2006; Wolkenstein 2018). While the traditional delegate model understands voters as principals and members of parliament as agents, recent research points out that such a model 'turns a blind eye to the internal life of parties' (Wolkenstein 2018, 440). Party members or a party congress usually select candidates, who are then available to the electorate for further delegation. Accordingly, party members and voters have to be conceived as 'co-principals' (Wolkenstein 2018, 440), and both members and candidates could arguably be conceived as part of the commonly known 'parliamentary chain of delegation' (Neto and Strøm 2006, 623).

Both theoretical frameworks – EVL and the chain of delegation – have similar implications, for instance, when party candidates' political preferences are not in line with those of members. But both first require one to assume that party members know about the *general* position of their own party candidates on major political issues. There are good reasons to think this might be the case. Candidates running for parliament have strong incentives to communicate their political positions. This is especially true for majoritarian electoral systems or those with open-list proportional representation, as in the three Scandinavian countries (Lijphart 2012). In addition, there is evidence from research on parliamentary voting behaviour that voters are able to obtain information about their candidates when it is useful to them (e.g. see Shugart , Valdini and Suominen 2005). If this is true, then we should expect party members to be quite good at obtaining information about their candidates as well since they both have an incentive for and interest in doing so. In particular, we do not expect that they will have detailed information about all candidates and on all issues, but we think it is more likely that members have a general sense of who the party nominated for election. We therefore conceptualize ideological disagreement between members and candidates as the distance between candidates' *central tendency* on the left-right dimension and party members' own self-placement on the same scale.

Our expectation is that party members who are more ideologically distant from the mean position of their party's parliamentary candidates will voice their dissatisfaction and be more likely to favour decision-making structures within the party that privilege party members. Several studies show that, in addition to other factors such as professional ambition, a major reason that citizens join political parties is to influence policy (Bruter and Harrison 2009; van Haute and Gauja 2015; see chapter 3 of this volume). If the issue preferences of a party member coincide or closely align with those of the candidates for parliament, that party member could be relatively confident that his or her policy preferences will be pursued by the party leadership and the party in parliament no matter the decision-making structure within the party or the style of representation of the candidates. However, if there is more ideological disagreement between the preferences of a party member and those of the party's parliamentary candidates, the member should be more inclined to forgo delegation altogether and prefer intra-party decision-making procedures that maximize the voice of party members in relation to other segments of the party, such as the leadership.

Greater decision-making power for individual members would be at the expense of individual candidates as well as the party leadership. Candidates enjoy a more prominent position within the party because they were chosen to be the public faces to win the national election. Those candidates that are successfully elected into parliament receive even more power, at least in relation to members. It means that even if candidates or elected candidates are still less powerful than the party leadership, they are more powerful than ordinary members. Therefore, we anticipate that ideological differences between members and the average candidates will lead members to demand a stronger role in the party's decision-making process to forgo delegation. This leads to our central hypothesis:

> *The larger the ideological distance between a party member and her party's parliamentary candidates, the more the member supports direct democratic features for party decision-making.*

DATA AND RESEARCH DESIGN

Empirically, our analysis relies on the most recent membership surveys from Denmark, Norway and Sweden as well as the Comparative Candidate Surveys in the same Scandinavian countries from a comparable time period. Party members are particularly difficult to survey because political parties often guard access to them. Therefore, coordinated cross-country efforts to survey members are difficult to achieve. However, the research community has recently started to harmonize existing data and has launched a new membership survey across Europe in order to arrive at a comparable data set (van Haute and Gauja 2015). For the current analysis, this means that the existing surveys are comparable across countries only to a limited extent. Nonetheless, survey researchers across the Nordic countries have paid particular attention to lining up their surveys to similar projects, such as national election studies or candidate surveys. We take advantage of these efforts and use a combination of party membership and party candidate surveys to test our individual-level party member expectations.

For Denmark, we use the 2012 Party Membership Survey (Kosiara-Pedersen 2017), which contains information on 22,415 members of nine political parties. Unlike in most other chapters for Norway, we use the 2009 Norwegian Party Membership Survey (Jupskås and Heidar 2009), which records a total of 3,315 members belonging to seven political parties. We use this survey and not the 2016 wave in order to maximize temporal comparability with the Norwegian candidate study. Finally, 10,392 respondents from seven political parties participated in the 2015 Swedish Party Membership Survey (Kölln and Polk 2017). This means that we can test our hypothesis in three countries with a total of twenty-three parties and more than 36,000 party members. For more information on the party membership surveys, see chapter 1.

The candidate data come from the Comparative Candidate Survey (CCS), Module 1 (CCS 2016) and Module 2 (CCS 2018). The survey measures candidates' genuine preferences as opposed to the electorally revealed preferences because it is an anonymous survey (Willumsen and Öhberg 2017). The same questionnaires were sent out to the entire population of candidates standing for national election in Denmark in 2011, Norway in 2009 and Sweden in 2014. The membership surveys in Denmark and Sweden were fielded after the candidate surveys, while the Norwegian membership survey preceded the candidate survey. Unlike the Danish and Swedish cases, the timing of the surveys in Norway means that our measurement point for the members precedes that for the candidates by about six months. While this is certainly not ideal from a research design perspective, there is reason to assume that candidates did not significantly change their attitudes during this period. First, these were the six months leading up to the national election and candidates most likely knew about their candidacy then and had possibly announced it – if not publicly, then at least within the party. Any major change in preferences even over the course of six months is less likely because it would signal inconsistency. Second, our measures of political preferences are either very broad, such as left-right self-placement, or very salient, such as opinions on immigration issues. While it is certainly conceivable that a candidate would change her position over the course of the six months leading up to the election on some issues, we think that – given the breadth and salience of our issues – major attitudinal change is less likely. Third, we do not measure individual candidates' positions but aggregate them to a common average. We therefore assume that Norwegian party members already had a good idea of their candidates' average position on major political issues six months before the candidate survey was conducted.

Response rates for the CCS are around 50 per cent for all three countries, and the number of respondents per country is sufficiently high to conduct meaningful analyses. The Danish sample includes 375 respondents, the Norwegian 1,015 and the Swedish 1,872.[2] The candidate survey in Sweden was conducted via Internet, while the Danish and Norwegian surveys were conducted with a written questionnaire.[3]

We use comparable operationalizations to test our hypothesis across the three countries. We begin with the idea that party members and candidates could report themselves at different positions on the general left-right ideological scale. This item is identical and available in all six surveys, ranging from 0 to 10. It means that we can directly compare the individual positions of candidates and members across and within countries. We operationalize ideological incongruence as the absolute distance between the self-placement of a party member on the 0 to 10 general left-right scale and the mean position of the parliamentary candidates from that member's party.

Left-right self-placement is a good and important first indicator for a general overview of ideological disagreement within a party (see chapter 5 in this volume).

However, this general disagreement between members and candidates might be the result of particular issues. To test for that possibility, we move, in a second step, over to individual political issues and measure the level of (dis)agreement on important political statements.

In particular, we are interested in the extent to which contentious issues of party competition also play a role in members' demands for intra-party democracy. In Scandinavia, as well as elsewhere in Europe, the issue of immigration has become one such contentious policy area. Despite the historical dominance of left-right party competition in the region, changes in the party system dynamics of Europe suggest that specific issues such as immigration or European integration are mobilized by challenger parties, which have enhanced their electoral prospects by doing so (Hobolt and de Vries 2015; Hobolt and Tilley 2016; Pardos-Prado 2015; van de Wardt 2014).

For the Norwegian and Swedish cases, a survey item asking about immigration attitudes is available that is comparable within and across countries. The strong relationship between attitudes towards immigration and the liberal-authoritarian dimension (e.g. Borre and Andersen 1997; Kriesi et al. 2006) helps us examine the effect of socio-cultural candidate-member incongruence. The Norwegian surveys asked respondents for their level of support on the statement 'It is important for immigrants to adapt to Norwegian customs and norms', while the comparable item in the candidate survey reads, 'Immigrants should be required to adapt to the customs of [country]'. The items are obviously not identical because the candidate survey's wording is stronger than that of the membership survey. However, these items are still sufficiently similar in meaning and direction that we can test our hypothesis on this item. A total of five response options are provided, ranging from 'agree completely' to 'disagree completely'. In Sweden, both the membership survey and the CCS asked respondents about their support for the following statement: 'Immigrants should be required to adapt to the customs of Sweden', with response options ranging from 'very good proposal' (= 1) to 'very bad proposal' (= 5). For the analysis, we reversed the coding of all items to measure support for this cultural immigration item, and we calculated the absolute distance measures for these questions in the same way that we described earlier for the general left-right dimension.

In addition to these concrete political statements and issues, we also consider an EU-related question, which was only available for both the membership and the candidate surveys in Sweden. Although party positions on European integration are interrelated with economic left-right and liberal-authoritarian positions, this varies substantially country to country, and in all member states, the inclusion of an EU-specific dimension adds explanatory power (Bakker, Jolly and Polk 2012). Additionally, voter-party incongruence on the EU dimension was associated with higher levels of vote switching in the 2014 European Parliament elections (Bakker, Jolly and Polk 2018). The EU has been a somewhat contentious issue in Scandinavia, as evidenced by, for example, the rejection of the euro in Denmark and Sweden. Specifically, we measure support for the statement 'Some think European integration should go further, others think it has already gone too far'. The original response options range from 0 to 10, and our measures for party members are simply derived from computing again the absolute distance between individual members and their candidates' mean position.

For our dependent variable, we require a measure that pertains to party members' satisfaction with internal democracy. This is a relatively new measure that is (not yet) standardized across the surveys. It means that we do not have a single measure that is the same across the three countries. However, all three surveys asked party members about their assessments of intra-party democracy in some form and so we were able to find appropriate survey measures in the three countries. Membership ballots are just one dimension of intra-party democracy, yet arguably a very important one that also regularly attracts media attention (e.g. see Bolin et al. 2017). For Norway, we take the share of members per party agreeing with the following statement on party policy: 'On major and important matters, the decision should depend on the results of a *binding ballot* in which all members may vote'. The alternative response options were that the national congress should have the final say (with and without an advisory ballot by members). And so we can take the share of members agreeing with the statement above as an individual-level measure of preferences for more intra-party democracy. The Swedish and Danish surveys contain a number of questions on intra-party democracy, and one in particular that is rather similar to the one found in the Norwegian survey. In Sweden, members were asked for their level of support for the following statement: 'The most important decisions should be taken directly by all members'. The Danish survey included a similar statement: 'Membership ballots are necessary to strengthen party democracy'. In both cases the five response options ranged from 'strongly disagree' (= 1) to 'strongly agree' (= 5), plus a 'don't know' option. The upper panel of figure 11.1 shows the distribution of our intra-party democracy variable for the Danish case, while the middle and lower panels document the distribution within and across Norwegian and Swedish parties, respectively.

Substantively, this first descriptive view of the dependent variable(s) shows that party members belonging to different parties hold very different views on how much direct power they should have. In Denmark, the highest support for more membership power can be found among members of the Left Socialist Party (Enhedslisten; EL), while several parties share similarly low levels of support for the same proposition, namely the Christian Democrats (KD), the Liberal Alliance (LA) and the Social Liberals (RV). In Norway, the highest and lowest levels of support are exhibited among members of the Progress Party (FrP) and the Conservative Party (H), respectively. Among Swedish parties, it is Green Party (Mp) members who show the highest level of support for direct power exerted by members. Perhaps surprisingly, the lowest level of support can be found among the Social Democrats (S).

In our models, we control for members' age, gender and level of activity within the party with the expectation that those that are more engaged will be more satisfied and less demanding of a greater voice within the party. We also expect activity

DENMARK

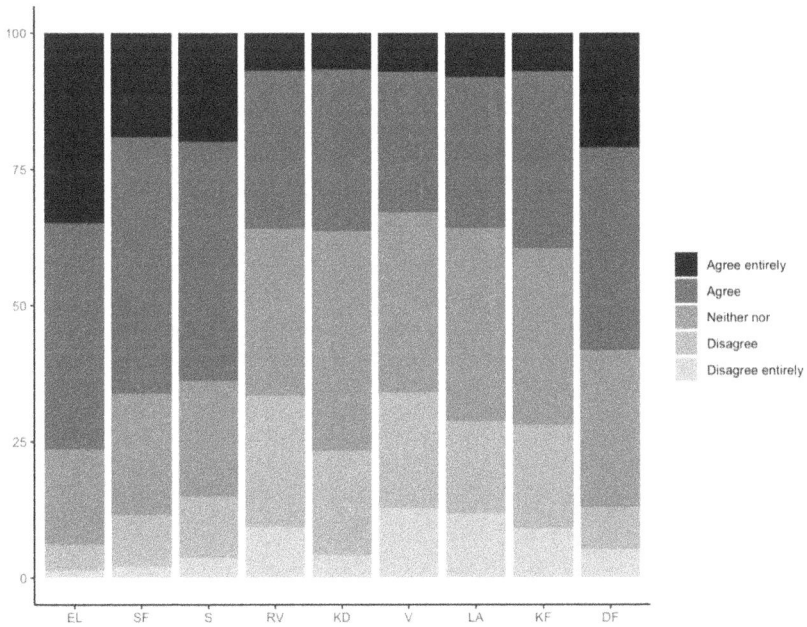

NORWAY

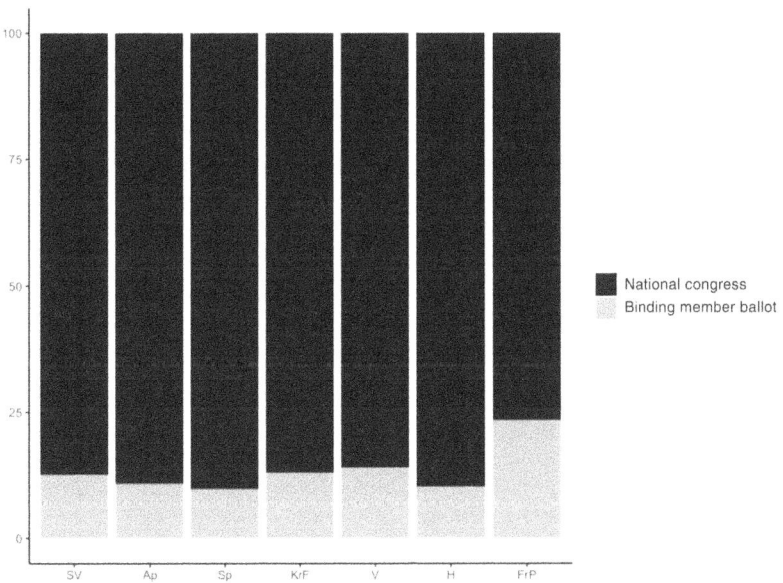

Figure 11.1. Distribution of members' intra-party democracy demands in Danish (upper panel), Norwegian (middle panel) and Swedish (lower panel) parties.

SWEDEN

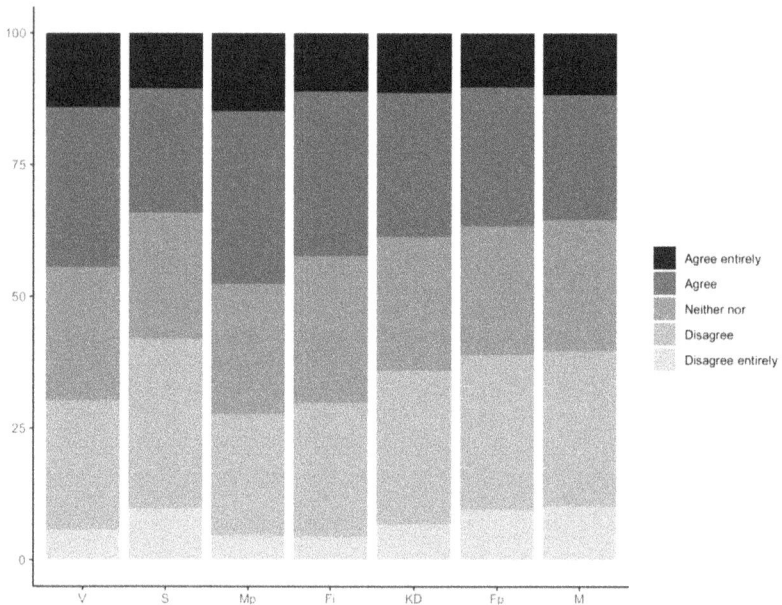

Figure 11.1. (continued)

levels to be negatively associated with preferences for more intra-party democracy because those who are more engaged in the party or even belong to the mid-level elite (because they hold a local office) would not gain more power if more rights were passed to ordinary members. In fact, they would potentially lose power. Age and gender serve as very basic demographic control variables. For Denmark and Sweden, the activity variable is an ordinal variable that measured the hours spent on party activity per month, while we have a different measure available in Norway. Activity levels here are measured through a question that asked members to indicate how often they had participated in 'branch meetings, seminars, gatherings, parties' during the past year. Responses were measured on a five-point ordinal scale ranging from once to more than twenty times.

RESULTS

Figure 11.2 first shows a portion of the data that was already presented in chapter 5. However, this figure is restricted to the positions of members and candidates alone and to the three countries of interest for this particular chapter. To quickly repeat, the results show that the average distances between candidates and members in Sweden

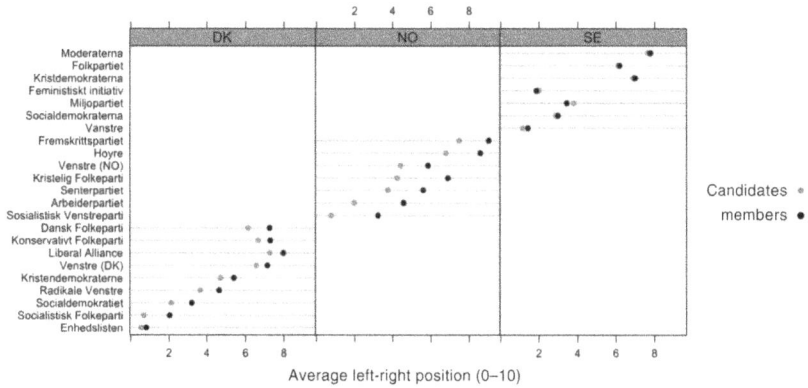

Figure 11.2.   Left-right self-placement of candidates and members across parties and countries.

seem to be generally smaller compared to differences in the other countries. Interestingly, among Danish and Norwegian parties, candidates seem to be consistently more left leaning than their own members – irrespective of the general political leaning of the party. Across all three countries, we see substantial variation in the level of ideological (dis)agreement between the average candidates' and members' positions.

But to what extent are these distances related to members' preferences for more power within the party? According to our hypothesis, members who are more ideologically distant from their party's candidate should prefer to forgo delegation and demand more direct power for members. We test our individual-level hypotheses by estimating several random intercept ordinary least square regression models (for the Danish and Swedish data) and general linear mixed-effects models (for the Norwegian data because of the binary nature of the dependent variable) with party as the grouping variable in order to deal with the nested structure of the data. With the exception of binary measures, we standardized all independent variables to a mean of 0 and a variance of 1 to facilitate comparisons (Gelman 2008).

We first test our hypothesis with respect to absolute ideological incongruence in all three countries with comparable variables across models. With respect to our central variable of interest, model 1 and model 3 on the Danish and Swedish data, respectively, show that ideological disagreement between a party member and the mean position of that party's parliamentary candidates has a positive and significant effect on the dependent variable. According to the models' results, it is also the strongest predictor of members demanding more influence. Although we cannot make any causal claims, this is consistent with our hypothesis that a larger ideological gap between a party member and the party's candidates will be associated with more support for membership-based decision-making within the party. And although the coefficient on incongruence is also positive in the Norwegian case, it is not statistically significant and thus does not support our hypothesis. Table 11.1

Table 11.1. Results of modelling support for party membership decision-making in Denmark, Norway and Sweden: Random intercept regressions with coefficients and standard errors.

	DK		NO		SE	
	B	Std. error	Log-odds	Std. error	B	Std. error
Fixed Parts						
(Intercept)	3.33***	0.12	–2.01 ***	0.14	3.09***	0.05
Age	0.11***	0.02	–0.58***	0.18	–0.09***	0.03
Female	0.07***	0.02	0.29	0.17	–0.06*	0.03
Activity	–0.05 **	0.02	–0.23	0.17	–0.07**	0.03
Incongruence left-right (abs.)	0.10***	0.02	0.30	0.17	0.20***	0.03
Random Parts						
Residual variance		1.036		–		1.309
Variance intercept$_{party}$		0.135		0.054		0.013
N$_{party}$		9		7		7
Observations		15,137		1,227		8,000
R^2 / Tjur's D		0.133		0.019		0.024
AIC		43,552.102		969.797		24,889.645

Notes: *** p<0.01, ** p<0.05, * p<0.1.
DVs: 'Membership ballots are necessary to strengthen party democracy' (DK); 'On major and important matters, the decision should depend on the results of a binding ballot in which all members may vote' (1 = selected, 0 = national congress final say [with and without advisory ballot by members]) (NO); 'The most important decisions should be taken directly by all members' (SE).

further shows that across all three countries, the only uniform pattern that emerges for the control variables is that activity levels are negatively correlated with support for more member power, and significantly so in Denmark and Sweden: more active party members are less likely to favour members taking the most important decisions. This could be related to role of those members within the party since members who report spending a lot of time on party work are also likely to hold an office in the party.

Some results change when we include other relevant variables in the model. In table 11.2, we estimate similar models based on the Norwegian data and Swedish data but this time making use of additional variables likely connected to intra-party disagreement and demands for more intra-party democracy available across the surveys: immigration attitudes and leadership dissatisfaction. We already know that dissatisfaction with leadership affects party members' exit and voice behaviour (Kölln and Polk 2017; Polk and Kölln 2018; van Haute and Carty 2012; see also chapter 7), and we therefore control for general leadership dissatisfaction, working from the expectation that less satisfaction with leadership will also increase

Table 11.2. Results of modelling support for party membership decision-making in Norway and Sweden: Random intercept mixed-effects with coefficients and standard errors.

	Model 1 (NO)		Model 2 (NO)		Model 3 (SE)		Model 4 (SE)	
	Log-odds	Std. error	Log-odds	Std. error	B	Std. error	B	Std. error
Fixed Parts								
(Intercept)	-2.03***	0.17	-2.17***	0.23	3.09***	0.05	3.09***	0.06
Age	-0.63***	0.18	-0.72***	0.19	-0.09***	0.03	-0.07*	0.03
Female	0.32	0.17	0.35*	0.18	-0.06*	0.03	-0.03	0.03
Activity	-0.23	0.17	-0.22	0.18	-0.06*	0.03	-0.05	0.03
Incongruence left-right (abs.)	0.28	0.17	0.36*	0.18	0.18***	0.03	0.17***	0.03
Incongruence immigration (abs.)	0.45*	0.18	0.41*	0.18	0.17***	0.03	0.15***	0.03
Dissatisfaction leader	–	–	1.22***	0.18	–	–	0.34***	0.03
Random Parts								
Residual variance	–		–		1.302		1.277	
Variance intercept$_{party}$	0.106		0.273		0.014		0.024	
N$_{party}$	7		7		7		7	
Observations	1,227		1,227		8,000		8,000	
Tjur's D/ R^2	0.026		0.081		0.029		0.048	
AIC	965.722		917.507		24,849.072		24,700.497	

Notes: *** $p<0.01$ ** $p<0.05$, * $p<0.1$. Data not available for Denmark.

demand for individual member influence. In the Norwegian survey, leadership dissatisfaction was measured with a five-point support scale for the statement 'The central party leadership is good at paying attention to the views of ordinary party members'. The Swedish membership survey asked directly about general satisfaction with the party leadership on a five-point scale. In both cases, we reversed the coding to measure dissatisfaction with the expectation that those members who are generally dissatisfied with the leadership will also be more likely to demand more influence and might see themselves as ideologically more distant from the next level of representation, that is, candidates. We again control for members' age, gender and activity levels, and include general dissatisfaction with the party leadership.

Despite some differences in survey items between the Swedish and Norwegian surveys, the results are surprisingly similar. Table 11.2 shows that older members tend not to support more grass-roots' decision-making power. But they also show for our variables of interest, first, that incongruence between members and candidates on the specific issue of cultural immigration has an independent effect on support for more membership power (models 1 and 3). It suggests that the contentious issue of immigration matters for members' demand for more influence within parties in these two countries. Second, the results of models 2 and 4 also show that this effect diminishes in size only slightly once we control for leadership dissatisfaction. What is more, model 2 on the Norwegian data also now shows a statistically significant effect of general left-right incongruence on more membership power within the party. On the basis of these most fully specified models on the Norwegian and Swedish data, it appears that members do take the chain of representation seriously and increase their support for more membership influence when their party candidates' have divergent attitudes on the general left-right dimension and immigration. These results are supportive of our hypothesis. In this context, it is worth mentioning that neither of these incongruence measures was the strongest predictor but that instead leadership dissatisfaction turned out to be the strongest correlate of members' desire to have more intra-party influence in Norwegian and Swedish parties.

Finally, and in order to potentially get more insight into the extent to which disagreement over particular issues is important, we bring a measure of incongruence on EU attitudes that is only available in Sweden in the fourth model. Table 11.3 documents that when we include the measure of EU incongruence, the sizes of the coefficients for the other substantive variables are reduced, and also that EU incongruence has a positive and statistically significant association with support for more intra-party influence for members. This further supports our hypothesis about the relationship between ideological disagreement and demand for more voice within the party from members because even when controlling for disagreement in individual issues, member-candidate incongruence on general ideology is still positively related to demand for more intra-party democracy.

Table 11.3. Results of modelling support for party membership decision-making in Sweden: Random intercept mixed-effects with coefficients and standard errors.

	SE	
	B	Std. error
Fixed Parts		
(Intercept)	3.08***	0.06
Age	–0.06*	0.03
Female	–0.02	0.03
Activity	–0.05	0.02
Incongruence left-right (abs.)	0.15***	0.03
Incongruence immigration (abs.)	0.13***	0.03
Dissatisfaction leadership	0.32***	0.03
Incongruence EU (abs.)	0.16***	0.03
Random Parts		
Residual variance	1.272	
Variance intercept$_{party}$	0.024	
N_{party}	7	
Observations	8,000	
R^2	0.052	
AIC	24,666.448	

Notes: *** $p<0.01$, ** $p<0.05$, * $p<0.1$.

DISCUSSION

This chapter set out to compare the ideological preferences of party members and candidates for parliament in Scandinavian countries. We combined party membership surveys from Denmark, Norway and Sweden with data from the Comparative Candidate Surveys in the same countries in order to examine the relationship between ideological disagreement (which we call incongruence) and party members voicing more demand for more intra-party democracy within their political party. Based on exit, voice and loyalty theory and institutionalist theory, our central proposition was that larger distances between a party member and the mean position of that member's parliamentary candidates would be associated with greater demand for membership-based decision-making within the party. The results of the analyses are consistent with our hypothesis on general left-right placement and for all three countries: with increasing ideological incongruence between members and candidates, party members are more likely to voice their dissatisfaction and express a preference for increased intra-party membership influence. Our more detailed analyses on individual issues in Norway and Sweden also indicate that larger distances between party members and candidates on immigration preferences (both countries) and a separate item on European integration (only Sweden) have independent associations with member preferences for more grass-roots' decision-making power.

The harmonization of party membership surveys in European countries is still in its early stages. In this chapter, we have wrestled with differences in question wording, survey mode and survey timing that complicate comparative analysis and substantially qualify the generalizability of our findings. Nevertheless, progress is being made on this front, and this chapter (chapter 1, pg. 2) presents a fuller comparison of members and candidates for parliament across these countries. The relationship between party members and parliamentary candidates remains a promising area for future research on party-based representation across Europe.

This book is centrally concerned with understanding the role of party members in contemporary political parties in four areas: reach, representation, activity and influence. These sub-topics all serve the more general purpose of examining whether or not 'parties organize effective member-based linkages between civil society and the state'. Our results speak most clearly to questions related to the themes of representation and influence and provide preliminary support for the idea that ideological disagreements between parties and candidates for office, and thus issues related to the representational function of parties, have consequences for how members view their connection to their party and how they choose to express themselves within the organization. Members' demands for more influence within their party also seem to be connected to how well the party works in representing their preferences.

NOTES

1. Authors are listed in alphabetical order; both authors contributed equally and to all parts of the chapter. The authors received funding from the Swedish Research Council project 2016-01810.

2. Table 11.A1 in the appendix lists the number of respondents per party and country.

3. For more information on the candidate surveys, please visit: http://www.comparative candidates.org.

BIBLIOGRAPHY

Andreadis, Ioannis and Yannis Stavrakakis. 2017. 'European Populist Parties in Government: How Well Are Voters Represented? Evidence from Greece'. *Swiss Political Science Review* 23 (4): 485–508.

Bakker, Ryan, Seth Jolly and Jonathan Polk. 2012. 'Complexity in the European Party Space: Exploring Dimensionality with Experts'. *European Union Politics* 13 (2): 219–45.

———. 2018. 'Multidimensional Incongruence and Vote Switching in Europe'. *Public Choice* 176 (1–2): 267–96.

Bolin, Niklas, Nicholas Aylott, Benjamin von dem Berge and Thomas Poguntke. 2017. 'Patterns of Intra-Party Democracy across the World'. In *Organizing Political Parties:*

Representation, Participation, and Power, edited by Susan E. Scarrow, Paul Webb and Thomas Poguntke, 158–86. Oxford: Oxford University Press.

Borre, Ole and Jørgen Goul Andersen. 1997. *Voting and Political Attitudes in Denmark: A Study of the 1994 Election*. Aarhus: Aarhus Universitetsforlag.

Bruter, Michael and Sarah Harrison. 2009. 'Tomorrow's Leaders? Understanding the Involvement of Young Party Members in Six European Democracies'. *Comparative Political Studies* 42 (10): 1259–91.

CCS. 2016. Comparative Candidates Survey Module I – 2005–2013 [Dataset – cumulative file]. Distributed by FORS, Lausanne, 2016.

———. 2018. Comparative Candidates Survey Module II – 2013–2016 [Dataset – cumulative file]. Distributed by FORS, Lausanne, 2018.

Clark, William Roberts, Matt Golder and Sona N. Golder. 2017. 'The British Academy Brian Barry Prize Essay: An Exit, Voice and Loyalty Model of Politics'. *British Journal of Political Science* 47 (4): 719–48.

Costello, Rory, Jacques Thomassen and Martin Rosema. 2012. 'European Parliament Elections and Political Representation: Policy Congruence between Voters and Parties'. *West European Politics* 35 (6): 1226–48.

Cross, William P. and Richard S. Katz. 2013. *The Challenges of Intra-Party Democracy*. Oxford: Oxford University Press.

Gelman, Andrew. 2008. 'Scaling Regression Inputs by Dividing by Two Standard Deviations'. *Statistics in Medicine* 27: 2865–73.

Hirschman, Albert. 1970. *Exit, Voice, and Loyalty: Responses to Decline in Firms, Organizations, and States*. Cambridge, MA: Harvard University Press.

Hobolt, Sara B. and Catherine E. de Vries. 2015. 'Issue Entrepreneurship and Multiparty Competition'. *Comparative Political Studies* 48 (9): 1159–85.

Hobolt, Sara B. and James Tilley. 2016. 'Fleeing the Centre: The Rise of Challenger Parties in the Aftermath of the Euro Crisis'. *West European Politics* 39 (5): 971–91.

Jupskås, Anders and Knut Heidar. 2009. Norwegian Party Member Survey 2009. Department of Political Science, University of Oslo.

Katz, Richard S. and Peter Mair. 1995. 'Changing Models of Party Organization and Party Democracy: The Emergence of the Cartel Party'. *Party Politics* 1 (1): 5–28.

———. 2009. 'The Cartel Party Thesis: A Restatement'. *Perspectives on Politics* 7 (4): 753–66.

Kölln, Ann-Kristin. 2016. 'Party Membership in Europe: Testing Party-Level Explanations of Decline'. *Party Politics* 22 (4): 465–77.

———. 2017. 'Has Party Members' Representativeness Changed over Time?' In *Larmar Och Gör Sig till. SOM-Undersökningen 2016, SOM-Rapport Nr 70*, edited by Ulrika Andersson, Jonas Ohlsson, Henrik Oscarsson and Maria Oskarson, 387–400. Gothenburg: SOM-Institut.

Kölln, Ann-Kristin and Jonathan Polk. 2017. 'Emancipated Party Members: Examining Ideological Incongruence within Political Parties'. *Party Politics* 23 (1): 18–29.

Kosiara-Pedersen, Karina. 2016. 'Why Are Members on the Way Out of Their Political Youth Organization?' University of Gothenburg Centre for European Research Working Paper Series, 2016:8.

———. 2017. *Demokratiets ildsjæle – Partimedlemmer i Danmark*. København: Djøf Forlag.

Kriesi, Hanspeter, Edgar Grande, Romain Lachat, Martin Dolezal, Simon Bornschier and Timotheos Frey. 2006. 'Globalization and the Transformation of the National Political

Space: Six European Countries Compared'. *European Journal of Political Research* 45 (6): 921–56.

Leimgruber, Philipp, Dominik Hangartner and Lucas Leemann. 2010. 'Comparing Candidates and Citizens in the Ideological Space'. *Swiss Political Science Review* 16 (J3): 499–531.

Lijphart, Arend. 2012. *Patterns of Democracy: Government Forms and Performance in Thirty-Six Countries*, 2nd ed. New Haven, CT: Yale University Press.

Lundell, Krister. 2004. 'Determinants of Candidate Selection: The Degree of Centralization in Comparative Perspective'. *Party Politics* 10 (1): 25–47.

May, John D. 1973. 'Opinion Structures of Political Parties: The Special Law of Curvilinear Disparity'. *Political Studies* 21: 135–51.

Müller, Wolfgang C. 2000. 'Political Parties in Parliamentary Democracies: Making Delegation and Accountability Work'. *European Journal of Political Research* 37: 309–33.

Müller, Wolfgang C. and Richard S. Katz. 1997. 'Party as Linkage'. *European Journal of Political Research* 31: 169–78.

Narud, Hanne Marthe and Audun Skare. 1999. 'Are Party Activists the Party Extremists? The Structure of Opinion in Political Parties'. *Scandinavian Political Studies* 22 (1): 45–65.

Neto, Octavio Amorim and Kaare Strøm. 2006. 'Breaking the Parliamentary Chain of Delegation: Presidents and Non-Partisan Cabinet Members'. *British Journal of Political Science* 36 (4): 619–43.

Pardos-Prado, Sergi. 2015. 'How Can Mainstream Parties Prevent Niche Party Success? Center-Right Parties and the Immigration Issue'. *The Journal of Politics* 77 (2): 352–67.

Poguntke, Thomas, Susan E. Scarrow, Paul D. Webb, Elin H. Allern, Nicholas Aylott, Ingrid van Biezen, Enrico Calossi et al. 2016. 'Party Rules, Party Resources and the Politics of Parliamentary Democracies'. *Party Politics* 22 (6): 661–78.

Polk, Jonathan and Ann-Kristin Kölln. 2018. 'Electoral Infidelity: Why Party Members Cast Defecting Votes'. *European Journal of Political Research* 57 (2): 539–60.

Scarrow, Susan E. and Burcu Gezgor. 2010. 'Declining Memberships, Changing Members? European Political Party Members in a New Era'. *Party Politics* 16 (6): 823–43.

Scarrow, Susan E., Paul Webb and David M. Farrell. 2000. 'From Social Integration to Electoral Contestation: The Changing Distribution of Power within Political Parties'. In *Parties without Partisans: Political Change in Advanced Industrial Democracies*, edited by Russell J. Dalton and Martin P. Wattenberg, 129–53. Oxford: Oxford University Press.

Schumacher, Gijs and Nathalie Giger. 2017. 'Who Leads the Party? On Membership Size, Selectorates and Party Oligarchy'. *Political Studies* 65 (IS): 162–81.

Shugart, Matthew Søberg, Melody Ellis Valdini and Kati Suominen. 2005. 'Looking for Locals: Voter Information Demands and Personal Vote-Earning Attributes of Legislators under Proportional Representation'. *American Journal of Political Science* 49 (2): 437–49.

van Biezen, Ingrid, Peter Mair and Thomas Poguntke. 2012. 'Going, Going, . . . Gone? The Decline of Party Membership in Contemporary Europe'. *European Journal of Political Research* 51 (1): 24–56.

van de Wardt, Marc. 2014. 'Putting the Damper On: Do Parties De-emphasize Issues in Response to Internal Divisions among Their Supporters?' *Party Politics* 20 (3): 330–40.

van Haute, Emilie and Anika Gauja, eds. 2015. *Party Members and Activists*. Oxon: Routledge.

van Haute, Emilie and R. Kenneth Carty. 2012. 'Ideological Misfits: A Distinctive Class of Party Members'. *Party Politics* 18 (6): 885–95.

Widfeldt, Anders. 1995. 'Party Membership and Party Representativeness'. In *Citizens and the State*, edited by Hans-Dieter Klingemann and Dieter Fuchs, 134–82. Oxford: Oxford University Press.

———. 1999. 'Losing Touch? The Political Representativeness of Swedish Parties, 1985–1994'. *Scandinavian Political Studies* 22: 307–26.

Willumsen, David M. and Patrik Öhberg. 2017. 'Toe the Line, Break the Whip: Explaining Floor Dissent in Parliamentary Democracies'. *West European Politics* 40 (4): 688–716.

Wolkenstein, Fabio. 2018. 'Membership Ballots and the Value of Intra-Party Democracy'. *Critical Review of International Social and Political Philosophy* 21 (4): 433–55.

Appendix

Table 11.A1. Frequency distribution of respondents per party and country in the Comparative Candidate Survey.

STUDY		N
Denmark	Enhedslisten	59
(2011)	Socialistisk Folkeparti	46
	Socialdemokratiet	35
	Radikale Venstre	35
	Kristendemokraterne	46
	Liberal Alliance	36
	Venstre	40
	Konservativt Folkeparti	36
	Dansk Folkeparti	42
Norway	Sosialistisk Venstreparti	155
(2009)	Arbeiderpartiet	150
	Senterpartiet	147
	Kristelig Folkeparti	140
	Venstre	136
	Hoyre	131
	Fremskrittpartiet	147
Sweden	Vanstre	328
(2014)	Socialdemokraterna	307
	Miljopartiet	289
	Feministisk initiativ	20
	Kristdemokraterna	189
	Folkpartiet	264
	Moderaterna	327

V

CONCLUSION

12

The Current State and Future Challenges of Nordic Party Membership Linkage

Marie Demker, Knut Heidar and Karina Kosiara-Pedersen

Political parties provide a unique linkage between the elected and the electors, between those who rule and those who are ruled. While party member organizations are not necessary for democracies to work, they have provided the backbone of most parties for the past 100 years. In particular, in the heyday of the mass party model, party membership organizations seemed essential to the workings of parties. However, parties as membership organizations are currently challenged by trends towards professionalization, personalization, individualization and digitalization of politics.

In recent decades, the Nordic countries have seen the rise of more parties while at the same time parties have suffered a loss of members. Old cleavages and interest-based politics have lost their supremacy, and electoral volatility has increased. Party democracy is, on the one hand, strengthened by the creation of new parties, which means that citizens' interests in society are better represented. On the other hand, the proportion of citizens who are members in a political party is decreasing. Politics has entered the digital age, the level of political interest is very high (Bergström and Oscarsson 2016), and there is no sign of decreasing trust in Nordic democracy (van der Meer 2017). At the same time, the will to join organizations for long-term projects, to further broad political agendas or to participate in the not-so-glamorous world of negotiations and meetings, is declining (van Biezen and Poguntke 2014). There is also a growing group of citizens expressing dissatisfaction with democracy and their own life prospect, both through elections and in opinion polls (Oskarson and Demker 2015; Rydgren 2013). The paradox is that, from a democratic point of view, we see signs of both a healthy party democracy and a party democracy in decline.

Hence, now is the time to take stock and analyse the current state of party membership linkage. In this book, we explore and describe how the political parties in the Nordic countries encounter these turbulent times for democracy and the party systems. From different angles, we analyse and discuss whether *members in political parties today, despite the fading of party membership numbers, provide Nordic party democracy with the kind of linkage that supports a sustainable democracy.*

The Nordic countries are old, well-anchored party-based democracies, more or less built on an ideal of society where democratic linkage is provided through parties' aggregation, articulation and canalization of voters' interests and members' engagement in party organizations. Despite great changes and transformative processes, the Nordic party democracies have been a stable foundation for parliamentary power and government. Studying the Nordic countries, and in particular the three Scandinavian countries, means that we analyse party membership linkage in similar but not identical systems. They are not exceptional cases compared to other European countries. Hence, the analysis of Nordic party membership linkage provides a transparent setting for discussions of the causal impact of a number of relevant factors, even if we are not able to control systematically for critical factors like public party finance, media structure and electoral system. While parties' participatory linkages have favourable conditions in the Nordic countries, they are not 'critical cases' in the sense that negative findings here indicate that linkage in other countries is impossible. However, due to the conditions favourable to party membership linkage in what are still predominantly traditionally organized 'mass' parties in the Nordic countries, it follows that if party membership linkage is crumbling here, it may also be at risk in most other developed democracies. Hence, we find that useful lessons may be drawn from the Nordic comparisons – lessons that are relevant for parties in other societies with a well-educated, affluent and highly volatile electorate.

In this chapter, we first draw conclusions about the current state of Nordic party membership linkage and thereby provide a response to the question of whether members in political parties today, despite declining party membership numbers, provide Nordic party democracy with the kind of linkage that will support a sustainable democracy. In the second part of the conclusion, we discuss the implications of these findings. What are the current challenges for party membership linkage in the Nordic countries?

THE STATE OF NORDIC PARTY MEMBERSHIP LINKAGE

The purpose of this first part is to pull the threads together and draw conclusions about the current state of Nordic party membership linkage. Hence, we respond to our overall question on whether members in political parties today provide Nordic party democracy with the kind of linkage that will support a sustainable democracy. The four themes through which we analyse party membership linkage will also structure this conclusion, namely (1) reach (membership, and recruitment), (2) representation (social and ideological), (3) activity (participation and activism) and, finally, (4) influence (decision-making and power relations).

Reach

The first aspect of party membership linkage analysed is primarily an organizational characteristic and indicates the level of party reach within civil society. Broader reach indicates a stronger potential and a stronger base for party membership linkage. Membership figures and the member/electorate ratio show the extent to which parties have recruited and kept members, and party member motivations for enrolment show the human base for party linkage.

In chapter 2, Bolin, Kosiara-Pedersen and Kristinsson analyse trends in the party membership figures in the Nordic parties. The main picture is one of decline. Between 3 and 5 per cent of the electorates in Denmark, Finland, Norway and Sweden are registered as traditional, dues-paying party members today. Iceland stands out from the overall Nordic trend, with an increasing membership since the 1990s and a current enrolment level of 30 to 40 per cent (M/E). The obvious explanation for the Icelandic exceptionalism is that the mass party never took root among Icelandic parties, and many of their members do not join to spend time at party events but only to select party candidates at public primaries. This is more of an American-type party affiliation, and the introduction of primaries has no doubt created a larger member reach for the Icelandic parties than for the other Nordic parties.

There are important differences between the parties. The old Nordic social cleavage parties – in particular social democrats and agrarians – have been declining, whereas newer (post-1960) parties, like green and radical right parties, are on the rise. Their rise, however, is moderate, not bringing them on par with the old parties in terms of M/E ratios. Still, we see a convergence in old and new parties.

Declining membership figures is a warning sign for the state of party membership linkage. Party democracy is affected by a yet smaller part of the citizenry participating in the party organizations. Old movement parties are the most exposed to this trend. However, with the growth of new parties, more – and possibly – different types of voters are attracted to join. Some parties also enable other forms of affiliation (at least on paper but, for most parties, not much in practice).

Turning to the 'why membership' question, in chapter 3, Heidar and Kosiara-Pedersen find that party members are recruited among all age groups, hence, even though parties are recruiting among the young in particular, a substantial proportion of party members enrol after turning fifty. We consider it a sign of relative strength when parties are able to recruit among different age groups. While members enrolled while young may provide the backbone of the party member organization for years to come, the recruitment of older party members indicates that parties serve as a channel of participation that politically interested citizens deem open and relevant. Party membership linkage is also sustained not only by the members who enrolled in the golden days of the classic mass parties, but also by more recently enrolled members.

The incentives to join parties are primarily ideology and political interests. This is especially so for the smaller parties, parties that are tailored for niche interests or special issues. In all Scandinavian countries, ideology is the most important motive for joining. In Denmark and Sweden, this motive is also stable between generations, while in Norway, younger generations are somewhat less motivated by ideology. There is no indication that career ambition is a growing motivation, a trend that could have strengthened a tendency towards professionalization and personalization of party membership linkage.

In Denmark and Norway, there is a limited inclination to join as an expression of passive support only. Within this group, this is more the case for the most recent intake of members compared to the older intakes. This, of course, could merely be an expression of not wanting to be integrated into party life from the start. Otherwise, it could potentially harm the activism dimension of party membership linkage. If members enrol merely as an expression of support, parties cannot sustain the participatory aspects of representative democracy.

The ties between social groups and parties have loosened, social mobility is up, and politics have become more individualized. Still, there is an element of heritage in party membership. In Denmark and Norway, the figures show that Four out of ten (DK) and Five out of ten (*N*) members already had a family member in a party. Children do not necessarily enrol in the same parties as their parents, but children of party members are more likely to enrol in a party. This heritage pattern is particularly strong among social democrats and christian democrats. In addition, the social milieu, taken as a whole including friends and work colleagues, is important for joining.

Declining membership figures no doubt narrow the reach of parties. However, the resilience of Nordic cleavage parties, the rise of new membership-based parties, and the members' motivation to participate and bring forward political issues suggest at least a continued linkage potential.

Representation

The social and ideological profile of party members is central to the issue of linkage as it shows how well parties are anchored socially and politically in society. Hence, we analyse both descriptive and substantive representation.

Heidar, Kristinsson, Saarinen, Koivula and Keipi analyse in chapter 4 who the Nordic party members are and the extent to which they are socially representative of their parties' voters. Analysing the members' socio-demographic background, they find large differences between the social profiles of the individual parties. This shows up in terms of gender, education, religious affiliations and occupational sector. In spite of these different party profiles, however, the members of individual parties largely mirror the profiles of the party voters. Exceptions are that men are over-represented in nearly all parties, especially in the parties on the right, and party members have higher education than the party voters. But apart from gender and education, most parties have a high or medium similarity to their voters. The Nordic party members are in fact fairly ordinary citizens; they do not appear to be particularly elitist. Icelandic parties have the highest level of member-voter congruence,

Norwegian parties have the lowest. There is no clear relationship between size of party membership and degree of member representativeness.

In chapter 5, Kölln and Polk compare political profiles of party voters, party members and party candidates on the general left-right dimension. They analyse patterns of relative agreement between the party levels in four Nordic countries, Finland excluded. Members and voters are by and large in agreement on their ideological preferences. Comparing candidates and members, there seems to be more variation, and candidates from all parties in Denmark and Norway place themselves to the left of the members. They do not find systematic evidence for May's law in the Nordic countries, although in some parties, the members are in fact more extreme. The agreement levels imply that party members seem to provide an adequate linkage and channel of communication. Party members do not seem to distort the political interests and policy positions of party voters.

In chapter 6, Blombäck, Hinnfors and Jupskås map the extent to which members in Scandinavian parties agree internally on 'old' and 'new' issues. The question is whether the member profiles send a clear (or blurred) political message on party policy intentions to the prospective voters. The chapter shows that party members basically agree on key political issues like economic policies, immigration, the environment, law and order and the EU. In terms of member unity, there are small differences between the countries and between old and new parties. Members in the different party families basically agree on issues they care about, but they are more diverse on issues that are not so central to the party (but which may be central to other parties). The social democrats are cohesive on economic issues but not on the new issues of immigration and the environment. Radical right parties are cohesive on immigration but divided on left-right issues. Parties towards the ends of the political dimensions are most cohesive; extreme parties are not catch-all.

In sum, the main conclusion is that, despite declining membership, Nordic political parties are representative of their voters along both descriptive and political dimensions. The member profiles signal clear political alternatives to the voters. Party membership linkage is not seriously skewed in regard to either descriptive or substantive representation.

Activity

Membership figures have traditionally been *the* measure of parties' participatory linkages. This rests on the premise, however, that signing up for membership actually indicates member activism within and for the party. As we have seen, not all members are active, and among those that are, party activism varies in degree, type and quality both within and among parties and over time. Some degree of member participation is clearly necessary to enable linkage between voters and party elites.

In chapter 7, Heidar and Kosiara-Pedersen analyse member participation within and outside of the parties. They find that about four out of five members in the Scandinavian parties are active in a range of internal and external party activities.

One in five do not participate at all (or at least do not report it in the surveys). A large majority of Scandinavian party members do attend party meetings and are active as ambassadors for their party. About two-thirds of the party members attend meetings or nomination processes.

The overall picture is that the old party families – like the conservatives, social democrats and liberals – have the most active members internally. Sweden appears to have party members who are somewhat less interested in internal party activities than Norway and Denmark. In terms of external activities, the pattern is different. Although the lion's share of party members discuss policies and promote their party among friends and non-members, the general level of external activity is much lower than for internal activities. Comparing the Scandinavian countries, party members in Denmark and Norway have a lower activity level in digital and social media than in Sweden. Handing out leaflets for the party is also more common for party members in Sweden than in Denmark and Norway. Studying change in Denmark and Norway, it is found that the share of active party members actually seems to increase slightly. This indicates that, as the overall membership numbers shrink, it is the inactive members who disproportionally disappear from the membership files.

In the follow-up chapter 8, Heidar and Kosiara-Pedersen analyse the main dimensions, or patterns, in member activism across the Scandinavian parties. They find that two dimensions come through in all the factor analyses. The main dimension in the participation of Scandinavian party members is termed 'party workers' and is characterized by a broad range of activities such as attending meetings, campaign activities, influencing policies and holding office. This party worker dimension is important in linking party and civil society. Second, they find a 'veteran' dimension that captures members who have held party or public office in the past. They also identify a 'party ambassador' dimension in most surveys, covering party activities directed at voters, such as to encourage them to vote for the party and to discuss party policies with non-members online or offline. While the online ambassadors (active in social media) make up a separate dimension in Norway and Sweden, this is not the case in Denmark, which may be explained by the 'older' survey in Denmark (2012 vs. 2015–2017).

Ambassador activities alone are not sustaining a comprehensive party membership linkage; these members do not by default link voters and party decision makers in person. Rather, they communicate the parties' political profiles to the voters; they 'speak for' parties as campaign organizations. In contrast, both the party worker and veteran dimensions are important when assessing the extent to which party members provide linkage. These types of activism make up different types of linkage that together perform vital tasks in linking parties and civil society through the memberships.

Turning to the trend over time, the Danish and Norwegian data show that the online ambassadors are on the rise but that the balance between internal and outreach member activism is about the same over time. Hence, this points towards a member linkage that does not show a transformation of parties into 'campaign machines' putting more emphasis on electoral activities and less on maintaining the membership organization.

In chapter 9, Jupskås and Kosiara-Pedersen analyse why Scandinavian party members participate. The 'why' question helps us understand who engages in various types of activism within party organizations and hence what creates the activist dimension of party membership linkage. They find some, but limited, support for the expectation that resources and participation are positively related. Older members participate less than younger members in all countries, and high education levels are connected to less activism. Among families with children, party activities are fewer and to a greater extent less time-consuming, like campaigning offline or online. Their overall conclusion is that party membership linkage is not further skewed at the activist level, hence pointing towards a stable rather than weak participatory linkage. Party members are a mixed bunch whom parties can mobilize to different types of participation.

Party membership linkage is impaired, however, if active members are merely there to support the leadership. It is also weakened if only those who are satisfied with intra-party democracy participate, as this will create a passive followership, not an engaged channel of participation. In the chapter, the authors find a weak link between supporting a 'mass party' participatory culture and participation, and mixed results on a link between satisfaction with intra-party democracy and participation. In sum, party membership linkage is not seriously harmed by participation dominated by 'party leadership pleasers'.

There is a strong link between parties and civil society organizations. Being integrated in civil society has a positive impact on party member participation; party members in all the Scandinavian countries are also very active in other organizations. The historical links between civil society organizations and parties can, in other words, also be found at the individual level. This is an important point in regard to party membership linkage.

Party members are broadly engaged citizens; their party activism generally supports traditional party linkage; and the participation is not skewed in favour of social elites. However, due to declining membership figures, it is a weakened linkage; the party reach is reduced.

Influence

A well-functioning participatory linkage requires some degree of intra-party democracy. Hence, whether party elites pay attention to and are willing to adjust their policies, on the basis of internal party decision-making processes, is essential. Formally, party members are increasingly included in core intra-party decision-making processes such as leader and candidate selections (Cross and Pilet 2014), and this could indicate an increased linkage through party member organizations. However, we need to know how changes in decision-making processes play out in practice, whether there is a correspondence between the formal and de facto intra-party democracy.

Bolin and Kosiara-Pedersen study in chapter 10 how party members perceive the level of intra-party democracy in the three Scandinavian countries. They find that members are generally satisfied with the level of intra-party democracy. Norwegian party members are more satisfied than the Swedes and the Danes. Norwegian parties also have a higher level of formal intra-party democracy. Possibly, both formal organization and party practice contribute to forming members' experiences.

Differences between party families are small. Not even the green parties, which typically seem to promote a more bottom-up type of organization, show any notable difference in members' satisfaction with intra-party democracy. However, members of the christian democratic parties are somewhat more content than others, while members of the social democratic parties seem a little less satisfied. There is also a tendency for members of parties to the right, together with the social democratic parties, to agree more with the idea of 'supporting the leadership', while the members in left parties and the liberal parties tend to want more influence.

With no large differences between countries and party families, individual-level factors seem to be important when explaining perceptions of intra-party democracy. First, party members' engagement with the party, that is, office holding and meeting attendance, does not strongly correlate with a positive perception of intra-party democracy. Party membership linkage is not made up only of satisfied members, which bodes well for sustaining a lively linkage. Second, party members' expectations of intra-party influence, however, seem to be important for perceptions of intra-party democracy. It is not only the formal level of intra-party democracy as found in the party statutes and the experience of party praxis that explain perception of intra-party democracy. Some party members *expect* more than others. Third, party members' political distance from the party mean is linked to how they perceive intra-party democracy: The greater the distance between party members' self- and party placement on the left-right dimension, the more dissatisfied they are with intra-party democracy. If they disagree with their party, they also seem to participate more, even if at the same time they are more likely to consider leaving their party. Political disagreement seems to have major implications for the character of party membership linkage. Finally, female members are generally more positive about intra-party democracy than male members. While the impact of this is not expected to be huge, it may point to more satisfied membership in parties with more women-friendly cultures and decreasing gender gaps, as seems to be more the case in Norway and Sweden than in Denmark (cf. chapter 9).

In the last empirical chapter (chapter 11), Kölln and Polk study the extent to which the chain of representation within parties is connected to demands for intra-party democracy. Their findings suggest that a high level of member-candidate disagreement on ideology and issues is associated with greater demand for more membership voice in internal party decision-making. Hence, while party members' disagreement is correlated with dissatisfaction with intra-party democracy (cf. chapter 10), Kölln and Polk show that this incongruence leads to party members asking for more intra-party democracy. Together, chapters 10 and 11 provide strong evidence that the demand for intra-party democracy is greater among party members somewhat out of line with the mainstream party, and hence also that there are likely to be policy implications of granting party members a larger say. If parties choose to enhance their party membership linkage with higher levels of intra-party democracy, it is likely that those who are more at odds with party policies will make use of it. However, political disagreement is also linked to exit considerations, hence, among party members who are somewhat out of line with their party, both voice and exit are feasible options.

In sum, party members seem sufficiently satisfied with the level of intra-party democracy for party membership linkage to work. We may also note, however, that there is some variation among members and parties. Being a demanding party member in a top-steered party and holding political opinions that are at a certain distance from the party's ideological position will make one dissatisfied. On the other hand, being a member with rather low expectations for influencing party decisions and feeling close to the left-right position of the party surely will make one more satisfied. For neither position does it matter how formal rules regulate members' influence.

Challenges of Party Membership Linkage

The Nordic countries are (still) party democracies, and their party organizations provide society and political institutions with democratic linkage through elections and members. While not without flaws, Nordic party membership linkage does seem to work even with reduced membership figures. Party membership linkage is not as strong as before, and it could be further challenged even in the short run. The purpose of this second, and final, part of the conclusion is to discuss the implications of our findings.

Nordic parties still provide a linkage that is necessary for party democracy as understood within the European 'two-pillar' democracy model. Most importantly, in spite of declining membership, the parties have managed to maintain their represent-ability vis-à-vis the voters. There are no signs that a declining membership implies that today's membership is unrepresentative of the parties' voters. However, there are concerns about how party linkage is affected by the relationship between modes of activity and claims of influence. New forms of party management, individualization, professionalization and, maybe, higher expectations among the members themselves may have a strong impact on how parties maintain their task of articulating and channelling voter interests.

Party Systems and the New Parties

Although the Nordic countries have seen the rise of some new party families during the late twentieth century – like the greens, populist right parties, Christian parties, feminist parties and pirate parties – the older parties hold on and are still the most likely to form government. However, older parties are losing ground and newer parties are gaining both electorally (Kosiara-Pedersen and Kurrild-Klitgaard 2018; Rocha 2018) and (relatively) in terms of membership. New parties improve membership linkage as they recruit members, a part of which would not otherwise sign up and be engaged in parties. Moreover, these new parties do not – at least in the Nordic parliamentary parties – form party membership linkage in a radically different way. Looking at the party systems in the Nordic countries, one could argue that these systems, taken as a whole, have improved in both *political* reach (which is not the same as numerical voter reach, cf. chapter 2) and representation, but maybe not so much regarding activity and influence. Most populist right parties in the Nordic countries have more hierarchical organizations than the older parties, and these parties have been the most electorally successful among the new parties (Hooghe and Marks 2018; Kriesi 2014). Hence, the membership challenges of older 'mass' parties also apply to newer parties, possibly with the exception of some of the newly formed parties such as the Danish Alternativet and the pirate parties.

Political Parties Adapt

Political parties adapt. As parties transform both their environment and themselves, they will be able to meet the challenge of declining traditional membership. Peter Mair has argued that political parties have an outstanding ability to change their environments in ways that make them sustainable, regardless of the demands and liabilities of democracy (Mair 1997). Parties are crucial in maintaining Nordic parliamentary democracy and – if threatened – will most likely meet the changing social environments with reorganized membership forms.

Linkage will be provided through candidate nomination and campaigning. That also takes place in parties that are more or less without members (Mazzoleni and Voerman 2017) and in highly leader-centred parties (Hopkin and Paolucci 1999; Kefford and McDonnell 2018). As noted in chapter 1, political parties have other ways than member activism to aggregate interests, formulate political proposals, recruit and train political leadership, communicate and campaign. Parties have tried to cope with the fading interests of citizens by developing alternative linkage mechanisms. Through advanced, well-organized opinion polls and work with focus groups, the parties can also learn about the voters' opinions, values and interests. With the help of professional employees (in the central party office and parliament), supporting actors (in friendly interest organizations and sympathizing 'think thanks' and among political stakeholders) and hired public relations consultants (in communications agencies, etc.), political parties can aggregate and articulate these views in concrete policy proposals (Garsten, Rothstein and Svallfors 2015).

The important question is whether, or to what extent, party adaptation will include the participation of members and supporters and the linkage to civil society that they provide – whether parties will sustain a channel of participation that is unique by giving participants a say on policy programmes and candidate nomination. This lies at the heart of electoral, participatory and representative democracy but will also sustain democracy between elections.

The trend towards a decreased focus on parties as channels of participation is far from new. It seems to be the long-term trend in party organization research and political practice as depicted in the party-type literature (Katz and Mair 1995; Kirchheimer 1966; Panebianco 1988). When fewer individuals engage in parties and parties are necessary for political decision-making, it is probably true that electoral-professional organizations are more attractive. Looking ahead, more electoral-professional political parties may try to attract members with low expectations in order not to challenge the authority of the party elite. Parties with a 'traditional' social movement agenda will probably attract members with high expectations that are willing to challenge elites. Whether the former or latter type of party will have the best chances of influencing a national policy agenda is not within the frame of this study, but it will most certainly affect the potential for a democratic linkage. This development may threaten democratic linkage by cutting off the important task of articulating policy demands anchored in specified interest groups.

New Forms of Participatory Linkage

In her book *Beyond Party Members*, Susan Scarrow (2015, 206) sheds light on recent changes in party organizations, including declining membership, and offers a sharp focus on the increase in party members' rights. Today parties have to be accountable, be able to prioritize among tasks, and keep the loyalty of their most devoted party workers – all with a view to being the most attractive team on the electoral market. These changes have made an impact on party organizations. They have not, however, changed the organizations from the bottom but instead added a new model on the top. Digital development has changed both the outreach and the mobilization activities of the party organizations; through social media and the web, it is possible to introduce news, changes and discussions both faster and with a wider reach than before. Digital tools make mobilization easier but at the same time also more individualized. Members are more often expected to participate in intra-party nomination/electoral processes, electing party leaders, nominating candidates and deciding on new electoral platforms (Cross and Pilet 2014; Scarrow 2015, 181–85).

In order to reverse the decreasing membership figures, there has been a tendency in traditional parties to increase the individual rights of members and decrease those of the active mid-level elite. This is particularly seen in regard to leadership selection (Cross and Pilet 2014). This trend has not yet reached the Nordic countries, Iceland excepted. However, such change would have an impact on party membership linkage as this individualizes activism and party member engagement in intra-party processes. While it may broaden participation, it may also limit the extent to which the party membership collectively responds to party leadership. This may provide the dissatisfied members, in particular those that find themselves out of step with their party, with more opportunities to influence party processes, but it is of a more tame nature since individual members are less likely to be able to act in unison to control party leadership than, for example, local officeholders.

The overall trend is to blur the distinction between members and other party supporters. While we initially argue the case of sustaining party membership linkage within the European democracy model, several developments point to parties' adaptation to a form that broadens but at the same time dilutes participation. Parties have opened up to light memberships that entail fewer rights and duties, social media followers, newsletter receivers and fundraisers (Faucher 2015; Gauja 2015; Kosiara-Pedersen and Kristiansen 2016; Kosiara-Pedersen, Scarrow and van Haute 2017; Scarrow 2015). This enables party supporters to affiliate themselves without signing up for full-party membership. With increased electoral volatility, individualization and digitalization of politics, a less demanding form of affiliation seems to fit present-day citizens better than the commitment inherent in traditional party membership. Parties seem to be able to affiliate more supporters when offering these lighter forms even if it implies lower membership figures (Kosiara-Pedersen, Scarrow and van Haute 2017). Although Nordic party members represent their voters reasonably well, cross-national studies show that representativeness may be improved by lowering the costs of party involvement (Achury et al. 2018). Hence, traditional party members – 'as we know them' – may become an endangered species.

Challenges to Democracy at Large

While intra-party democracy and participation are not necessary requirements for representative democracy, the lack of channels of influence and participation may challenge long-term interests, democratic satisfaction, external efficacy and political trust. Between elections, the large majority of voters are (more than) happy to leave party involvement to others. However, in the long run, the link between citizens and parties is crucial for the vitality and sustainability of democracy. It is only through the articulation, formulation and development of policy aimed at addressing social problems that parties offer voters real political alternatives. If the voters as some sort of 'collective average' dominate the parties' image of the citizens, politics become more obliterated and less challenging. If the parties chase the same voters with different interchangeable labels, in social media arenas as well as in the traditional ones, the struggle between the parties becomes a struggle – or 'game' – in its own right (Bjereld et al. 2018). It may be more interesting to watch but less effective in solving social problems.

BIBLIOGRAPHY

Achury, Susan, Susan E. Scarrow, Karina Kosiara-Pedersen and Emilie van Haute. 2018. 'The Consequences of Membership Incentives: Do Greater Political Benefits Attract Different Kinds of Members?' *Party Politics*. Online. https://doi.org/10.1177/13540688187546.

Bergström, Annika and Henrik Oscarsson, eds. 2016. *Swedish Trends 1986–2015*. Report, SOM-Institute, Gothenburg University.

Bjereld, Ulf, Sofie Blombäck, Marie Demker and Linn Sandberg. 2018. *Digital demokrati? Partierna i en ny tid*. Stockholm: Atlas förlag.

Cross, William and Jean-Benoit Pilet 2014. *The Selection of Political Party Leaders in Contemporary Parliamentary Democracies: A Comparative Study*. London: Routledge.

Faucher, Florence. 2015. 'New Forms of Political Participation: Changing Demands or Changing Opportunities to Participate in Political Parties?' *Comparative European Politics* 13: 409–59.

Garsten, Christina, Bo Rothstein and Stefan Svallfors. 2015. *Makt utan mandat. De policyprofessionella i svensk politik*. Stockholm: Dialogos.

Gauja, Anika. 2015. 'The Construction of Party Membership'. *European Journal of Political Research* 54 (2): 232–48.

Hooghe, Liesbet and Gary Marks. 2018. 'Cleavage Theory Meets Europe's Crises: Lipset, Rokkan, and the Transnational Cleavage'. *Journal of European Public Policy* 25 (1): 109–35.

Hopkin, Jonathan and Caterina Paolucci. 1999. 'The Business Firm Model of Party Organisation: Cases from Spain and Italy'. *European Journal of Political Research* 35: 307–39.

Katz, Richard S. and Peter Mair. 1995. 'Changing Models of Party Organizations and Party Democracy: The Emergence of the Cartel Party'. *Party Politics* 1 (1): 5–28.

Kefford, Glenn and Duncan McDonnell. 2018. 'Inside the Personal Party: Leader-Owners, Light Organizations and Limited Lifespans'. *The British Journal of Politics and International Relations* 20 (2): 379–94.

Kirchheimer, Otto. 1966. 'The Transformation of the Western European Party System'. In *Political Parties and Political Development*, edited by Joseph Lapalombara and Myron Weiner. Princeton, NJ: Princeton University Press.

Kosiara-Pedersen, Karina and Amalie Munkner Kristiansen. 2016. 'Alternativt partimedlemskab'. In *Statskundskab i praksis. Klassiske teorier og moderne problemer*, edited by Karina Kosiara-Pedersen, Gustav Nedergaard and Emil Lobe Suenson. Copenhagen: Karnov Group.

Kosiara-Pedersen, Karina and Peter Kurrild-Klitgaard. 2018. 'Change and Stability in the Danish Party System'. In *Party System Change, the European Crisis and the State of Democracy*, edited by Marco Lisi. London: Routledge.

Kosiara-Pedersen, Karina, Susan E. Scarrow and Emilie van Haute. 2017. 'Rules of Engagement? Party Membership Costs, New Forms of Party Affiliation, and Partisan Participation'. In *Organizing Representation: Political Parties, Participation, and Power*, edited by Susan E. Scarrow, Paul D. Webb and Thomas Poguntke. Oxford: Oxford University Press.

Kriesi, Hanspeter. 2014. 'The Populist Challenge'. *West European Politics* 37: 2, 361–78.

Mair, Peter. 1997. *Party System Change: Adaption and Interpretations*. London: Clarendon Press.

Mazzoleni, Oscar and Gerrit Voerman. 2017. 'Memberless Parties: Beyond the Business-Firm Party Model?' *Party Politics* 23 (6): 783–92.

Oskarson, Maria and Marie Demker. 2015. 'Room for Realignment: The Working-Class Sympathy for Sweden Democrats'. *Government and Opposition* 50 (4): 629–51. doi:10.1017/gov.2014.41.

Panebianco, Angelo. 1988. *Political Parties: Organization and Power*. Cambridge: Cambridge University Press.

Rocha, Frederico Pedroso. 2018. 'Soul Searching and Political Change in the Name of the Swedish Welfare Model'. In *Party System Change, the European Crisis and the State of Democracy*, edited by Marco Lisi. London: Routledge.

Rydgren, J., ed. 2013. *Class Politics and the Radical Right*. London: Routledge.

Scarrow, Susan E. 2015. *Beyond Party Members: Changing Approaches to Partisan Mobilization*. Oxford: Oxford University Press.

van Biezen, Ingrid and Thomas Poguntke. 2014. 'The Decline of Membership-Based Politics'. *Party Politics* 20 (2): 205–14.

van der Meer, Tom W. G. 2017. 'Political Trust and the "Crisis of Democracy"'. In *Oxford Research Encyclopedia of Politics*, edited by William R. Thompson, doi: 10.1093/acrefore/9780190228637.013.77. Oxford: Oxford University Press.

Index

Achury, Susan, 92
age: gender and, 80–83; and member
    enrolment, 54–55; membership
    activism and, 184; and member-voter
    congruence, 80, 82; party, 42–43, 47n4,
    112–14; representativeness and, 80–83;
    of Scandinavian party members joining
    their party, 55; socio-demographic
    profiles and, 80–83
agrarian parties, 10, 32, 40, 89, 125
agrarians (Ag): caucus-style party
    organization and, 37; Danish liberal
    parties, 60; membership in Nordic
    countries, 40; Norwegian, 66;
    Norwegian agrarian parties, 60
alternativet (Danish party), 41, 47
amateur-activist parties, 179–80
'ambassadors to the community,' 159–60
authoritarian parties, 114, 119
'authoritarian social democrats,' 119

Bengtsson, Åsa, 77, 129n4
bias: gender and age, 93; member
    recruitment, 87, 93; representative, 80
binding ballot, 232
Blondel, Jean, 113
British Conservative Party, 159
British Labour Party, 100

campaigning, 138–40; capital-intensive,
    177; external, 167; financial resources
    for, 32; labour-intensive, 5; and
    'party worker' dimension, 177; rise of
    permanent, 138; use of technology, 140
campaign linkage, 3
candidates, 160; Danish party member
    participation, 160–61; left-right
    self-placement across parties and
    countries, 235; mean left-right
    ideology positions in Denmark, 103;
    mean left-right ideology positions in
    Norway, 105; mean left-right ideology
    positions in Sweden, 103; members
    and ideological preferences, 226–29;
    nomination for public office, 11;
    Norwegian party member participation,
    162; in party primaries, 38; in Swedish
    parties, 102–3
capital-intensive campaigning,
    5, 177
capital-intensive campaign methods, 5
cartel party model, 3, 31–32, 44, 149
cartel party theory, 77, 152
Christian democratic parties (Cd), 40, 83,
    85, 89, 254
Christian parties, 10, 51, 58, 63, 66, 85,
    92, 255

Moderates (Moderaterna), 104, 121
movement parties, 60, 63, 65, 66

Narud, Hanne Marthe, 99
National Coalition Party, 79
National Revolution, 76
'net generation,' 179
new political parties: enrolment of
    members, 42–43; member/electorate
    (M/E) ratios, 42–43; *vs.* old political
    parties, 14–15, 32
Nordic countries: comparing voters,
    members and candidates within,
    97–107; ideological representation
    of candidates in, 97–107; ideological
    representation of members in, 97–107;
    ideological representation of voters
    in, 97–107; opinion structures within
    political parties in, 97–106
Nordic exceptionalism, myth of, 11–12
Nordic party membership linkage: activity,
    251–53; challenges of, 255; challenges
    to democracy at large, 258; influence,
    253–55; new forms of participatory
    linkage, 257–58; party systems and the
    new parties, 255–56; political parties
    adapting, 256–57; reach, 249–50;
    representation, 250–51; state of, 248–58
Nordic party membership trends, 29–47
Nordic political parties and systems, 12–15;
    differences and similarities, 11–12;
    five-party system, 10–11; old and newer,
    14–15; parties, 12–15; party family and
    left-right order, 13
Norway, 157; customs and norms, 231;
    elections of 1973, 31–32; external
    activities by members in, 145, 147,
    149; external or 'outreach' activities,
    151–52; factor loadings for Norwegian
    party member activism, 162–63; forms
    of membership activism in Norway,
    185; internal activism, 150–51; internal
    activities by members, 143, 144;
    intra-party democracy across party
    family, 211; member/electorate (M/E)
    ratio, 34–37; memberships decline
    in Socialist Left Party (SV), 43–44;

members' perception of intra-party
    democracy, 212; modelling support
    for membership decision making, 208,
    237; party member survey of 1991, 15;
    party member surveys, 15–17; social
    democratic parties, 10
Norwegian agrarian parties, 56, 60, 66
Norwegian Centre Party, 128, 144
Norwegian Christian party, 65
Norwegian Greens, 56, 60, 63, 65
Norwegian Labour Party, 33
Norwegian Left Socialist Party, 80
Norwegian Liberals, 14, 56
Norwegian members: party division
    among, 119–20; party unity among,
    119–20
Norwegian Progress Party, 13–14, 41, 113,
    119, 120
Norwegian Socialist Left, 181

occupation: education and, 87–91; level of,
    and region, 87–91
old political parties, 42; enrolment of
    members, 42–43; member/electorate
    (M/E) ratios, 42–43; *vs.* new parties,
    14–15, 32
'one-pillar' democracy models, 6, 7
online ambassadors, 140, 162
Önnudóttir, Eva H., 113
opinion structures: analysis of, within
    political parties in Nordic countries,
    97–106; intra-party, 97–98, 100, 227
opposition, and government, 43–44

Partei voor de vrijheid, 7, 29
participation: and activism of political
    party, 8–9; dimensions in, 137–53; and
    linkage, 138–40, 149–52
participatory linkage, 3, 8–9, 12, 29, 138,
    141, 158, 160, 168
participatory types of party members,
    158–59
party activism, 158; citizens and, 253; civil
    society organizations and, 176, 182–83;
    definition of, 138
party activities, 138–40, 149–52;
    campaigning, 138–40; external, 139–40,

Authors

Sofie Blombäck is Lecturer in political science at Mid Sweden University. Her main research interests are political parties and party systems, with a particular interest in new parties and European Parliament elections. Her work has been published in *Scandinavian Political Studies*, and she has contributed a chapter in *The European Union in a Changing World Order* (eds. Bakardjieva Engelbrekt, Bremberg et al. 2018/2019).

Niklas Bolin is Associate Professor at Mid Sweden University. His main research interests are parties and elections with a focus on party organization, party leadership, intra-party democracy, radical right parties and green parties. He has published in journals, including *West European Politics*, *Party Politics*, *Journal of Elections*, *Public Opinion and Parties* and *Scandinavian Political Studies*.

Marie Demker is Professor of Political Science at University of Gothenburg. Her main interests are political parties, political ideologies, nationalism and public opinion. She has published in journals, including *Scandinavian Political Studies*, *Party Politics*, *Government & Opposition* and *Ethnicities*. Her most recent book in English is *Sweden Unparadised?* (ed. with Leffler and Sigurdson, 2014) and, in Swedish, *Digital Demokrati. Partierna i en ny tid (Digital Democracy? Political Parties in a New Era*, with Bjereld, Blombäck and Sandberg 2018).

Knut Heidar is Professor of Political Science at the University of Oslo. His main interests are parties and parliaments. He has published in journals, including *Scandinavian Political Studies*, *West European Politics*, *Party Politics* and *Representation*. His most recent books are *After the Mass Party* (with Allern and Karlsen 2016) and *Do Parties Still Represent?* (ed. with Bram Wauters 2019).

Jonas Hinnfors is Professor of Political Science at the University of Gothenburg. Recent publications concern multi-level governance (with Bucken-Knapp, Spehar and Zelano) in *Nordic Journal of Migration Research*, 2017, and in *Between Mobility and Migration: The Urban Consequences of Intra-EU Migration* (eds. Scholten and van Ostaijen 2018). He is a coauthor of books in Swedish concerning parties and democracy – *Förhandla eller DÖ* (*Negotiate or Agree*, with Bjereld and Eriksson 2016) and theory of science – *Varför vetenskap?* (*Why Science?* with Bjereld and Demker 2018).

Anders Ravik Jupskås is Deputy Director at the Center for Research on Extremism and Lecturer at the Department of Political Science at the University of Oslo. His main interests are political parties, right-wing extremism and ideologies. He has published in *Scandinavian Political Studies*, *Swiss Political Science Review* and *Norsk statsvitenskapelig tidsskrift*, and he has contributed chapters in several recently published edited volumes on radical right politics.

Teo Keipi is Senior Researcher of Economic Sociology at the University of Turku. His current research focus is on political ideology and trust, digitally-mediated social networks, social media use patterns and societal risks related to inequality. He has recently published in *Party Politics*, *Journal of Youth Studies*, *Journal of Risk Research* and *Cyberpsychology, Behaviour and Social Networking*.

Aki Koivula is Instructor and Senior Researcher in Economic Sociology at the University of Turku. His research focuses primarily on party members and supporters, social networks and the use of information and communication technologies. He has recently published in *Party Politics*, *Telematics and Informatics*, *Environmental Politics* and *Comparative European Politics*.

Ann-Kristin Kölln is Associate Professor in Political Science at Aarhus University. Her research interests focus on political parties, public opinion, theories of political representation and survey methodology. In 2018, she won the Emerging Scholar Award and the Jack Walker Award for the best article from the American Political Science Association's section on Political Organizations and Parties.

Karina Kosiara-Pedersen is Associate Professor at the University of Copenhagen. She studies parties, party membership, candidate recruitment, campaigning, elections and party systems, sometimes with a focus on gender. Her recent work is published in *West European Politics*, *Party Politics*, *Journal of Elections, Public Opinion and Parties* and in the Danish book *Demokratiets Ildsjæle* (*The Fiery Souls of Democracy* 2017).

Gunnar Helgi Kristinsson is Professor of Political Science at the University of Iceland. His main research interests include political parties, the politics of the executive and the relationship between politics and administration in public policymaking.

He has published in journals such as the *European Journal of Political Research*, *Party Politics*, *West European Politics* and *Scandinavian Political Studies*.

Jonathan Polk is Associate Professor in the Department of Political Science and Centre for European Research at the University of Gothenburg. His research focuses on party competition, political parties and European integration, and political representation. In 2018, he won the Jack Walker Award for the best article from the American Political Science Association's section on Political Organizations and Parties.

Arttu Saarinen, DSocSci, is Assistant Professor of Economic Sociology at the University of Turku. His current research focus is on party members and supporters, social policy, social and institutional trust, and social networks. He has recently published in *Party Politics*, *Telematics and Informatics*, *International Journal of Sociology and Social Policy* and *Comparative European Politics*.